OCCUPATIONAL HEALTH FOR HEALTH CARE WORKERS

A Practical Guide

OCCUPATIONAL HEALTH FOR HEALTH CARE WORKERS

A Practical Guide

Edited by

Hans-Martin Hasselhorn
Karolinska Institutet, Department of Public Health Sciences,
Division of Psychosocial Factors and Health,
Stockholm, Sweden

Allan Toomingas and Monica Lagerström
National Institute for Working Life,
Stockholm, Sweden

1999

ELSEVIER

Amsterdam - Lausanne - New York - Oxford - Shannon - Singapore - Tokyo

ELSEVIER SCIENCE B.V.
Sara Burgerhartstraat 25
P.O. Box 211, 1000 AE Amsterdam, The Netherlands

First edition 1999

Library of Congress Cataloging in Publication Data
A catalog record from the Library of Congress has been applied for.

Cover Photography: Lasse Wigur

ISBN: 0-444-50335-8

♾ The paper used in this publication meets the requirements of ANSI/NISO Z39.48-1992 (Permanence of Paper).
Printed in The Netherlands.

Preface

In Stockholm during the summer of 1994, the International Commission on Occupational Health (ICOH) held a 2nd International Conference on Occupational Health for Health Care Workers. During the discussions, the Scientific Committee uncovered the need for a practical and comprehensive, but concise, book covering the broad range of occupational hazards facing health care workers. This was the first step towards production of the present book, under the auspices of the ICOH and the National Institute for Working Life in Sweden.

This book is intended to give guidance and advice to those dealing with occupational health issues in the health care sector. It is largely written for occupational health practitioners, such as occupational health physicians, nurses, and safety engineers. However, it may also be useful to administrators and managers in the health care sector and to medical students.

Our target group is thus mainly health care and dental staff in contact with patients, or in different supporting roles, such as laboratory personnel. Major issues in occupational health in the health care sector are covered, including biological, chemical, physiological and psychosocial hazards. The book provides an up-to-date overview of risk assessment and describes pathways in problem solving and risk management. Suggestions for further reading are included for those with special interests. The book does not review scientific studies in detail nor seek to reproduce basic established knowledge in the field of occupational health.

Our intention is to provide support for health care institutions in the industrialised world. Specific occupational health conditions encountered in the developing countries would require separate treatment in a dedicated publication. The occupational health advice given here should be adapted to local requirements and national regulations as well as to prevailing medical and epidemiological conditions.

This book has brought together over 45 international experts from different fields. All their contributions have been peer reviewed. The editorial group wishes to thank the authors for their contributions and also the scientific reviewers, language editors and others, named in the acknowledgement for their valuable help. We would like particularly to thank the Swedish National Institute for Working Life for financial support, and professor Christer Hogstedt, head of the Department for Work and Health for valuable advice and support in the production of this book. Without all their contributions, this book would not have been published.

Stockholm, June 1999

Hans-Martin Hasselhorn　　　　Allan Toomingas　　　　Monica Lagerström

Acknowledgements

Scientific reviewers
Sweden
J. Albert, B. Arnetz, R. Carlsson, M. Granström, B. Gustavsson, P. Gustavsson, K. Hedén, A. Knutsson, U. Kvist, U. Landström, W. Leitz, A. Linde, L.O. Magnius, C. Malmberg, K.E. Myrbeck, G. Nise, U. Rydberg, H.P. Söndergaard, S. Svenson, B. Wistedt

Germany
W. Bredt, F. Hamann, F. Hofmann, M. Kist, H. Martiny, D. Neumann-Haefelin, L. Pöllmann, T. Schwarz, U. Stössel, M. Weiss

UK
I. Dale, A. Forsyth, N. Gill, I. Symington

USA
T.K. Hodous, C. Muntaner

Spain
M.P. Arias, X. Guardino

France
J.F. Gehanno

Finland
G. Wikström

Language editors
UK
I. Dale, S. Elder, J. Morrison, I. Symington, D. Watt, J. Wilford

Sponsors
Arjo Limited, Gloucester, UK; Pasteur Mérieux MSD; SmithKline Beecham; National Institute for Working Life (Sweden) for financial support.

Others
Barbro Rönsch-Hasselhorn for the final layout and technical editing.

Foreword

"If you ever wondered how people can manage to work with the sick and always stay healthy themselves, the answer is – they can't!"
(Stellman JM. Women's work, women's health: Myths and realities. New York: Pantheon, 1976)

Working in health care is one of the oldest professions, and the occupational risks for some categories have already been described and commented upon in the classic book "Diseases of workers" written in 1700 by Bernardino Ramazzini. Today, health care is a labour intensive industry and, in most countries, health care workers constitute a major sector of the work force, usually predominantly female. Most of the classical occupational hazards still occur among different categories of health care worker as is evident from this new guide.

At the same time, modern concepts in the organisation of work and the working environment such as temporary jobs, outsourcing, downsizing, shiftwork, nightwork, "just-in-time employment", and teamwork are all conditions that are prevalent in hospitals and are considered to be "natural ingredients" in the organisation of health care work.

Health care workers will always be exposed to potential hazards, like infections from contagious patients, back pain from lifting patients or violence from psychotic patients. Most risks can, however, be minimised with the right precautions and a well thought out prevention strategy which puts a particular emphasis on occupational safety and health for both employers and employees in health care facilities.

One of the current challenges for the health care system in many countries is the ageing work force. It is therefore important for governments and health care employers to make sure that a sufficient number of young health care workers are trained to substitute for the "baby boom generation". It is equally important to make sure that health care workers can continue to work until the time of retirement – or even after. In these circumstances, the working conditions must secure "sustainable work ability" by facilitating good ergonomic solutions, keeping the work organisation reasonably staffed and providing a safe work environment.

Developments during the 90's, however, have been counterproductive. The trend to make drastic rationalisations in the health care sector as well as other sectors has meant an increased work load, longer working hours and higher patient/staffing ratios. In many countries, health care workers are among the professions that report the highest percentages of complaints caused by negative stress and related disorders. This factor is particularly worrying, as it must have an adverse influence on the quality of care for patients and reduces the opportunities for health care workers to participate in preventive activities such as "workplace health promotion". In addition, there is a risk of burn-out developing among the health care workers themselves.

Workplace health promotion is a modern concept that tries to combine traditional occupational safety and health practice with modern health promotion strategies directed towards changing unhealthy lifestyle practices. Such health promotion can be particularly successful among health care workers who have the necessary knowledge about health risks and also the obvious opportunities and responsibility to inform and influence patients on subjects such as smoking, drugs and prevention of sexually transmitted disorders. The motivation to become involved is to a large extent dependent on how well the occupational health and safety factors are taken into consideration for the health care workers themselves.

For many years, the Swedish National Institute for Working Life (NIWL) and its predecessors have had the main responsibility for training occupational health personnel in Sweden. During the 90´s, NIWL has also organised many international courses on occupational health and safety for colleagues from developing countries. NIWL, therefore, enthusiastically accepted the invitation to cooperate with the Scientific Committee on Occupational Health for Health Care Workers within the International Commission on Occupational Health in the production of this guide. Organisational as well as health and safety aspects of work in human service professions is a high priority for research and training in the NIWL. We feel that it has been appropriate to develop a modern, relatively short, international, practical guide of this kind and hope that it will be widely used to promote safe work environments and sustainable work ability among all health care workers.

Christer Hogstedt, MD
Professor of occupational health
National Institute for Working Life, Stockholm

The Scientific Committee "Occupational Health for Health Care Workers" of the International Commission on Occupational Health was founded in 1990 in Montreal. One of its responsibilities is to identify occupational hazards which affect the health, wellbeing and work ability of health care workers. Another responsibility is to disseminate information about such hazards and how to prevent them by taking action at both a strategic and a workplace level. The initiation of this guide has taken both aspects – identification and dissemination – into consideration.

Hazards at work among health care workers are extremely diverse. They are found in all countries of the world even though their relative importance may differ between regions and between types of health care institution. Many of the occupational hazards are mainly encountered in the health care sector.

Patients with severe and hazardous infections are aggregated at health care institutions. Infectious hazards tend to reflect the epidemiological panorama in the society. There is, for example, a world wide spread of HBV, HCV and HIV and the return of tuberculosis and diphtheria in eastern European countries poses an obvious risk to staff. These risks have to be identified quickly and adequate preventive actions such as vaccinations, hygienic measures, and the use of different protective barriers must be implemented.

Another factor that adds to the uniqueness of occupational risks among health care workers is the fact that the diagnostic, therapeutic and hygienic arsenal intended for patients, makes use of methods that are deliberately designed to have potent effects on biological systems, including the human body. Examples of such methods include the use of ionising radiation for radiotherapy, cytotoxic drugs for treatment of cancers and germicides for prevention of spread of microbes. Health care workers are at risk of repeated exposure to these agents with subsequent, and sometimes serious, harmful effects to their own wellbeing.

The health care sector is dominated by female personnel. Women generally have a somewhat lower muscular strength, which can put heavy demands on their physical capacity e.g. when performing manual patient transfers. This factor is even more accentuated among older female health care workers. Among younger female staff there are specific risks for pregnant women and their unborn children, such as rubella, parvovirus infections or ionising radiation.

A further aspect of health care work is that human beings, patients or clients, are in focus for the caring efforts. Patient care cannot be rationalised or automated as in a factory. Health care workers will therefore continue to be needed in the future to provide care for people. Health care workers are generally committed to their mission of helping sick people and are keen to produce a high quality of care. The fear of making mistakes that could hurt or even kill a patient has a much more serious dimension in health care than in other work. In addition, health care workers must not let their work be dominated by their own emotions or reactions to patients' circumstances, comments or behaviour, whether anguished or aggressive. These are examples of situations that put heavy demands on health care workers' empathy and professionalism. Good support and working conditions are essential for prevention of ill health from such psychosocial demands.

Preventive actions have proved to be fruitful and effective in many situations involving the safety and health of health care workers and their patients. The prevention of hepatitis B infection through hygienic measures, immunoglobulin and vaccinations is just one excellent example. This progress must continuously be maintained through identification of new health hazards, evaluation of the preventive work, and education and information of personnel. This is a major task for the occupational health system. The health care sector, however, like other economic sectors in society, is also put under heavy pressure to reduce costs. Demands for increased productivity are a reality in the health care sector and it must be a priority for the occupational health system to ensure that these new developments do not led to new or increased occupational health hazards. It will be important to show that healthy and well-motivated health care workers will increase the quality of health care work.

There is a wealth of scientific research and literature in this field, both on risk identification and on preventive actions. However, it is not easy to make the scientific knowledge accessible to those active in occupational health practice. The members of the Scientific Committee identified a need for a comprehensive but condensed book giving practical guidance on these issues for an international audience of practitioners active in occupational health in the health care sector. The present book "Occupational health for health care workers – a practical guide" can fulfil this purpose.

Friedrich Hofmann MD, PhD

Professor of occupational health,
work physiology and infectiology
University of Wuppertal
Wuppertal, Germany

Ian S. Symington, MBCLB, FFOM, FRCP

Consultant in Occupational Medicine
North Glasgow University Hospitals NHS
Trust
Glasgow, UK

Chairman

Secretary

of the Scientific Committee "Occupational Health for Health Care Workers" of the International Commission on Occupational Health

Contents

Impact of occupational health hazards in health care work

Allan Toomingas, Hans-Martin Hasselhorn

Occupational health risks for health care workers (HCW) are manifold. They span a wide range from needlesticks, physical overload leading to back strain to the emotional consequences of working in a demanding environment. There are also risks from transmission of infectious organisms such as tuberculosis bacteria and from exposure to toxic agents like cytostatic drugs, or allergens like acrylates. Many HCW experience mental stress due to multiple and sometimes conflicting demands from patients and colleagues. Economical constraints, ethical "rules" and concerns about making mistakes create added pressures.

Injuries, occupational diseases, work related disorders and their significance

These occupational health risks can cause injuries through accidents, e.g. a bruise or fracture caused by violence from a patient in a psychiatric ward. Hazards can also be associated with "occupational diseases" (OD) or "work related disorders" (WRD). OD includes diseases that are *caused* by work, such as hepatitis B infection following a needlestick injury or allergy due to use of latex gloves. In WRD work is a *contributing* factor linked with other components to the development, aggravation or persistence of the disorder. Examples of WRD are low-back pain among nurses performing patient transfers without aids or skin disorders due to frequent hand washing. Both OD and WRD can be related to a single exposure or to insidious or multiple exposure episodes.

The significance of different injuries, OD or WRD can be evaluated by a range of characteristics:
* *Occurrence* or *frequency* of the injury, OD or WRD.
* *Severity* of the injury. More severe injuries, OD or WRD are those that are (potentially) lethal (e.g. HIV infection), become chronic or are non-curable (e.g. hepatitis C infection), give major function loss or handicap (e.g. severe exzema), or give reproductive hazards (rubella infection). The suffering of the diseased HCW adds to the severity, but is difficult to evaluate.
* *Cost* the injury, OD or WRD is causing the diseased HCW, the employer or the society and the insurance system. The cost will be high for the society and the insurance system if its frequency is high, if the duration is long (chronic), and if it is associated with sick-leave. Costly treatment, rehabilitation or a need for change of work place or even profession may further add to the costs.

Data about reported injuries, OD or WRD do not reflect the total occupational health risk for the employee. Many exposures lead to diseases commonly thought of as "not worth reporting", such as the common cold and many other infectious diseases. In addition, many diseases may not be recognised as OD in some countries, even although the association between occupational exposure and health outcome seems obvious. This is the case for "stress related diseases" which may be reported and recognised as WRD in Sweden and the Netherlands, but not in other countries, like Germany. Many injuries, OD or WRD are not reported due to fears of negative consequences, including concern about loss of employment. In addition to varying hazard situations, the reporting habits, registration practices and compensation rules, may also explain the variation in statistics between many countries.

Occurrence of occupational diseases and work related disorders

In 1997, about 4 per 1000 HCW in Sweden and Germany reported an OD or WRD to the occupational insurance system. This is somewhat above the national average (3 per 1000). The most common *reported* OD or WRD were skin diseases (53% of all cases in Germany and 7% of all cases in Sweden) and strain on the musculoskeletal system (15% of all cases in Germany and 52% of all cases in Sweden, whereof 2/3 were located to the neck or upper extremities and 1/4 to the low back). Other common reported OD were allergic airways diseases (9% of all cases in Germany) and infectious diseases (6-9%). About 14% of all Swedish reports were due to psychosocial and organisational factors. Psychosocial factors are not formally recognised in Germany, whereas they are in Sweden, hence this difference. About one case in ten of reported OD or WRD were *approved* by the insurance system in Germany, with the same relative ranking between causal agents. The rate of approved cases was somewhat lower in healthcare (0.4 per 1000 HCW) compared to the national average (0.7 per 1000 workers).

Occurrence of injuries due to accidents at work

During 1997 there were about 7 reports per 1000 HCW in Sweden and 17 in Germany of occupational injuries *with subsequent sick-leave* caused by accidents. This was lower than in most other occupational sectors and the national averages of 9 and 40 respectively. Among the most common causes in Sweden were injuries due to overstrain (36% of all, whereof 3/4 were caused by lifting patients or other loads). About 17% of all injuries were caused by violence (1.2 report per 1000 HCW). In addition there were about 100 reports per 1000 HCW of minor injuries *without* sick-leave. Most common were reports caused by violence and threats (15% of all) and needle-sticks (8% of all). Work related accidents accounted for 0.1 (Sweden) and 0.7 days (Germany) lost per year and per HCW, which is exactly half of the national averages.

This relatively low rate of injuries due to accidents may be partly due to the type of work and the relatively safe conditions in the health care sector but also due to the fact that many injuries can be treated at the workplace and are therefore not reported.

Lethal accidents or occupational diseases

Death due to accidents or OD are uncommon among HCW. The rate in Sweden and Germany is about 1 death per 100 000 HCW. Violence is the cause in some cases. Usually other occupational sectors have higher rates, and the national average is about 3.5 deaths per 100 000. High suicide-rates however, have been found among Swedish HCW. Rates 2.1-3.4 times higher than expected in relation to other people of same gender and age have been reported e.g. among dentists, doctors, nurses, and psychiatric-care staff.

Somewhat increased rates of cancer among HCW have been reported in Sweden e.g. among physicians, pharmaceutical and laboratory personnel. No substantially increased rates of reproductive hazards have been reported among Swedish HCW.

Costs of occupational injuries, diseases and work related disorders

In 1997 skin disease was the OD within the private health care sector with the highest cost to the occupational health insurance system in Germany. From a total budget of 169 Million DM, 82 Million was paid to 10 500 HCW with occupational skin diseases and about 38 Million DM was paid for infectious diseases. The OD with the highest costs per case (apart from a few expensive rare diseases) were diseases due to exposure to radiation (19 000 DM), allergic and toxic lung diseases (15 000 DM), and infectious diseases (12 000 DM). Skin diseases averaged 8 000 DM and were below the average cost of 9 000 DM. However, the costs for injuries that led to retraining of the HCW could exceed 100 000 DM per case.

Sick-leave

Information about sick-leave and sickness pensions among HCW may provide further evidence of the significance of occupational health hazards for HCW. The absolute magnitude of sick-leave and sickness pension data differs, however, between different countries and even within the same country between different time periods due to variations and changes in the health insurance system, levels of benefits, and unemployment rates.

In 1996, German hospital personnel were on sick-leave for an average of 22 days per year, and 60% of HCW were on sick-leave at least once. Apart from public administration, no other economic sector has such a high rate of sick-leave. The total cost for all German hospitals due to sickness absence was calculated around 3.7 billion DM per year. Larger hospitals or public hospitals had somewhat higher rates of sick-leave. Long-term sick-leave (>6 weeks) caused about 44% of all sick-leave days. About half of all sick-leave episodes lasted up to one week only, causing 13% of all sick-leave-days.

The highest sick-leave rates were found for service workers, cleaning, laundry and kitchen staff. Also auxiliary nurses were above average (24 days), whereas registered nurses and physicians showed a lower rate (13 and 5 days, respectively). The same sick-leave pattern between different professions has been observed in Sweden. It should be noted that in contrast to younger HCW, female nurses above 59 years of age were much more often on sick-leave (41 days) than other working women of the same age (28 days).

Musculoskeletal diseases (MSD) counted for 28% of all sick-leave days. Registered nurses were on sick-leave due to MSD on average 3 days per year and auxiliary nurses for 7 days, compared to 5 days among all working women. Mental diseases or psychological disorders accounted for a somewhat higher percentage of days lost among HCW (6.7-8.4%) than in other economic sectors (4.8%). Physicians were 0.3, registered nurses 0.9 and auxiliary nurses 2 days on sick-leave per year, whereas the average in the working population was 1 day. Contrary to expectations, the number of sick-leave days per year due to airway disease is rather lower among HCW compared to the general working population (physicians 0.8 days per year, registered nurses 2.3, auxiliary nurses 3.5, and general population 3.1).

Sick-leave data support the impression that doctors and registered nurses have good health. It should, however, be borne in mind that many groups of HCW are somewhat reluctant to take sick-leave, even when they judge that they should do so. In fact, HCW have among the highest rate of "sickness presence" (contrary to sickness absence) compared to all other sectors. More than 50% of Swedish HCW reported sickness presence twice or more during 1997, and in Germany 64% of the HCW stated that they would work even when they felt that they were sick.

On the other hand, the sick-leave data highlights one particular risk group - auxiliary nurses. They are more often sick and suffer more from MSD, airway diseases and psychological diseases than the general population. This group needs extra attention and support from all involved including the occupational health units.

Sickness pensions

Sickness pensions and early retirements among Swedish HCW are about as frequent as among other workers, and are mainly due to musculoskeletal disorders (60% of total). The highest rates were seen among female occupational therapists (12 per 1000), auxiliary nurses (10 per 1000), and dentists (7 per 1000).

Past, present and future occupational health hazards

When looking at serious accidents or deaths the risk in the health care sector is low compared to other occupational sectors in industrialised countries. On the other hand there is a somewhat increased rate of OD, WRD and sick-leave in the health care sector. Musculoskeletal and skin disorders are common among HCW and health problems related to psychosocial load or violence and threats are also frequently encountered.

During the past twenty years, reports about the working conditions and health status of HCW have emphasised various developments. Looking back to the 1980's, disorders in the musculoskeletal system and abuse of alcohol or drugs among HCW became increasingly recognised. During the 1990's, reactions to violence, threats, harassment and other unfavourable psychosocial working conditions and organisation of work have been highlighted. Attention has been placed on stress-related disorders, like "burnout" and "post-traumatic stress disorder". Patients are becoming more "demanding" and well-informed about their diseases and their rights. Fears and reactions to making mistakes or being sued or otherwise questioned are increasing problems among doctors and other professional groups. There is also an emerging consciousness about the problems of the ageing HCW in a demographically ageing industrialised world.

These changes may reflect a real transition in the working conditions of the health care system, but may also mirror a change in expectations or a consciousness in society of what constitutes good work and good health. An increased proportion of the health care work has to be performed in the homes of the patients where the ergonomic conditions are less favourable than in hospitals. About 70% of the Swedish HCW describe an increase of tempo at work during the five first years of the 1990's. About 35% indicated that the amount of physically heavy work had increased and 25% that the risk of being harmed by violence had increased. Cut-backs in budgets and increased costs have caused a downsizing of the number of HCW in many countries, leaving an increased demand on productivity on those remaining. Such a situation can also cause ethical and psychological conflicts together with feelings of insufficiency among HCW, who have to try to fulfil the demands of the needy patients.

It can be assumed that these evolving changes will be reflected in future occupational injuries, OD and WRD. The occupational health units in the health care sector should therefore be alert to these phenomena and plan for adequate preventive actions.

Data sources

Data for this chapter have been collected mainly from:
- Official statistics of Sweden. Occupational diseases and occupational accidents 1996. National board of occupational safety and health, Statistics Sweden. Stockholm 1998 (In Swedish with English summary and legends)
- Vetter C. Krankheitsbedingte Fehlzeiten in Krankenhäusern. In: Arnold M, Paffrath D (Eds). Krankenhaus-Report'97. Stuttgart/Jena/Ulm: Gustav Fischer Verlag, 1997:207-220 (German sick-leave)
- Dr. Butz, Hauptverband der gewerblichen Berufsgenossenschaften, St. Augustin, Germany (German OD/WRD)

Occupational Health for Health Care Workers - A Practical Guide
H.-M. Hasselhorn, A. Toomingas and M. Lagerström (Editors)

The organisation and scope of occupational health services in the health care sector

John Harrison

Healthcare settings, including hospitals and community health clinics, are workplaces. The health, safety and well being of the staff that work there is the responsibility of their employers. This can be achieved only through an organisational commitment to good occupational health. To achieve this requires a multi-disciplinary team approach which will include the involvement of the occupational health service. There will be a statutory framework governing the responsibilities for assessing hazards and risks to health and the level of health monitoring that should be carried out. This will vary from country to country. For example, there may be primary legislation describing general duties of employers supplemented by more specific secondary legislation covering a variety of workplace hazards, such as noise, manual handling and hazardous substances.

The occupational health team is responsible for the clinical assessment and interpretation of the health status of workers and the relevance of workplace risks to health. An example of the organisation of a healthcare occupational health service can be found in the series "State of The Art Reviews" [1]. The precise roles of the respective team members will vary according to the composition of the team, the organisation in which it is based and the professional relationships that are the norm in different national states. The activities of occupational health professionals are driven by several potentially conflicting influences. In addition to statutory duties, the requirements of employers as "the paymaster" will feature large in the shaping of the service. Occupational physicians and other occupational health professionals must remember that they are bound by ethical codes of practice. Countries such as the U.K. have published ethical guidance [2]. Guidance is also available from ICOH [3]. Ethical codes are concerned with issues such as confidentiality of information, duties to individual employees vs the organisation or society and professional conduct. However, ethical codes at an international level must take into account cultural and religious differences. Nonetheless, there is probably agreement that it is wrong to hurt people, either by omission or commission, and that the prevention or minimisation of harm to individuals is a fundamental responsibility of doctors and nurses [4].

There are continual pressures on public organisations to deliver cost-effective services. This can mean that the relationships between the healthcare worker and the employee, the Trades Union official and the hospital management are tested repeatedly. Legal and ethical duties are not always coterminous. There is often a need to educate people within the organisation about the respective roles of the members of the occupational health team and to explain the necessity of analysing problems holistically. What is the best overall solution to the problem for the organisation, rather than what is the most expedient. Cost-efficiency is not always synonymous with cost-effectiveness and the analysis of cost-effectiveness may be flawed. As a professionally independent source of advice, the occupational health specialist should be seen as a key resource for the hospital, someone who is balancing the needs of individuals against the needs of the organisation to secure long-term benefit for both. As hospitals are usually large employers, occupational health in the health care sector is being seen increasingly as part of the public health.

Occupational health and risk management

Healthcare organisations are concerned with managing risks. There are many types of risks but it is often useful to divide them into clinical and non-clinical risks. Clinical risks focus on patient safety and covers aspects of clinical practice and the environment in which patients are treated. Non-clinical risks include health and safety at work, fire safety, security and financial probity. Occupational health is important in most aspects of risk management. It should not be seen, therefore, as an add-on service. As a preventative specialty it is founded on the assessment of risks to health of workers that may arise from workplace hazards. This approach facilitates advice to be given to assist organisations in the formulation of strategic policies to minimise the risks of work-related ill health and accidents involving the public using healthcare facilities. As a rehabilitative specialty the assessment of clinical illness or disability, in the context of an appreciation of workplace risks, forms the basis of managed individual care that is intended to reintroduce people back into the workplace without risking their safety, or that of others.

When reviewing the necessary functions of an occupational health service this can be done from a risk assessment/risk management perspective [5]. Healthcare sector occupational health services should work closely with health and safety, security, infection control, pharmacy, estates and the human resources departments in devising and implementing policies. There should be an occupational health presence on health and safety and infection control committees. Effective management of health and safety is an essential component of an overall risk management strategy. Health and safety is the responsibility of every worker and every organisation should endeavour to create a culture that emphasises this. Communication of risks to all levels of the organisation is a key role for the occupational health service. Notwithstanding this, organisations should ensure that there is clarity of responsibilities for health and safety at all levels and that there are clear lines of accountability. The occupational health team has a role to facilitate and support the management of health and safety by acting as a repository of knowledge with respect to the evaluation of workplace hazards, by providing expert advice during the performance of risk assessments and by assisting in the education and training of workers.

Organisation of health and safety policies

Healthcare organisations have a legal duty to make health and safety arrangements. Within the European Union member national states must comply with the requirements of Directive 391, the Framework Directive [6]. However, the translation of the Directive into national health and safety laws has resulted in some variation in the requirements for the organisation of occupational health services. The approach to the organisation of health and safety policies is that general duties for proactive risk assessment, control of workplace hazards and the health surveillance of workers are described in legislation. There are requirements for organisations to produce a health and safety policy and this must be accessible in every workplace. The policy must describe how health and safety will be managed and clarify individual roles and responsibilities. The International Labour Organisation (ILO) is a good source of information and guidance. The ILO can now be accessed via the internet at http://www.ilo.org/ [7]. An excellent resource is the ILO/CIS Occupational Safety and Health Information Centre, (http://www.ilo.org/public/english/90travai/cis/) [8], whose major objective is to be a world-wide service dedicated to the collection and dissemination of information on the prevention of occupational diseases and accidents. The CIS bimonthly review bulletin *Safety and Health at Work* is published in English and in French and is available as an ILO-CIS bulletin, on-line as CISDOC, or on a CD-ROM (OSH-ROM) also containing NIOSHTIC, HSELINE and MHIDAS (SilverPlatter). A good alternative is the SafetyLine service provided by Work-Safe Western Australia, http://www.wt.com.au/safetyline [9]. An index of occupational safety and health resources on the internet can be found at http://oshweb.me.tut.fi/cgi-bin/oshweb.pl [10]. This site is hosted by the Institute of Occupational Safety Engineering at Tampere University of Technology in Finland. (http://turva24.me.tut.fi/english/front_page/index.html) [11, 12]. The WHO/ICOH publication Occupational Health Policy, Practice and Evaluation contains papers on general occupational health issues, as well as specific topics including some of direct relevance to healthcare occupational health services [13]. There is also a full-text on-line publication available from the University of Alberta, Canada, entitled "Occupational Health Services: A practical approach" (http://www.ualberta.ca/~gjhangri/ohp/contents.htm) [14].

In addition to general duties, there may be specific duties with respect to health and safety, either statutory or corporate. For example, in the EU there will be specific requirements to make provisions for controlling carcinogens [15], biological agents [16], manual handling [17], exposure to display screen equipment [18], noise at work [19] and hours of work [20]. Special arrangements must be made to protect the health of women who are pregnant, breast-feeding, or after childbirth [21]. In most countries health surveillance for workers is usually a statutory requirement for at least some workplace hazards. However, the range and type of health surveillance varies from country to country. There may be guidelines from national departments of health that will influence occupational health activity, in addition to compliance with statutory duties. In the Netherlands there are guidelines on infection prevention, based on professional consensus [22]. In Germany the medical examinations required for different groups of workers have been specified. In Italy regional guidelines from the Department of Health exist, in the main, although the guidelines vary between regions. The guidelines issued by the management executive of the National Health Service, in England, have the status of guidance only. Consequently, within a national framework of regulations and guidelines, there is likely to be room for a significant range of occupational health practice.

Monitoring of potential hazards and risk assessment

The implementation of a risk-based health and safety programme is a good example of a multi-disciplinary team approach. It is a management responsibility to carry out assessments of workplace hazards and to evaluate the likely risks to health for workers and other people. This may be a complex operation bringing in expert advice from safety officers, occupational hygienists, occupational physiotherapists and psychologists, in addition to the involvement of occupational physicians and occupational health nurses. Estimates of risks will be based on assessment of real or potential exposures (physical, chemical, biological and psychological) and on assessments of individual susceptibilities, where this is possible.

    Information about chemical hazards may be obtained from packaging information and the classification of the chemicals, e.g. very toxic, toxic, harmful, corrosive or irritant. There should also be safety data hazard sheets. A similar approach may be taken with biological agents, distinguishing those micro-organisms which are unlikely to cause human disease, from increasingly infectious agents that may ultimately cause serious outbreaks of infection in the community. An example is the approach taken by the Health and Safety Executive in the U.K. in the guidance issued to accompany the Control of Substances Hazardous to Health Regulations 1994 [23]. However, risk assessment relies not only on knowledge about the hazards, but also on how they will be used. The generation of aerosols that may be inhaled, or the production of mists, fumes or gases will be associated with greater risks to health than the handling of solid materials. Information about the potential for exposure may be obtained by direct observation of the workplace, or by asking workers to complete a questionnaire. Routine safety inspections could complement the risk assessment process by providing additional information about what actually happens in the workplace.

    This approach should enable the identification of individuals requiring health surveillance, the aim of which is to detect the occurrence of ill-health effects that might arise if the control of hazards fails, or if some workers are unduly sensitive to specific workplace exposures. Useful information can also come from an accident and incident reporting system, which will encourage the investigation of untoward events and which will provide statistics giving an overview of how successfully risks are being controlled. Analysis of sickness absence data may be helpful, if there is an effective occupational health assessment of the reasons for absences. The information collected should provide important feedback to managers about their control measures. It should be combined with further monitoring of exposures to determine whether the measures themselves are adequate, or whether the occupational exposure standards are appropriate.

Preventive programmes

The first priority in the prevention of ill health is the identification of hazards, followed by their removal from the workplace. An example might be the evaluation of activity requiring the lifting and handling of patients. If the activity is unnecessary, or if it can be carried out using mechanical aids, staff should be instructed to avoid lifting. Many hospitals have adopted minimal handling policies to reduce the risks of low back pain amongst the staff. Unfortunately, the pressures on hospitals to contain their costs often lead to inadequate staffing levels, or the failure to provide sufficient lifting aids. Such constraints mitigate against successful preventive programs. Screening of applicants for jobs requiring lifting and handling has been tried for many years, without much success. The use of ergonomic assessments, based on a thorough understanding of the job activities, should help to prevent musculo-skeletal injuries, such as low back pain [24]. However, the importance of psychosocial factors in the development of chronic problems should not be overlooked [25].

Immunisation of staff against diseases such as tuberculosis, hepatitis B, rubella, tetanus, polio and typhoid, is another example of a preventive programme, although in this case there is an acceptance that it is not possible to remove the hazards completely. Nonetheless, immunisation does not remove the need to ensure safe working practices in line with control of infection recommendations. General advice about vaccinations is available from the Centers for Disease Control and Prevention, in the U.S.A.. The most recent guidelines published in Morbidity and Mortality Weekly Report [26] strongly recommend immunisation against hepatitis B, influenza, measles, mumps, rubella and varicella. A review of exposure-based biological hazards [27] also highlights the importance of vaccination programmes in healthcare settings, but notes that practices may vary between countries. For example, the U.K. offers healthcare workers Bacillus Calmette-Guerin (BCG) vaccination against tuberculosis, but this is not popular elsewhere in Europe, nor in many parts of the U.S.A.

Noise may be a hazard in hospitals, particularly in laundries where the washing machines and dryers may emit noise levels in excess of 90 dB(A) if they are poorly maintained. Reduction of noise levels at source must be attempted, supplemented by the wearing of hearing protection devices and audiometric programmes.

Education and training are important aspects of any prevention programme. Staff need to understand the nature of the hazards with which they are working and how to work safely. They must understand what to do in the event of an accident, or an untoward occurrence. For example, prompt action is required following a needlestick injury. Staff must be familiar with the first aid measures that should be taken as well as the need to report the incident so that a risk assessment may be made of the nature of the injury, taking into account the immune status of the staff member and the health status of the patient on whom the needle has been used. Considerable amounts of training may be undertaken in lifting and handling and, increasingly, in recognising and managing stress at work.

If workplace hazards cannot be controlled by any other means, it may be necessary to rely on personal protective equipment, such as gloves, masks and gowns. For example, the reconstitution of cytotoxic drugs should be carried out in laminar airflow cabinets, such that any aerosol generated is drawn away from the breathing zone of the worker. However, it is not possible to exclude the chance of drugs coming into contact with the skin and so pharmacy technicians are also required to wear gloves, masks goggles and gowns. In a healthcare setting many substances may come into contact with the skin and the hands are often put into water. Once again, it is necessary to evaluate such working practices and, where possible, eliminate the hazard or substitute something that is less hazardous. Latex allergy has become an important issue in recent years. This means that the gloves themselves may be the cause of a skin or more serious health problem, rather than preventing it. It should be possible to introduce non-latex gloves for workers with this problem. In the future, a more general reduction in the use of latex will probably be required. A key element to a good skin care programme is a robust reporting mechanism to ensure that problems may be assessed early and advice and treatment given. This may be organised using a hierarchical approach, starting with the worker's supervisor, followed by an occupational health nurse and, where appropriate, an occupational physician.

Monitoring of health status

Surveillance of the health of workers complements the implementation of preventive programmes. Health surveillance should begin at the pre-employment or pre-placement stage, when a baseline data set can be gathered. Clinical assessments of workers should be linked to the possible health effects associated with exposures to workplace hazards. There should be a definite disease for which there is a method of measuring its occurrence. Detection of a positive result should lead to a clinical or workplace intervention that will benefit the person being monitored. An example of health surveillance carried out in a healthcare setting is the monitoring of workers exposed to respiratory sensitisers. The cold sterilising agent glutaraldehyde is used to disinfect endoscopes. Healthcare staff may develop dermatitis or asthma if exposures are not controlled. Regular surveillance, using respiratory questionnaires, is aimed at identifying workers who develop upper respiratory tract or mucosal symptoms. These may herald the onset of symptoms of bronchial hyperreactivity and possible asthma. The development of symptoms will trigger further assessments using spirometry, serial peak flow assessments and possible bronchial provocation tests [28]. Workers developing dermatitis will require a dermatological assessment to confirm the diagnosis of contact dermatitis and to identify the likely cause [29]. Allergy to latex has been recognised increasingly in recent years. Numerically musculo-skeletal and psychological health problems account for most work-related diseases in the healthcare sector and they present via routine surveillance, reporting mechanisms, altered performance at work or absence from work. Many industrial organisations have introduced screening for drugs and alcohol in the workplace, including random testing. Whilst being drunk at work cannot be condoned, there appears to be a general unwillingness to introduce such procedures in hospitals, or other health care settings. Consequently, the identification of workers with alcohol use problems requires education and awareness raising and a culture that encourages workers to come forward for rehabilitation [30]. Workers who develop symptoms must have their workplaces and working practices assessed with a view to minimising exposures. If it is not possible to alleviate the symptoms redeployment may have to be considered.

 The organisation of health surveillance programmes depends on national criteria for professional practice and responsibilities. It is likely that many workers who are assessed will have no symptoms or signs of illness. A cost-effective method for assessment is the use of questionnaires, possibly administered by occupational health nurses. Protocols and procedures can be devised to assist nurses identify potentially serious symptoms and to take the appropriate action. Referral criteria making it clear when workers should be assessed by an occupational physician mean that medical time can be used effectively. In some countries it is possible for occupational health nurses to sign fitness forms, without reference to a doctor. In others, this would not be possible. Whatever the outcome of a health surveillance assessment, it is important to ensure that the information is communicated to the managers. Occupational health records detailing the dates and the type of assessments, and the results, must be maintained and there should be a recall system.

Clinical occupational health practice

Occupational health is a clinical specialty. In some instances it is practised at a population level, in others it is concerned with the management of illnesses or disabilities in individuals.

Follow up of accidents and diseases

It is an unfortunate reality that any system of management of safety involving people will fail. The consequences of this are that accidents and work-related diseases will occur. This is particularly likely in healthcare organisations because the safety and welfare of staff may be secondary to that of patients. Part of the management of health and safety should involve the reporting of incidents and dangerous occurrences and the early involvement of the occupational health service. There may be a first aid requirement of the service, although staff who are seriously injured or ill should be assessed in accident and emergency, unless the occupational health department is appropriately staffed and equipped to treat staff safely. A clinical assessment following an accident or a dangerous occurrence is concerned with establishing the state of health and fitness for work of the individual concerned. It may highlight the need for further treatment or that the worker should spend time away from work. It will usually be linked with a workplace assessment, carried out by a safety officer and/or the occupational physician or occupational health nurse.

In the case of an apparent occupational or work-related disease, the diagnosis is based on the combination of a medical diagnosis, using the accepted process of obtaining a medical history, medical examination and investigations, and an assessment of workplace exposures. The latter may be based on the occupational history, supplemented by any objective measurements of exposure. In some instances it may be necessary to undertake invasive testing to establish an accurate diagnosis. For example, bronchial provocation tests may help to distinguish a respiratory sensitiser from several possible candidates. Alternatively, patch testing may assist in making a diagnosis of skin sensitivity in cases of contact dermatitis. Experts should perform such specialised procedures and so there should be arrangements in place for staff to be referred for testing. Making a precise diagnosis of occupational disease is not merely for academic interest. It will assist the rehabilitation of workers by ensuring that they are not reintroduced into hazardous work environments. Such information may also be required in legal cases if negligence is alleged.

Rehabilitation and back to work programmes

It is an established principle of rehabilitation that the process begins at the time of an accident or at the time of onset of an illness. Occupational health departments have an opportunity to play a key role in the rehabilitation of workers, therefore. In fact, the occupational health department has a central role in the rehabilitation process and can be likened to a spider in a web co-ordinating the actions taken by employers, fellow workers, and the health care system. In some countries it will interface with the health insurance system. It is important for occupational health professionals to adopt a positive attitude towards rehabilitation and to impart information and instructions regarding what will happen to the worker whilst absent from work and about the process of reintroduction into the workplace. It should be possible to draw on the relationship that has been established between the occupational health professional and the worker to contact him/her whilst at home to monitor progress and to prevent the worker from feeling isolated and forgotten. Occupational health nurses are well placed to do this. Arrangements can be made for the worker to visit the occupational health department at regular intervals for a formal medical assessment. At the appropriate time a return to work may be attempted, possibly facilitated by temporary or permanent modification of duties. However, the scope for doing this will depend on the type of work involved. An initial reduction in working hours may be helpful, gradually increasing the time at work over a number of weeks until normal working hours have been reached.

Assessment of "sickness absence" is often seen as a core function of an occupational health service. Although the management of absenteeism is not the responsibility of occupational health, it does have an important role to play in the clinical assessment of healthcare workers. Fitness for work is an important consideration in terms of possible work-related problems and their causes and also patient safety. Healthcare organisations should formulate policies that give clear guidance on the management of short-term and long-term absenteeism. There should be a delineation of the role of the occupational health service in diagnosing underlying health problems that may be contributing to repeated short-term absenteeism, such as anxiety and alcohol use disorders. Conditions leading to long-term absences need to be assessed in the context of work-related disability, with an emphasis on rehabilitating workers back into the working environment. This requires planning and co-ordination of the involvement of the treating agencies and healthcare managers. Temporary or permanent adjustment of the working arrangements may be necessary, including hours of work, type of shift, work activities, ergonomic revisions, access to workplaces or toileting arrangements. In some countries this may be a legal requirement for workers deemed to be disabled. On-going support from the occupational health service may be beneficial during the return to work phase, to titrate modifications in working arrangements with the effects on health.

Occupational health promotion (general)

The term health promotion can include a wide range of initiatives. Workplace health promotion is often focussed on measures that will lead to the reduction of sickness absence or accidents. It is also concerned with the reduction of morbidity and mortality from diseases such as ischaemic heart disease, strokes, cancer, respiratory illnesses and mental illness. Many healthcare organisations are implementing, or have implemented, no smoking policies in the workplace. Occupational health services can play an important role in drafting such policies and in supporting those workers who decide to stop smoking. They may also support other initiatives such as anti-cancer campaigns, World AIDS day and promoting health amongst ethnic minorities. Occupational health professionals can encourage the promotion of physical fitness, healthy eating and sensible drinking of alcohol.

References

1   Lewy R. Organization and Conduct of a Hospital Occupational Health Service. In: Emmett E. (Ed). Health Problems of Health Care Workers. Philadelphia, USA: Hanley & Belfus, INC., 1987:654
2   Guidance on ethics for occupational physicians. Royal College of Physicians, Faculty of Occupational Medicine. London, 1997
3   International Code of Ethics for Occupational Health Professionals. International Commission on Occupational Health. Singapore, 1992
4   Goodman K. Ethical Challenges. In: Herzstein J. Bunn III W. Fleming L. Harrington J. Jeyeratnum J. Gardner I. Eds. International Occupational and Environmental Medicine. St. Louis, USA: Mosby, 1998:86-96
5   Sadhra S, Rampal K. Occupational health Risk Assessment and Management. London: Blackwell, 1999:492
6   Council Directive 89/391/EEC. The Framework Directive European Commission, 1989
7   ILO Web Site Home Page. International Labour Organization. http://www.ilo.org/
8   Occupational Safety and Health Information Centre. International Labour Organization. http://www.ilo.org/public/english/90travai/cis
9   SafetyLine. WorkSafe Western Australia. http://www.wt.com.au/safetyline
10   Index of Occupational Safety and Health Resources. Institute of Occupational Safety Engineering, Tampere Univeristy of Technology, Finland. http://turva24.me.tut.fi/english/front_page/index.html
11   Institute of Occupational Safety and Health Front Page (English). Tampere University of Technology, Finland. http://turva24.me.tut.fi/english/front_page/index.html
12   Uusitalo T, Takala J. Internet resources, News Groups, and Home Page Addresses. In: Herzstein J. Bunn III W. Fleming L. Harrington J. Jeyeratnum J. Gardner I. Eds. International Occupational and Environmental Medicine. St. Louis, USA: Mosby, 1999:703-709
13   "Occupational health policy, practice and evaluation," presented at 2nd International Conference on Health Services Research in Occupational Health (WHO Regional Office for Europe), Bremen, Germany, 1994
14   Occupational Health Services: A practical approach. University of Alberta, Canada. http://www.ualberta.ca/~gjhangri/ohp/contents.htm
15   Council Directive 90/394/EEC. Protection of workers from the risks related to exposure to carcinogens at work European Commission, 1990
16   Council Directive 90/679/EEC. Protection of workers from risks related to exposure to biological agents at work European Commission, 1990
17   Council Directive 90/269/EEC. Minimum health and safety requirements for the manual

handling of loads where there is a risk particularly of back injury to workers European Commission, 1990

18   Council Directive 90/270/EEC. Minimum safety and health requirements for work with display screen equipment European Commission, 1990

19   Council Directive 86/188/EEC. European Commission, 1986

20   Council Directive 93/104/EC. Concerning certain aspects of the organisation of working time European Commission, 1993

21   Council Directive 92/85/EEC. Introduction of measures to encourage improvements in the safety and health at work of pregnant workers and workers who have recently given birth or are breastfeeding European Commission, 1992

22   Bedryfsartsen Inde Gezondheidszog. National Guidelines on Infection Prevention, The Netherlands

23   Control of Substances Hazardous to Health. U.K. Government, HM Stationary Ofice. London, 1994

24   Borenstein D, Wiesel S, Boden S. Low Back Pain. Medical Diagnosis and Comprehensive Management, second ed. Philadelphia, USA: WB Saunders, 1995:732

25   Wynn P, Pilling K. Risk Management and manual handling. In: Sadhra S. Rampal K. Eds. Occupational Health. Risk Assessment and Management. London: Blackwell Science Ltd., 1999:390-404

26   MMWR, Immunization of Health-care Workers. Recommendations of the advisory committee on Immunization Practices (ACIP) and the hospital infection control practices advisory committee (HICPAC). Centers for Disease Control and Prevention. Atlanta Georgia, Recommendations and Reports RR-18, December 26 1997

27   Aw T-C, Harrison J. Exposure-based hazards:Biological. In: Herzstein J. Bunn W. Fleming L. Eds. International Occupational and Environmental Medicine. St. Louis, USA: Mosby, 1998:768

28   Burge P. The management of occupational asthma and hyperreactive airways disease in the workplace. In: Waldron H. Edling C. Eds. Occupational Health Practice. Oxford U.K.: Butterworth-Heinemann, 1997:200-214

29   Coenraads P-J, Timmer C. Occupational skin diseases. In: Waldron H. Edling C. Eds. Occupational Health Practice. Oxford U.K.: Butterworth-Heinemann, 1997:215-230

30   Kelly D. Burnout and Alcohol problems. In: Lichfield P. Ed. Health risks to the healthcare professional. London: Royal College of Physicians, 1995:63-75

Quality assurance of occupational health services for health care workers

Raymond Agius

Introduction, and fundamental concepts

The delivery of a high quality Occupational Health Service (OHS) for health care workers (HCW), is based on the principles described in the preceding chapter by John Harrison. An important first step is an explicit documented statement of the purposes and objectives of the OHS, based on a comprehensive 'needs assessment' agreed by the purchasers, users and providers of the OHS. The next step is to establish specific and detailed statements on the structures, resources, staff competencies, policies and procedures essential to assure quality. Finally audit of the quality of the above, as well as of the outputs of the OHS (e.g. advice) and of their outcomes (e.g. risk reduction, rehabilitation) is needed using evidence based criteria [1-5]. These are fundamental obligations of the OHS which should ensure that it has appropriate mechanisms in place to deliver quality in the following aspects of the service:

Structure and resources

- Clear management and reporting structure with appropriate budget and financial management.
- Appropriate range, numbers and competencies of staff, with ongoing training.
- Essential office and consulting facilities with comfort and confidentiality.
- Appropriate maintained clinical and other equipment, and record storage.

Although auditing the quality of structures, by determining whether or not they comply with the agreed standard, is relatively cheap and easy it might have little bearing on the effectiveness and efficiency of OHS, and hence on the quality delivered to the HCW.

Process

This includes administrative processes such as the handling of requests for appointments and booking of appointments, scheduling of routine health surveillance, and workplace assessments.

However the most important processes are the workplace risk assessment processes and the clinical processes. It is essential to follow agreed, and where possible evidence-based, protocols and guidelines including assessment at commencement of employment, health surveillance or other periodic medical surveillance, immunisation, and rehabilitation.

Ensuring the quality of process is very valuable if it addresses important determinants of outcome, and has many advantages. Thus it can be cheaper, more sensitive and permit quicker remedial action than evaluating outcome.

Outcome

A few outcomes of great importance to HCW can be easily assessed directly, quantitatively and objectively, e.g. post-immunisation antibody titres.

Assuring outcomes such as long term morbidity and mortality intuitively appears more valuable than focussing on the quality of process but it may entail high expense, and certainly requires a longer time scale if a demonstrable reduction in health risk is taken as an outcome quality standard. Moreover the work of the OHS itself does not often produce an outcome independent of other factors outside the OHS. Nevertheless the advice or other activity of the occupational health service can be considered as an intermediate - output, the quality of which can be assured: for example the advice given by OHS to managers.

Practical application and guidance

Steps towards achieving and maintaining quality are common to all issues [2-5]:

- Determine the most crucial areas, focussing on high 'cost' to health, employment, or service delivery (e.g. reduction of risk at source, health surveillance, sickness absence and rehabilitation).
- Review the evidence-base for the relevant area(s).
- Debate and agree the protocols and practice guidelines for the above.
- Educate practitioners and then proceed with implementation of the guidelines.
- Develop audit criteria based on the practice guidelines.
- Audit a representative sample of practice against the quality criteria.
- Implement change and close the loop.

In the context of important issues of quality assurance in OHS for HCW, a few important key areas with specific guidance and advice are presented hereunder.

Exposure reduction and health surveillance

The following table 1 illustrates how starting from an evidence base can lead to steps to assure a quality standard for occupational health [2].

Table 1. Connection between evidence base and practice guideline – an example based on the application of health surveillance for respiratory sensitisation

Scientific evidence base	Derived practice guideline to ensure quality
The degree of exposure to sensitisers is a very important determinant of the risk of adverse health effects.	Systematic hazard identification is needed together with steps to substitute sensitisers, e.g. latex antigen, and in any case measures to reduce personal exposure.
Atopy *per se* has a poor predictive value in relation to pre-employment assessment	Applicants for jobs exposed to respiratory sensitisers should not be excluded on the basis of atopy alone.
Defined questions on respiratory symptoms e.g. wheeze and dyspnoea improving when off work are a sensitive way of identifying occupational asthma.	The first line of health surveillance of employees with significant exposure, e.g. to glutaraldehyde, should consist of a questionnaire with the appropriate items administered at intervals e.g. six monthly, and then yearly thereafter.
Specificity of diagnosis can be achieved through means such as lung function tests before and after exposure.	Positive respondents to the questionnaire should be followed up by work exposure related lung function tests, workplace re-assessment and advice.

In order to ascertain whether a high quality has been achieved in the delivery of Occupational Health in the context of this example (i.e. Exposure reduction and health surveillance) an audit consisting of some or all of the elements in the following Table 2, can be undertaken.

Table 2. Connection between element and method of audit

Element to be audited	Method of audit
Identification of exposures significant enough to warrant action	Occupational hygiene professional review of sample of risk assessments completed by line managers, or by professional peers
Identification of target population	Review of sample of workplaces, and of tasks undertaken there, and comparison with lists of employees subjected to health surveillance
Health surveillance protocol	Review of sensitivity and specificity of the questionnaire, calibration of diagnostic tools
Health assessment of employees	Peer review audit of stratified random sample of records of health surveillance
Reporting of cases as required by statute or policy	Confidential comparison of random sample of positive cases from peer review audit of health surveillance against actual reports
Managerial response to results of health surveillance	Review of workplaces with high frequency of adverse effects for evidence of implementation of change
Trends in frequency of adverse health effect (e.g of respiratory or skin sensitisation)	Review of validated frequency rates against time, classified by category of employees, workplace and task

Sickness absence and rehabilitation

These are very important issues for which quality needs to be assured at a group level for the organisation as a whole, and at an individual level. Thus it is important to be able to ensure that the OHS has satisfactorily addressed questions such as the following[6]:

Does the organisation as a whole, have a policy and procedures which include the following?
- Recording of numbers, dates, method of certification, diagnosis or description of attributed causes of sickness absence by employee, job type, age and department.
- Means of readily presenting contemporary statistics and trends of sickness absence, over time both for individuals and for sub-groups classified by the above categories.
- Guidelines on action to be taken by manager. Indications for management referral or self referral to OHS, including information to be provided by manager.
- Requirement for explicit managerial response to OHS advice.

Does the OHS advice in respect of the individual HCW indicate the following?
- Current level of fitness for work.
- Likely date of return to work.
- Specific limitations in redeployment of the employee.
- Likelihood of the employee to render regular and efficient service in the future in terms of attendance, performance and safety.
- Likely duration of any residual disability.
- Advice on whether work could be affecting the employee's health.
- Specific advice on rehabilitation, including steps to be taken, targets to be set, and plan for monitoring progress.

Both the quality of the OHS 'output' i.e. the advice given, as well as the managerial response can be evaluated by comparing them with the subsequent experience of return to work in the time interval indicated, implementation of the OHS advice on redeployment and rehabilitation, as well as possible recurrence of the original reason for referral. Some causes of sickness absence are of particular concern for HCW, such as back pain, and psychological stress, and specific tools have been described to audit and evaluate the management of these and other important clinical problems [2, 4].

Immunisation

Similar principles to the ones described above can be applied to any of a wide range of OHS issues. Immunisation is another example. Salient quality issues need to be addressed by effectively and efficiently fulfilling all the following steps:
- Identification of infections for which immunisation may be part of a control strategy is the first step.
- A full detailed evaluation is then needed for each of the possible immunisations based on information such as background frequency of the infection or of the carrier state, job specific risk assessment (including implications for HCW as well as patients), effectiveness of the specific immunisation procedure, side effects, and finally health economics. By addressing these issues in the context of each other and of the whole control strategy, the appropriate immunisation priorities are set.
- Identification of the target HCW population for each immunisation follows.
- Methods are needed for calling HCW for immunisation, logging of relevant employee and immunisation details, provision of information to HCW, and to management (in summary form).
- Mechanisms for recording, investigating and reporting apparent unwanted effects need to be in place.
- Subsequently means are needed for recall of HCW for completion of immunisation and/or for post immunisation serology (where relevant).
- Review of OHS immunisation activity and outcome, e.g. confirmed side-effects, and post immunisation serology (where relevant) is essential to complete the quality assurance process.

Relationships with other parties, and conclusion

Since international quality standards of the ISO 9000 type are gaining in popularity and in application in industry it is not surprising that employers of HCW and providers of OHS may seek their extrapolation to the health care sector [3]. However, the extension of such quality management systems to OHS requires careful consideration. The focus should be on those aspects which are crucial to occupational health and not merely those that can be easily measured and audited. Thus the strategy and tactics for workplace environment monitoring, the identification of workers at significant risk, the purpose, sensitivity and specificity of health surveillance questionnaires and those for initial health assessment [7], are all vital components of quality OHS for HCW. However, confirming the calibration of spirometers or of other equipment is not enough. Therefore certified quality management systems which do not address the scientific, epidemiological and clinical validity of the practice of Occupational Health could be an exercise of limited value. Internal methods of assuring quality within the OHS need to work hand in hand with other mechanisms the ongoing assurance of professional quality and of client satisfaction:

- Review of compliance with the Service Level Agreement binding the OHS provider and the purchaser (such as the hospital or other employing health authority).
- Review by a 'Users' Committee' which would include the purchaser as above but also representatives of the HCWs who utilise the OHS.
- External professional peer review to address issues such as the conformity of practice with the scientific evidence base.

References

1   http://www.agius.com/hew/resource/quality.htm Quality and Audit in Occupational Health
2   Agius RM, Lee R, Fletcher GM, Uttley J. Quantitative methods in evaluation - the medical audit. In Westerholm P, Menckel E (Eds). Evaluation and Development in Occupational Health. Butterworth-Heinemann. London 1999 (in press)
3   MacDonald EB (Ed.). Quality and Audit in Occupational Health. London: Faculty of Occupational Medicine of the Royal College of Physicians of London, 1995
4   van der Weide WE, Verbeek JHAM, van Dijk FJH, Doef J. An audit of occupational health care for employees with low-back pain. Occup Med 1997; 47:294-300
5   Agius RM, Lee RJ, Symington IS, Riddle HFV, Seaton A. An audit of occupational medicine consultation records. Occup Med 1994;44:151-157
6   Agius RM, Seaton A, Lee RJ. Audit of sickness absence and fitness-for-work referrals. Occup Med 1995;45:125-130
7   Whitaker S, Aw T-C. Audit of pre-employment assessments by occupational health departments in the National Health Service. Occup Med 1995;45:75-80

Occupational Health for Health Care Workers - A Practical Guide
H.-M. Hasselhorn, A. Toomingas and M. Lagerström (Editors)

Inspections in health care institutions

Heléne Harder, Friedrich Hofmann

In order to work successfully and effectively, the occupational health service (OHS) should know a) the workers, b) the specific occupational hazards, c) the working conditions and d) the work environment. This implies that the OHS personnel should be acquainted with the work place. Both spontaneous and regular inspections are important in achieving such knowledge. In this contribution, we present different types of workplace inspections aimed at improving the working conditions. National laws and guidelines may in many countries regulate similar or differing procedures.

Two different types of inspections are presented here:
- *Internal inspections* where only staff of the respective health care institution participate
- *External inspections* where representatives of institutions outside the hospital participate

The employer is responsible for the work environment and usually delegates risk assessment to other institutions, usually to the OHS which has the necessary expertise. Still, the employer remains responsible for organising regular internal and all external work place inspections. This should not become the task of the OHS. The participants should be selected in a way that a renders a comprehensive assessment possible of the different aspects of the total working environment (e.g. infectious, chemical, physical, psychosocial hazards, risks of accidents). It is fundamental that hospital management itself be represented.

Internal inspections

Commonly, internal inspections of work sites are performed as part of a systematic evaluation of all work areas within the institution (including administration). These inspections should take into account all potential hazards to staff working there. These may even include psychosocial hazards. The employer should call the following members to join the inspection: an OHS physician/nurse, safety engineer, safety delegate, representative of management and workers or labour union, medical representative of the department, and other people with special knowledge about the local working conditions or special risks. It may be useful to perform internal inspections on average once a year. Visits of high risk departments (e.g. intensive care, oncology, pathology, technical service, laundry) may be more frequent than inspections of low risk units (e.g. administration, schools).

At the beginning of an inspection, common and specific problems of the respective unit should be discussed. Thereafter all rooms (including cellar-, loft-, storage- and technical rooms) should be inspected and hazards should be noted. Examples might include:

- *ergonomics*: architecture of workplaces, space, seating (chairs), height -adjustable patient beds (+ functional check), patient hoists (+ functional check)?
- *floors, stairs*: skid-proof, hand rail, illumination?
- *illumination*: optimal intensity, presence of glare?
- *climate*: ventilation, temperature, humidity, planned preventative maintenance of e.g. airconditioning?
- *electrical installations*: plugs/wall sockets damaged, number of plugs/wall sockets sufficient, visible cables correctly and safely positioned?
- *escape routes*: marked, illuminated, emergency doors unlocked?
- *fire doors*: always closed, closing area of automatic doors always kept free?
- *fire extinguishers*: visible, easy access, sufficient number, correct classification, regularly checked, regular staff training on handling and use?
- *emergency plans*: visible, correct?
- *waste disposal procedures*: organised, followed?
- *sharps disposal procedures*: enough and appropriate disposal containers, well distributed, used?

Many more common as well as unusual, specific hazards have to be inspected depending on the particular characteristics of the worksite. Staff working in the respective areas may be asked about the working conditions including psychosocial aspects and even work organisation may be discussed.

The hospital management is responsible for production of an inspection report and usually will delegate this task to one of the participants, e.g. the OHS. The inspection report should

- give a general description of the working conditions in the respective area,
- document the observations made (establishment of hazards and risks),
- identify possible means of control,
- decide on the need for further investigations,
- designate persons responsible for improvements arising out of each observation,
- lay down a deadline for enacting the measures,
- make sure that the measures are carried out (which is the responsibility of the management).

A reliable recall system for the necessary measures is essential. Those responsible for the improvement have to inform the person in charge of the inspection report about the steps taken. A second and more informal inspection may verify effective improvement. A short final report to all involved and the management will discuss whether and how the control of hazards mentioned earlier has been improved.

External inspections

National institutions responsible for supervising working conditions usually have the right of access to working areas where hazardous conditions are suspected. Such "external inspections" may concern the whole hospital, but are usually restricted to specific work sites. They are carried out by Labour Inspectors (LI) who must have good knowledge about the respective working conditions as well as specific legislation.

External inspection may be performed
- on demand by employees of the hospital (e.g. safety representative, OHS staff),
- in investigating a serious accident at work,
- as part of district-wide investigation of specific working conditions (e.g. all emergency units known to have increased work pressure),
- as part of a nation-wide supervision project aimed at specific work sites. (e.g. to reduce overexertion injuries),
- because a statute may need to be revised (e.g. because of changed working conditions due to a new technical development or because new EU-legislation needs to be incorporated),
- because new knowledge about working conditions has emerged from e.g. work injury statistics, current research, contacts with the trade unions, media or other authorities.

In Sweden, almost all external inspections are announced to management a good time ahead and unannounced inspections are only accomplished in exceptional cases. The aim is to secure the co-operation of all parties involved and not to confront.

External inspections may focus on the physical working environment (e.g. worksite and ventilation, exposure to cytotoxic drugs, lifting and handling) or on both physical and psychosocial factors.

System inspections

"System inspection" is a method of external inspection of big companies and hospitals that has been developed by the Labour Inspectorate to investigate the employer's internal control [1] of the working environment. The method is also especially suitable when examining psychosocial aspects of the working environment. System inspections are carried out in several stages in which several inspectors take part. After a first contact between the inspector and the management a working group is appointed. The inspectors have special competence and expertise for example the physical or the psychosocial environment.

A system inspection usually begins with an introductory meeting with the employer and the representative of the workers or trade union where the reason for the inspection and the proceedings are presented. At this meeting a plan for the inspection is drawn up. A system inspection may last several days depending on the size and complexity of the department.

Next, the departments of interest are visited and discussions held between different groups of staff and the inspectors. The risks encountered are analysed and presented at a meeting with the directors of the clinic and representatives of the workers or trade union.

A system inspection almost always results in an inspection report to the employer. In this report, the Labour Inspectorate delivers an opinion on the working conditions of interest and formulates specific demands to the employer for improvement. The employer's response to the demanded improvements is made in a written reply to the Labour Inspectorate or through a new visit to the place of work. If the employer omits to undertake the measures demanded by the Labour Inspectorate judicial proceedings can be instituted and fines may result. Decisions of the Labour Inspectorate can be appealed both by the employer and by the trade union.

Reference

1   Statute Book of the Swedish National Board of Occupational Safety and Health.Internal Control of the Working Environment.(AFS:1992:6), Solna, Sweden

Occupational Health for Health Care Workers - A Practical Guide
H.-M. Hasselhorn, A. Toomingas and M. Lagerström (Editors)

Occupationally acquired infectious diseases - general aspects

Hans-Martin Hasselhorn, Allan Toomingas

Infectious diseases pose a constant occupational hazard for health care workers (HCW). Hygienic measures, such as the use of standard and universal precautions, isolation measures, vaccination and screening as well as diagnosis in early stage of disease have dramatically reduced the occupational health risk for HCW in industrialised countries. Still, the occupational health service (OHS) has to deal with (possible) occupational exposure to numerous common as well as rare infectious agents. Those infectious diseases with most importance for occupational health in health care are described in separate chapters in this book. In this chapter, a proposal for an "Infectious diseases prevention programme" and vaccinations as one part of such a programme are presented, together with specific aspects on pregnancy and other topics.

Infectious diseases prevention programme

An effective infectious diseases prevention programme is an ongoing multidisciplinary activity, which can be organised by the OHS and operates as part of the hospital's management strategy. The activities need to be co-ordinated among hospital administration, hygiene, medical staff, union/workers representatives, occupational health authorities and other associated programmes such as waste management and needlestick prevention. The overall aims of an infectious diseases prevention programme are to effectively reduce the disease burden on the employees and, in turn, the level of absence and resultant costs. Three key aspects of the programme will be considered.

Programme development and evaluation
- The occurrence of infectious diseases needs to be monitored and analysed in relation to frequency, health effects, absenteeism and costs.
- Personnel at risk have to be defined in terms of care and non care professions, permanent, temporary, voluntary, contractual and out-of-hospital personnel.
- Legal requirements should be reviewed. These include laws and/or guidelines concerning hospital hygiene, vaccination, exclusion from duty, record keeping and confidentiality. Fulfilment of legal requirements and responsibilities needs to be evaluated.
- The aims of the programme such as reduction of infection-related sick leave and costs need to be determined.
- Responsibilities need to be defined in relation to organisation, costs and authority over definition and enforcement of measures such as work restrictions or exclusion from duty.

- All activities related to infection control need to be documented.
- The aims, methods, results and responsibilities of the programme need to be reviewed as part of a continuing quality assurance system, with modifications made as necessary.

Contents of programme, medical evaluation and treatment
- The occupational health examination of staff should include a pre-employment/pre-placement interview and immune status check for previous infections, a vaccination update (Table 1), and a health inventory to assess risk factors for acquiring/transmitting infections. Follow-up of protection may be necessary such as a PPD skin test or booster immunisation against diphtheria every ten years. Vaccination and immunity records need to be documented.
- Adherence to hygienic precautions needs to be promoted.
- Vaccination campaigns can be performed.
- Continuous access to postexposure prophylaxis needs to be provided to protect against infections such as HIV, HBV or meningococcal meningitis.
- Treatment of infections may be an identified component within the programme.
- Counselling of staff by OHS should be part of the programme to cover concerns such as those in relation to pregnancy and exposure to infectious diseases, and to give advice to the HCW who becomes infected.

Information and education
- Understandable and adapted information should be provided to HCW about risks and their prevention covering subjects such as infection control policies, vaccination, postexposure prophylaxis, and reporting procedures for occupational diseases.
- The OHS should inform the hospital management about infection risks, epidemiology and prevention.
- An awareness of the responsibility of the employer as well as employees should be promoted.
- OHS expertise should be considered when planning/installing new work places.

Establishing a vaccination programme

European Union directives (90/697/EWG; 93/88/EWG) and very often national legislation demand that an employer must offer susceptible employees free vaccination against infectious agents when vaccination and occupational exposure is possible. Whether a HCW should be classified as "possibly exposed", however, may be difficult to define for a specific disease in a specific working location. Conflicts due to different views may arise between employees, hospital management and the OHS. It can be helpful to set up a "vaccination programme" for the hospital which combines knowledge of epidemiology and infectious diseases (Table 1). Within this programme, it should be determined separately for each working area, which vaccinations should be compulsory (e.g. hepatitis B), which should be *strongly* recommended or recommended and to whom they should be given (including volunteers, students and other staff not employed by the hospital). Informative vaccination campaigns may lead to higher vaccine acceptance among personnel. The programme should be approved by hospital management and unions or workers' representatives.

Table 1. Vaccinations and post exposure measures for health care personnel

d=day(s); w=week(s); mo=month(s); y=year(s); vacc=vaccination; Pv=primary vaccination; Bd=booster dose

Infectious agent	Who should be vaccinated?	Vaccination scheme	Immunity check after vacc?	Immunity begins after Pv/Bd	Post exposure measures
Diphtheria	all HCW	Pv: mo 0,1,6-12 Bd: every 10 y In case of epidemic: one Bd to all whose last vacc >5 y ago	no	Pv: 14 d after 2nd dose Bd: 4 d	antibiotics, antitoxin
Hepatitis A	HCW at increased risk (e.g. in infection wards, emergency, paediatrics, travelling HCW)	Pv: mo 0,6-12 Bd: every 10 y	no	Pv: 2 w after 1st dose	immuno-globulin within 2 w +/-vacc; possibly vacc alone*
Hepatitis B	all (susceptible) HCW with possible contact with blood or blood-contaminated material, including cleaning and janitorial staff	Pv: mo 0,1, 6-12 rapid course: mo 0,1,2,12 Bd: differing proposals - no booster - every 10 y	Yes >4-12 w after last dose	Pv: 2 w after 2nd dose (85% of all vaccinees)	vacc simul-taneously with specific hepatitis B immuno-globulin within 48 hours
Influenza	all HCW, especially gerontology, infectious diseases, oncology	yearly vacc	no	2 w	antivirals within 2 d of onset of ill-ness (reduce severity and duration)
Measles	all (susceptible) HCW	at least one vacc to HCW suspected to be unprotected	no	4 w	none

to be continued on page 29

continued
Table 1. Vaccinations and post exposure measures for health care personnel

d=day(s); w=week(s); mo=month(s); y=year(s); vacc=vaccination; Pv=primary vaccination; Bd=booster dose

Infectious agent	Who should be vaccinated?	Vaccination scheme	Immunity check after vacc?	Immunity begins after Pv/Bd	Post exposure measures
Meningococcal disease	HCW exposed to strains A, C, Y and W-135 (esp. laboratory)	Pv: 1 dose Bd: need unknown	no	1-2 w	rifampicin or ciprofloxacin; ceftriaxone (in pregnancy)
Mumps	all (susceptible) HCW	at least one vacc to HCW suspected to be unprotected	no	4 w	none
Poliomyelitis	all HCW (different regulations worldwide, usually inactivated polio vaccine, IPV)	Pv: IPV mo 1,3,6-12 Bd: IPV or oral polio vaccine (OPV)	no	Pv: 14 d after 2nd IPV dose Bd: 4 d after IPV	possibly Bd: OPV
Pertussis	possibly all HCW once acellular vaccine licensed for adults	possibly every 10 y	no	14 d after 2nd dose Bd: 4 d	antibiotics (macrolides)
Rabies	personnel working with animals with potential exposure	depends on vacc	no	14 d after 2nd dose Bd: 4 d	course of antirabies treatment
Rubella	all (susceptible) HCW	at least one vaccination to persons suspected to be unprotected	possibly in women of childbearing age	2 w	none
Tetanus	all HCW	Pv: mo 0,1,12 Bd: every 10 y	no	2 w after 2nd dose	hyperimmuno globulin + simultaneous vacc

to be continued on page 30

continued
Table 1. Vaccinations and post exposure measures for health care personnel

d=day(s); w=week(s); mo=month(s); y=year(s); vacc=vaccination; Pv=primary vaccination; Bd=booster dose

Infectious agent	Who should be vaccinated?	Vaccination scheme	Immunity check after vacc?	Immunity begins after Pv/Bd	Post exposure measures
Tuberculosis	none, some, or all HCW (different regulations world-wide)	Pv: BCG one dose Bd: none	no	6-8 w after Pv	(possibly) INH prophylaxis
Typhoid	stool handling laboratory staff	depending on vacc	no	2 w	none
Varicella	all (susceptible) HCW or seronegative HCW with contact to risk patients	Pv: w 0,4-8 **	no	2 w after 2nd dose	immunoglob-ulin within 3d if susceptible and pregnant, immuno-compromised, or HIV-infected

*   not accepted indication for vaccine alone in Sweden due to poor clinical documentation of effect
**   Exclusion from work with high risk patients following vaccination may be considered, although risk of transmission seems minimal

Personnel preparing to work in countries with different epidemiological and hygienic conditions should receive the necessary vaccinations and advice on preventing ill health that is relevant to that country.

Special considerations

Bloodborne transmission

The most commonly discussed bloodborne infections with occupational risk for HCW are hepatitis B, hepatitis C and HIV. A variety of other infectious diseases may also be transmitted by the same route, e.g. tuberculosis, blastomycosis, brucellosis, cowpox, cryptococcosis, diphtheria, gonorrhoea, leptospirosis, malaria, Marburg virus disease, non-HIV-retrovirus infections, staphylococcus infections, streptococcus infections, syphilis, and trypanosomiasis. Syphilis and tuberculosis may be prevalent among AIDS patients, and follow-up after a needlestick injury should take possible transmission into consideration.

Exclusion from duty

It may become necessary to exclude infected or potentially infected (exposed) HCW from duty to prevent further transmission. It must be clear which authority decides about this. Such decisions should be made using appropriate expertise in and knowledge of infectious disease and epidemiology. The OHS may be well placed to co-ordinate this process. This requires much effort, because such measures are often met with little understanding among HCW and their managers. This is especially so when no symptomatic disease is apparent, for example, when a varicella (VZV) negative HCW has had contact with a VZV patient. All personnel as well as hospital administration should know the diseases or symptoms among HCW which must be reported, the time scale for reporting and the manager to whom they should report. A non-judgemental atmosphere is very helpful in assisting HCW to openly disclose a possible infection. No financial or other disadvantages should result from such disclosure or exclusion from duty. Exclusion measures must be enforceable. When public laws require exclusion from work (e.g. in case of salmonella infection), in some countries the health care institution may receive financial compensation for the loss of the employees work force.

Exclusion from duty may also require that contact should also be avoided with susceptible people in private life. Conditions for return to work after exclusion must be clearly defined.

Pregnancy

Pregnant women do not seem to be more susceptible to infectious agents than others but some diseases like VZV infection may be more severe in this group [1]. Furthermore, infections during pregnancy may also affect the unborn child. Rubella and varicella are diseases associated with congenital diseases and malformations. The aim should be to vaccinate all seronegative women in childbearing age.

Currently, the most important problem in this respect is cytomegalovirus (CMV) infection. An increased risk of foetal neuronal damage exists when seronegative (and rarely seropositive) pregnant women are infected. This risk is very low but cannot be estimated exactly. Parvovirus (B19) infection in the mother may – in a few cases – lead to spontaneous abortion, but again, not much is known about the real risk (see respective chapters). When counselling pregnant women after close exposure to CMV or B19, occupational health personnel should inform the women about the risks in a sensitive manner, but at the same time prevent undue worry in favour of a positive attitude to the pregnancy. These two aspects may be difficult to combine.

The question, as to whether CMV or B19 negative pregnant women need to be excluded from work in paediatric care to minimise risk of infection is being discussed. The benefit of such measures is likely to be extremely low. Universal solutions of these problems are not possible and individual evaluation may be the best way of dealing with them.

In some countries, the law puts restrictions on working tasks for pregnant women. One example is in Germany, where pregnant women are not formally allowed to perform invasive procedures that bear an increased risk of acquiring infectious diseases. It is therefore practically almost impossible for a pregnant woman to work as a dentist in Germany.

Limitations

In most chapters in this book which relate to specific infectious diseases, preventive measures are proposed. In different countries, however, there may be different prevalences of disease, different legislation, and different levels of risk awareness. The health care resources available and varying attitudes towards preventive measures are additional factors that will affect what can be achieved. Taking these aspects into consideration, the readers may integrate the proposed measures into their practice within whatever constraints apply.

Practical guidelines for infection control relating to HCW have been published in the USA by the Centers for Disease Control and Prevention (CDC). These may provide additional information to occupational health personnel [1, 2].

References

1   CDC. Guideline for infection control in health care personnel, 1998. AJIC 1998;26:289-354
      (http://www.cdc.gov/ncidod/hip/Guide/infectcont98.htm)
2   CDC. Immunization of Health-Care Workers: Recommendations of the Advisory Committee
      on Immunization Practices (ACIP) and the Hospital Infection Control Practices Advisory
      Committee (HICPAC). MMWR 1997;46(RR-18):1-44

Occupational Health for Health Care Workers - A Practical Guide
H.-M. Hasselhorn, A. Toomingas and M. Lagerström (Editors)
© 1999 Elsevier Science B.V. All rights reserved.

Hygienic infection control

Thomas Kistemann

In this chapter, barrier protection is discussed as a substantial component of infection control for health care personnel. Barrier protection often called barrier nursing includes measures such as hand washing and hand antisepsis, use of gloves, gowns, masks, protective eye-wear, etc, safe working devices and procedures, ventilation processes, rooming including isolation and transport restrictions for patients, cleaning and disinfection protocols. Education of staff is essential.

Routes of transmission are similar and often overlap for patients and staff. Thus, control of infection in health care personnel has to be integrated into the general program for infection control in any health care setting. Current isolation precautions should also be applied for the protection of staff from patients with infections [1].

Isolation protocols are many and may differ considerably from country to country. In this chapter, we present the recommendations of the Centers for Disease Control and Prevention (CDC) for U.S. hospitals. However, national and local hospital guidelines should be observed where they exist.

Initially, isolation recommendations by the CDC were *category-specific* [2], comprising seven categories of isolation and precaution and an alternative *disease-specific isolation* system in its last update [3].

Universal precautions

After previous recommendations in 1985 and 1986, largely because of the HIV epidemic and initial reports of hospital personnel becoming infected with HIV through needlesticks and skin contamination with patients' blood, the CDC published recommendations for prevention of HIV transmission in health-care settings in 1987 [4]. In acknowledgement of the fact that many patients with bloodborne infections are not identified, these new guidelines recommend the application of blood and body fluid precautions *universally* to all patients, which led to the name of Universal Precautions (UP). UP apply to blood, semen, vaginal secretions, cerebrospinal fluid, synovial fluid, pleural fluid, peritoneal fluid, pericardial fluid, amniotic fluid, and any body fluid containing visible blood.

UP include the following measures:
- Appropriate barrier protection should routinely be followed to avoid skin and mucous membrane contamination with blood or body fluids from *any* patient.
- Gloves are required for contact with blood and body fluids, mucous membranes, or non-intact skin, when handling surfaces or items soiled with blood or body fluids.

They should be used for performing vascular access procedures, when the HCW has breaks in the skin; when hand contamination with blood is anticipated (uncooperative patients, children); when staff are receiving phlebotomy training.

- Gloves should be changed after every patient contact. They should not be washed or disinfected.
- Masks and protective eyewear or face shields shall be worn when procedures are likely to generate aerosols or droplets of blood or body fluids.
- Gowns are required when splashes of fluid might soil clothing.
- Hands or skin contaminated with blood or body fluids shall be washed immediately.
- Hands should be washed after removing gloves. (For hand disinfection see below.)
- Precautions should be taken to prevent sharps or needlestick injuries. Needles should not be recapped, removed from disposable syringes; sharp instruments should immediately after use be placed in a puncture-resistant container.
- Mouthpieces and resuscitation bags or other ventilation devices should be readily available for use in areas where resuscitation procedures may be anticipated.
- HCW with exsudative skin lesions or weeping dermatitis should not be involved in direct patient care or handle patient care equipment.
- Pregnant HCW should be especially familiar with and should strictly follow the concepts of UP.

In 1988, an update [5] emphasises especially that blood is the single most important source of bloodborne pathogens, and that therefore infection control efforts must focus on preventing exposures to blood, as well as on delivery of HBV immunisation.

UP protect HCW against unidentified bloodborne pathogens and have superseded previous blood and body fluid precautions. They have the advantage of simplicity, as the blood and body fluid category applies to all patients. But on the other hand, it is often difficult at the bedside to decide where a body fluid comes from and whether it contains blood.

Body Substance Isolation

Body Substance Isolation (BSI) has been outlined as an alternative to CDC recommendations since 1987 [6, 7]. This system designates *all patients* as potentially infectious and is in this similar to the UP concept, but it differs in that barrier precautions are used to prevent contact with *all body substances*. The central statement is, that gloves should be used for anticipated contact with blood, mucous membranes, nonintact skin, secretions, and moist body substances of all patients.

New guideline for isolation precautions

Summarising the various previous guidelines, the CDC published a new guideline for isolation precautions in hospitals in 1996 [8]. This guideline contains two tiers of procedures. The first tier incorporates the major features of UP and BSI and decreases the risk of transmission from diagnosed as well as unrecognised infections and is called *standard precautions*. These apply to all patients and the following body substances: Blood, all body fluids, secretions, excretions (except sweat), nonintact skin and mucous membranes.

Standard precautions

They comprise the following recommendations:
- *Hand washing* should be performed to remove soiling after touching blood, body fluids, secretions, excretions, and contaminated items; if gloves have been worn, immediately after removal; between patient contacts and whenever transfer of micro-organisms to other patients, to other body sites of the same patient or to environments is to be feared. (Many national and local guidelines differ in this from the CDC proposals and recommend hand disinfection instead of hand washing for all purposes.)
- *Hand disinfection* should be performed to remove transient microbial flora under specific circumstances, as defined by the hospitals infection control program (see contact precautions below).
- *Gloves* should be worn when in contact with blood, body fluids, secretions, excretions, and contaminated items; removal promptly after use, before touching uncontaminated items and environmental surfaces.
- *Mask, eye protection, face shield* should be worn during procedures and patient-care activities that are likely to generate splashes or sprays of blood, body fluids, secretions, and excretions onto mucous membranes of the eyes, nose, and mouth.
- *Gowns* should be worn during procedures and patient-care activities that are likely to generate splashes or sprays of blood, body fluids, secretions, and excretions onto skin and clothing.
- *Patient-Care equipment, linen* should be handled in a manner that prevents skin and mucous membrane exposures, contamination of clothing, and transfer of micro-organisms to other patients and environments, if soiled with blood, body fluids, secretions, and excretions.
- *Environmental control* has to be ensured by appropriate procedures for the routine care, cleaning, and disinfection of environmental surfaces.
- *Sharp instruments and needles* should be handled with care to prevent injuries. Used needles should never be recapped or otherwise be manipulated using both hands or directing the point of a needle toward any part of the body. When recapping is necessary, either a onehanded scoop technique or a mechanical device should be used. Used needles should not be removed from syringes or otherwise be manipulated by hand. Used sharp items should be placed in appropriate puncture-resistant containers for disposal or transport to the reprocessing area.
- *Mouthpieces and resuscitation bags or other ventilation devices* should be readily available for use in areas where the need for resuscitation is predictable.
- *Private rooms* should be available for patients who contaminate the environment or cannot assist in maintaining appropriate hygiene or environmental control.

Transmission-based precautions

The second tier summarises *transmission-based precautions*. They are designed for patients with documented or suspected infection with highly transmissible or epidemiologically important pathogens. The former category-specific and disease-specific isolation precautions have been merged into three types of transmission-based precautions:

- *Airborne precautions*: for patients known or suspected to have serious illnesses transmitted by airborne droplet nuclei (especially pulmonary tuberculosis): private room or cohorting, negative air pressure, 6-12 air changes per hour, appropriate discharge of air outdoors or high-efficiency filtration before circulation; closed door, transport of the patient limited to essential purposes, with surgical mask; respiratory protection for HCW in case of tuberculosis, and for susceptible HCW entering the room;
- *Droplet precautions*: for patients known or suspected to have serious illnesses transmitted by large particle droplets (invasive Haemophilus influenzae type b disease, invasive Neisseriae meningitidis disease, diphtheria, pertussis, influenza, rubella etc): private room or cohorting, at least spatial separation of 3ft; transport of the patient limited to essential purposes, with surgical mask; mask within 3ft of the patient;
- *Contact precautions*: for patients known or suspected to have serious illnesses transmitted by direct patient contact or by contact with items in the patients environment (gastrointestinal, respiratory, skin, or wound infections or colonisations with multidrug-resistant bacteria of special clinical and epidemiological significance; enteric infections with a low infectious dose or prolonged environmental survival; RSV, parainfluenza virus, or enteroviral infections in infants and young children; skin infections that are highly contagious; viral/haemorrhagic conjunctivitis; viral haemorrhagic infections): private room or cohorting, transport limited to essential purposes, patient-care equipment dedicated to one patient (or cohort); gloves, when entering the room, change of gloves after contact with infective material, removal of gloves before leaving the room, immediate handwashing with an antimicrobial agent; gowns when soiling is anticipated.

Training and education

In-service training and education on infection control is necessary annually and whenever the need arises. It should be appropriate and specific for the work assignments, so that personnel can maintain accurate and up-to-date knowledge about the essential elements of infection control. The following topics have to be included in the initial training on infection control [1]:

- Hand washing and disinfection;
- Modes of transmission of infections;
- Importance of complying with standard and transmission-based precautions;
- Importance of reporting certain illnesses or conditions;

- Tuberculosis control;
- Importance of complying with reporting procedures in case of exposure to blood and body fluids to prevent transmission of bloodborne pathogens;
- Importance of co-operating with infection control staff during outbreak investigations;
- Importance of staff screening and immunisation programs.

All staff should be aware if they suffer from medical conditions or are receiving medical treatment that may render them more susceptible to or more likely to transmit infections. Specific written policies and procedures for control of infection in healthcare personnel have to be readily available to all personnel.

References

1   CDC. Guideline for infection control in healthcare personnel. Infect control Hosp Epidemiol 19;1998:407-493 (http://www.cdc.gov/ncidod/hip/guide/infectcont98.htm)
2   CDC. Isolation Techniques for Use in Hospitals. DHEW publication no. (PHS) 70-2054. Washington, D.C.: U.S. Government Printing Office, 1970
3   Garner JS, Simmons BP. Guideline for isolation precautions in hospitals. Infect Control 1983;4:245-325
4   CDC. Recommendations for prevention of HIV transmission in health-care settings. MMWR 1987;36(suppl.2S):1S-18S (http://www.cdc.gov/epo/mmwr/preview/mmwrhtml/00023587.htm)
5   CDC. Perspectives in disease prevention and health promotion update: universal precautions for preventing of transmission of human immunodeficiency virus, hepatitis B virus, and other bloodborne pathogens in health-care settings. MMWR 1988;37:377-388 (http://www.cdc.gov/epo/mmwr/preview/mmwrhtml/00000039.htm)
6   Lynch P, Jackson MM, Cummings MJ, Stamm WE. Rethinking the role of isolation practices in the prevention of nosocomial infections. Ann Intern Med 1987;107:243-246
7   Lynch P, Cummings MJ, Roberts PL, Herriot MJ, Yates B, Stamm WE. Implementing and evaluating a system of generic infection precautions: body substance isolation. Am J Infect Control 1990;18:1-12
8   Garner JS and the Hospital Infection Control Practices Advisory Committee. Guideline for isolation precautions in hospitals. Infect Control Hosp Epidemiol 1996;17:53-80 (http://www.cdc.gov/ncidod/hip/isolat/isolat.htm)

Further Reading

- Patterson JE. Isolation of patients with communicable diseases. In: Mayhall CG (Ed). Hospital Epidemiology and Infection Control. Baltimore: Williams&Wilkins, 1996:1032-1051
- Beekman SE, Henderson DK. Controversies in isolation policies and practices. In: Wenzel RP (Ed). Prevention and control of nosocomial infections. Baltimore: Williams&Wilkins, 1997:71-84
- Doebbeling BN. Protecting Healthcare Workers from infection and injury. In: Wenzel RP (Ed). Prevention and control of nosocomial infections. Baltimore: Williams&Wilkins, 1997:397-435

Occupational Health for Health Care Workers - A Practical Guide
H.-M. Hasselhorn, A. Toomingas and M. Lagerström (Editors)

Management of needlestick injuries

Ian S. Symington

Needlestick injuries occur frequently in health care workers (HCW) but many go unreported. The term is used when needles and other sharp objects that have been in contact with blood, puncture the skin and present a risk of blood borne infection. These risks also occur when blood splashes on to broken skin surfaces; when there is contamination of the mucous membranes of the eye, nose or mouth; and when a human bite breaks the skin. In this chapter, the term needlestick injury will be used to cover all these circumstances.

Sharps-injury rates vary among different groups of hospital staff, with high rates (between 25 and 80%) reported [1] in medical students and junior doctors during their first year in post. High-risk situations occur during surgical procedures and when medicines are being injected, but the sharps disposal phase is also critical. Re-sheathing needles has been identified as a potentially hazardous practice and failure to use robust receptacles for disposal can lead to serious risks for laundry workers, cleaners and sterile supplies staff.

Adverse health effects

Transmission of blood borne viruses, (BBV's) is the main concern although bacteriological causes should also be borne in mind. Hepatitis B virus (HBV), Human Immunodeficiency virus (HIV) and hepatitis C (HCV) are all recognised as having been transmitted to HCW through occupational injury. The approximate risk of transmission from a confirmed infected source is estimated as:
- 30% for HBV when detectable e antigen (HBeAg) is present,
- 3% for HCV infection, and
- 0.3% for HIV infection.

While most needlestick injuries do not lead to transmission of infection, the uncertainty about the outcome can also cause considerable distress and anxiety for many HCW. Consequently prompt assessment and treatment is of importance in the management of these injuries.

During the assessment, the possibility of other viruses, bacteria or parasites should be considered. Herpes simplex, syphilis, and malaria are all treatable conditions, which have potential for transmission. The susceptibility of AIDS patients to tuberculosis should raise awareness of this additional infection in a seriously ill patient.

First aid measures

All HCW should be familiar with the first aid measures to be taken immediately after a needlestick injury:
- Encourage bleeding by gentle squeezing but do not suck the area.
- Wash with soap and warm running water.
- Treat mucosal surfaces such as the mouth or conjunctivae of the eye by rinsing with warm water or saline.

Following first aid all injured employees should immediately seek further advice from the occupational health service or other departments designated to provide advice and treatment.

Risk assessment

Those providing advice and treatment should first of all have access to a risk assessment of the key factors involved before recommending a particular course of action. An assessment of the injury should record the procedure involved (such as suturing or giving an injection) and should focus on those factors known to affect the likelihood of transmission:
- Type of needle: Hollow bore needles and longer needles have higher risk.
- Depth of injury: Deeper injuries have higher risk
- Presence of blood in syringe or needle: The bigger the volume the higher the risk

An assessment of the source blood can, if negative for BBV's, give the most specific reassurance available to the injured HCW although there is still a chance of a high risk subject being seronegative while incubating an infection. If the result is positive, this can ensure the treatment given is appropriate to the risk. In practice, the assessment is best undertaken by the clinicians directly involved in the source patient's care. It will involve establishing whether that patient comes into any group at high risk of contracting a BBV infection. The list of questions normally used by blood transfusion services to exclude potentially infected donors is a helpful checklist for clinicians to use:
- Have you ever been told you are positive for HBV, HIV or HCV?
- If you are a man have you ever had sex with another man?
- Have you ever injected yourself with drugs?
- Have you ever lived in countries with a high prevalence of HIV, HBV, or HCV?
- Have you ever been with a prostitute at any time?
- Have you ever had sex with a person in any of the above groups?

If the source blood is traced to an individual who is already known to be positive for a BBV, further confirmation for that infection may not be needed. If not, all those identified should be asked if they would be willing to have blood tested for BBV's. Such enquiries should be handled with the utmost sensitivity and without undue pressure on the individual to comply. To meet ethical guidelines, no testing should be undertaken without obtaining fully informed consent, and appropriate confidentiality should be maintained.

When it is not possible to identify the source blood, the risk assessment becomes less precise. In these situations there is still an opportunity to up-date the hepatitis B immunisation status of the injured HCW but, as described in the following section on prophylaxis, it is unlikely that HIV prophylaxis will be indicated without clearer information on the source.

Prophylactic treatment

The information obtained from the risk assessment will enable those treating the individual to make a reasonable judgement on what action to take. The three main BBV's will be dealt with separately.

Hepatitis B

A high proportion of HCW will have been immunised with hepatitis B vaccine. Those with a proven immunologically satisfactory ($\geq$100 IU/L) response after a full course of vaccine will have long standing protection and following needlestick injury no further action against hepatitis B may be required
While no universally accepted protocol has been agreed many practitioners consider it good practice to give a booster dose of HBV vaccine to those considered incompletely protected following a needlestick injury. This group may include:
- those who have not had a hepatitis B surface antibody (anti-HBs) check after a full primary course or on whom results are not known
- those who reached 10-99 IU/L (anti-HBs) after a full primary course but had the last dose more than two years ago

Similarly no universally accepted protocol has been agreed to define those who are unprotected. They may be expected to include:
- those who have not been immunised
- those who failed to reach 10 IU/L (anti-HBs) after a full primary course
- those who have started but not completed a full primary course.

For this unprotected group a booster dose of HBV vaccine should be given or the first dose of a rapid schedule course (three injections within 2 months) for those previously unimmunised. In addition, specific hepatitis B immunoglobulin should be given if the source blood is considered high risk or proven to be infectious (HBsAg positive $\pm$ HBeAg positive). (see chapter "Hepatitis B and D")

Human Immunodeficiency Virus

No vaccine is currently available but a case control study [2] has shown that post exposure prophylaxis with Zidovudine may reduce transmission of HIV by around 79% in cases where the source blood was known to be HIV positive. It is thought that a combination of 2 or more anti-retroviral drugs will give better protection and should be considered when a) the source patient is known to be HIV positive or considered to be at high risk and b) when the injury has been significant (see earlier paragraph) or when the source patient has acute or end stage HIV infection

Time is of the essence and ideally therapy should commence within 1 hour of the injury, although in practice this represents a tight timescale. When the HIV status of the source blood is unknown but the history suggests high risk factors, prophylactic treatment can be started prior to the result of the HIV test being available. It is helpful, therefore, if "starter packs" of prophylactic medication can be made available with clear instructions on dose schedules, side effects, and contra-indications. Drugs currently in use for this purpose include Zidovudine, Lamivudine and Indinavir. It is advisable to draw up protocols and arrange treatment in conjunction with medical colleagues who are familiar with the use of these drugs and who can also take into account any variations required by the current medication regime of the source patient. Those who are started on prophylactic treatment will require to be followed-up at regular intervals to ensure that there are not problems related to the medication and to check HIV status to ensure that they are free from infection 6 months after the injury. Those who have received significant needlestick injuries but have not been able to receive reassurance by testing the source blood, can be offered follow-up testing of their own blood at 3 months and 6 months to ensure that they have not become HIV positive. (see chapter HIV/AIDS)

Hepatitis C

No vaccine or prophylactic treatment of proven value is currently available for hepatitis C. Anecdotal case reports [3, 4] on the use of Interferon following needlestick injuries involving HCV positive blood have demonstrated contradictory responses, but effective assessment of prophylaxis would require carefully structured clinical trials. Follow-up assessment for HCV infection [5], can, if negative, provide reassurance that no infection has occurred and, if positive, provide those who are infected with the opportunity to receive counselling regarding their risk of transmission to others and to be evaluated for treatment of established disease.

Health surveillance arrangements to identify early effects of HCV infection may include liver function tests (alanine aminotransferase) at 6 weeks, 3 months and 6 months with additional follow-up tests at 3 months and 6 months for HCV antibody. If access to a polymerase chain reaction (PCR) technique is available, assessment at 6 weeks may be helpful if liver function tests are abnormal or if the source blood is known to be HCV positive. (see chapter Hepatitis C)

Preventing needlestick injuries

Most needlestick injuries are preventable but educational efforts to achieve this goal have had limited effectiveness in producing behavioural change. Responsibility for tackling sharps injuries among HCW is often unclear. It is, however, the employer's obligation to make the clinical workplace as safe as realistically possible. By achieving this, not only is the risk of infection – and often the considerable anxiety for HCW - significantly reduced but so also is the potential liability on the healthcare organisation.

It may be possible to reduce the number of needlestick injuries in HCW when measures are being taken at different levels. In addition to ongoing education, a continuous and systematic review of hazardous working devices and working procedures is necessary. This should occur under the responsibility of the hospital management and requires close multidisciplinary co-operation. The following paragraphs give examples for interventions at different levels.

Education and training

If all HCW remained alert to the hazards arising from sharps, the frequency of needlestick injuries could be significantly reduced. The introduction of universal precautions has led to some behavioural changes affecting protective behaviour (e.g. use of gloves) but this has been less successful in other areas (e.g. resheathing). Although educational measures seem to have had limited effect, intensive training is necessary to ensure that all those involved are aware of the risks and are fully conversant with what is required. All personnel should know when needlestick injuries are likely to occur and how to prevent the development of these situations. Knowledge about the appropriate use of personal protective equipment such as gloves and masks and the need to cover cuts or broken skin with waterproof plasters, should be widespread. Compliance with universal precautions may be improved if each department established basic protective requirements for common types of invasive procedures. Before unskilled personnel perform venous access procedures, competency based training is imperative. Education includes providing comprehensive information about reporting procedures following a needlestick injury and such procedures must be kept as uncomplicated as possible and guarantee confidentiality.

Review of devices

Needleless devices, protected needle devices and shielded safety syringes or catheters are known to reduce the risk of needlestick injuries by > 70%. The use of equipment such as retractable lancets and vacuum tube blood collection systems should all be considered. In surgery, the use of electrocautery, vascular clips, staplers, blunt needles, scissors and free ligation may replace the use of sharp needles and scalpels. A multidisciplinary product evaluation team comprising representatives of management, the occupational health service, clinical staff with good knowledge of procedures, central supply, waste management and control of infection may review recent device developments and select new products [6]. In this way, features such as the product's efficacy, its safety for employees and patients and its costs are taken into account. Provisional testing in a selected user population provides the team with feedback about safety, practicability, and acceptance.

Review of procedures

A change of working procedures may effectively reduce the exposure risk. For example, double gloving reduces the amount of blood transferred in a needlestick injury. Instead of securing central venous catheters with sutures, this may be achieved by adhesive skin attachment devices. The use of needles for application of local anaesthetics may be replaced by use of a local anaesthetic cream. Unexpected patient movements during vascular access are known to lead to needlestick injuries. They may be reduced by use of local anaesthetics before placement of the intravenous device. It should be normal practice for all sharps to be disposed of into robust, needle-proof one-way containers at the point of use. These containers should be readily accessible in patient rooms and in nursing stations. They should not be overfilled.

Follow up of needlestick injuries

Although the number of reported needlestick injuries can be as low as 15% of all incidents, an analysis of these reports gives useful information for additional preventive measures. Consequently, for each reported event, information about the job category of the injured HCW, type and size of sharp, location and time of incident, location of injury, special procedures performed, and potential reporting delay should all be documented. "Carelessness" is often reported to be a "cause" of needlestick injuries, but – when thoroughly examined – the cause of the incident is often found to be a preventable factor such as time pressure, restricted work space, or the lack of a disposal container. Transmission of blood borne pathogens is disproportionally associated with venesection and other intravenous access procedures. These types of procedures should therefore be given high priority.

References

1   O'Neill TM, Abbott AV, Radecki SE. Risk of needlestick and occupational exposures among residents and medical students. Arch Intern Med 1992;152:1451-1456
2   CDC. Update: Provisional Public Health Service Recommendations for prophylaxis after occupational exposure to HIV. MMWR 1996;45:468-472
3   Nakano Y, Kiyosawa K, Sodeyama T, Tanaka E, Matsumoto A, Ichijo T, Mizokami M, Furuta S. Acute hepatitis C transmitted by needlestick accident despite short duration interferon treatment. J Gastroenterol Hepatol 1995;10:609-611
4   Noguchi S, Sata M, Suzuki H, Ohba K, Mizokami M, Tanikawa K. Early therapy with interferon for acute hepatitis C acquired through a needlestick. Clin Inf Dis 1997;24:992-994
5   CDC. Recommendations for follow-up of healthcare workers after occupational exposure to hepatitis C virus. MMWR 1997;46(26):603-606
6   Chiarello LA. Selection of needlestick prevention devices: a conceptual framework for approaching product evaluation. Am J Infect Control 1995;23:386-395

Further reading

•   Gerberding JL. Management of Occupational Exposures to Blood-Borne Viruses. N Engl J Med 1995; 332:144-151

Occupational Health for Health Care Workers - A Practical Guide
H.-M. Hasselhorn, A. Toomingas and M. Lagerström (Editors)

The hepatitis B, hepatitis C or HIV infectious health care worker

Hans-Martin Hasselhorn

Occupational transmission to patients of hepatitis B virus (HBV), hepatitis C virus (HCV) and HIV from an infected health care worker (HCW) shares common features, and prevention demands similar measures. When dealing with the question of work restrictions for infectious HCW, the occupational health service (OHS) may have a central role: often, the OHS is the first to become aware of the serological status of the HCW. In addition, occupational health physicians who are governed by rules of strict confidentiality, may serve as an advocate for the infected HCW. Thereby, they may play a key role in the decision-making process concerning whether or which working restrictions are imposed on an infectious HCW. This paper aims to give an overview of the size and significance of this topic and includes proposals for how to proceed when this situation arises.

HBV

HBV transmissions from infected HCW to patients were more common before the introduction of HBV vaccine but do still occur even in countries with high vaccination coverage of medical personnel. An analysis of internationally published reports of 31 respective cases (dating from 1971 to 1996 and including transmissions to at least 289 patients) shows that the circumstances of transmission are often very similar, suggesting the key areas for preventive measures:

- The medical professions involved are almost always surgeons, especially cardiothoracic and gynaecological. Transmissions from other HCW are exceptional.
- Transmission from dentists have not been reported since 1987, which may be due to a higher vaccination coverage, increased use of standard precautions and especially the use of gloves [1].
- Most HBV transmissions occurred from HCW with chronic HBV infection, but transmission has also occurred in the prodromal stage of the disease and after acute disease has resolved.
- Hepatitis B e antigen (HBeAg), indicating active and highly infectious disease, is found in almost all HCW who have transmitted HBV to patients. But several recent reports about transmissions from HBeAg negative personnel exist. In all cases a mutation of the HBV precore region was found which prevents the expression of HBeAg whereas antibodies against HBeAg may be present [2].

- HBV transmission was found to have occurred in up to 13% of all susceptible patients treated by the infectious HCW [3].

HCV

HCW-to-patient transmission of HCV is rare and little is known about this topic. Only 2 reports of cardiothoracic surgeons infecting one [4] and five patients [5] respectively exist. One case was examined extensively, revealing five transmissions among 222 patients investigated. The transmissions occurred during valve replacement surgery over the course of five years. The surgeon involved had very high titres of HCV-RNA.

A third report about HCW-to-patient transmission concerns a drug addicted anaesthesiologist who infected over 200 patients. Reports indicate that in this case, standard precautions were not adhered to at work.

HIV

In the early 1990's it became known that an HIV infected dentist had transmitted the virus to 6 of about 1100 patients [6, 7]. Another case of HIV transmission was reported in 1997 whereby a orthopaedic surgeon transmitted HIV to a patient (1 of 983 patients examined) during an operation lasting 10 hours. It is very likely that the surgeon was already suffering from AIDS at the time of transmission [8].

No HIV transmission was found in extensive "lookback investigations" examining 22171 patients of 51 HIV infectious doctors and medical students [9].

Transmission

HBV, HCV and HIV transmissions from medical personnel to patients share common features. Apart from the HIV-infected dentist and the i.v. drug addicted anaesthesiologist, surgeons have accounted for all reported transmissions of HBV, HCV or HIV since 1987. It may therefore be justified to apply some observations concerning HBV transmission to HCV and HIV too, although the *probability* of transmission seems to be much lower in the latter.

The route of transmission from HCW to patient during surgery remains unknown. Investigations found correct surgical techniques used by the surgeons involved. However, it is likely that transmission occurs by needlesticks penetrating the glove and skin of the surgeon. The continued use of thereby contaminated needles or scalpels or blood leaking through the puncture may lead to infection of susceptible patients.

Certain surgical procedures are associated with a higher risk for transmission such as hysterectomy, caesarean section and cardiac surgery. Here, transmission rates of above 20% were found. HBV transmissions occurring during procedures with low risk for injury of the surgeon are extremely rare but have been described (forceps delivery with episiotomy and manual removal of placenta respectively). Cardiothoracic and gynaecological surgery seem to be of special risk for transmissions.

It can be concluded that only a small group of HCW, namely those performing "exposure prone procedures" (EPPs) as defined below pose a possible risk for patients, provided that all HCW adhere to general infection control measures (see chapter "Hygienic infection control"). HCW who are infected with HBV (and are HBeAg positive) or HIV must not perform EPPs. Whether even HCV infected HCW should be excluded from performing EPPs is a matter of intense debate.

EPPs have been defined by the Centers for Disease Control and Prevention in the USA [10]:

"Characteristics of EPPs include digital palpation of a needle tip in a body cavity or the simultaneous presence of the HCW's fingers and a needle or other sharp instrument or object in a poorly visualized or highly confined anatomic site. Performance of EPPs presents a recognized risk of percutaneous injury to the HCW, and – if such an injury occurs – the HCW's blood is likely to contact the patient's body cavity, subcutaneous tissues, and/or mucous membranes."

Is screening of health care personnel necessary?

A *general* HBV-, HCV- and HIV-screening of HCW with the aim of preventing HCW-to-patient transmissions is not necessary and not justified. In practice, however, a HBV screening is being performed for HCW in the course of HBV basic vaccination (see chapter "Hepatitis B and D"). It should be noted that it is absolutely necessary to investigate whether HCW who are found to be anti-HBs negative after basic HBV vaccination are chronic HBV carriers. Several clusters of HBV transmissions from chronically infected physicians to patients have occurred because the vaccinated anti-HBs negative physicians were never tested for other HBV markers and were believed to be non-responders to the HBV vaccine.

HCV and HIV screening may be advisable for HCW who perform exposure prone procedures. Whether this screening should be compulsory or voluntary depends on epidemiological and cultural circumstances. In the USA, such personnel should know their HIV and HB status [10]. In Great Britain, HCW are advised to seek advice and appropriate testing if they consider they may be HIV positive or have particular risk factors for HIV infection, and to seek occupational advice accordingly. There, restrictions imposed upon HBeAg positive personnel are also applied to those who refuse HB vaccination or subsequent monitoring [11, 12].

What should be done in the case of an infectious HCW?

All HCW who are infected with HBV, HCV or HIV must seek counselling. Since occupational health physicians are obliged to keep strict confidentiality it is advisable that they serve as the contact person in such situations. HCW with impaired immune systems resulting from HIV infection (or other causes) are at increased risk of acquiring infectious diseases. Whether changes in their duties are necessary should be decided on an individual basis.

If there is reason to believe that a risk of infection for patients exists, has existed or will arise or if there is any doubt about this question, an "expert review panel" should be set up.

Expert review panel

A local expert panel should be set up in a way that it is able to:
- investigate and evaluate the present, past and future risk for patients,
- determine under which conditions the HCW may continue working,
- determine whether lookback investigations are necessary,
- determine whether public health authorities should be informed,
- determine if and when reviews of their decisions may become necessary.

The expert panel should represent a balanced view and may consist of:
- the HCW's personal physician and/or his or her occupational physician,
- an infectious diseases specialist,
- a health professional with expertise in the HCW's working procedures,
- a hospital epidemiologist,
- possibly a public health official.

The panel should ensure confidentiality for the HCW. In some countries (e.g. Great Britain and Germany) national expert advisory panels exist for additional consultation.

Work restrictions

Work restrictions as a consequence of infection may lead to a change of workplace and even retraining. The occupational health physician may have a central role in this process. The employer should ensure that the infected HCW has no or as few as possible employment disadvantages as a consequence of the infection.

Confidentiality

Confidentiality of the HCW and his family should be ensured at all stages of investigation. The obligation to confidentiality may become a problem, when lookback investigations become necessary or the respective HCW is not willing to co-operate and patients or others are or have been at risk. At that point, it may be necessary to breach confidentiality. In Great Britain, physicians and occupational health practitioners are officially encouraged to do so where this is in the public interest [11, 12]. Even allowing for this, it may be helpful to seek professional or legal advice before taking such steps.

Lookback investigations

When a lookback investigation needs to be performed it may be helpful to seek advice from people with experience of similar exercises. Many parties are involved in such an investigation, which can be complex and demanding. The important role of the public relations/press officer should not be overlooked as dealing with the media and relaying information to the public are critical functions. A telephone helpline for the public is usually essential when the lookback involves significant numbers of former patients.

Information, education and responsibilities

All HCW should be informed regularly about the risk of transmission of infectious diseases to patients and to whom they should report when they know or suspect they are infective. HCW should also be aware of their duty to remain fully informed about professional conduct and modes of transmission of infectious diseases. They should be reminded that they bear ethical responsibilities towards their patients.

Several HCW who have infected their patients were assumed to have acquired the disease occupationally. HCW should be educated to adhere to standard hygienic guidelines in order to protect themselves.

As part of their responsibility towards patients, health care institutions should ensure that medical practices and devices bearing a risk of infection are constantly being reviewed. Health care institutions should ensure that standard hygienic measures are being applied and that HBV vaccination is provided. They should promote an atmosphere that encourages personal disclosure in cases of infection.

References

1   Bell DM, Shapiro CN, Ciesielski CA, Chamberland ME. Preventing Bloodborne Pathogen Transmission from Health-Care Workers to Patients - The CDC Perspective. Surg Clin North Am 1995;75:1189-1203

2   Anonymous. Transmission of hepatitis B to patients from four infected surgeons without hepatitis B e antigen. The Incident Investigation Teams and others. N Engl J Med 1997;336:178-184

3   Harpaz R, Von Seidlein L, Averhoff FM, Tormey MP, Sinha SD, Kotsopoulou K, Lambert SB, Robertson BH, Cherry JD, Shapiro CN. Transmission of Hepatitis B Virus to Multiple Patients from a Surgeon without Evidence of Inadequate Infection Control. N Engl J Med 1996;334:549-554

4   Anonymous. Hepatitis C virus transmission from health care worker to patient. Communicable Disease Report 1995;5:121

5   Esteban JI, Gomez J, Martell M, Cabot B, Quer J, Camps J, Gonzalez A, Otero T, Moya A, Esteban R, Guardia J. Transmission of hepatitis C virus by a cardiac surgeon. N Engl J Med 1996;334:555-560

6   Ciesielski C, Marianos D, Ou CY, Dumbaugh R, Witte J, Berkelman R, Gooch B, Myers G, Luo CC, Schochetman G, Howell J, Lasch A, Bell K, Economou N, Scott B, Furman L, Curran J, Jaffe H. Transmission of human immunodeficiency virus in a dental practice. Ann Intern Med 1992;116:789-805

7   Anonymous. CDC identifies sixth case in Florida. Hospital Infection Control 1993;20:74

8   Lot F, Seguier JC, Fegueux S, Astagneau P, Simon P, Aggoune M, van Amerongen P, Ruch M, Cheron M, Brucker G, Desenclos JC, Drucker J. Probable transmission of HIV from an orthopedic surgeon to a patient in France. Ann Intern Med 1999;130:1-6

9   Robert LM, Chamberland ME, Cleveland JL, Marcus R, Gooch BF, Srivastava PU, Culver DH, Jaffe HW, Marianos DW, Panlilio AL, Bell D. Investigations of patients of health care workers infected with HIV. The Centers for Disease Control and Prevention Database. Ann Intern Med 1995;122:653-657

10   CDC. Recommendations for Preventing Transmission of Human Immunodeficiency Virus and Hepatitis B Virus to Patients During Exposure-Prone Invasive Procedures. MMWR 1991;40(No.RR-8):R1-R9

11   Expert Advisory Group on Hepatitis. Protecting Health Care Workers and Patients from Hepatitis B. London. UK Health Department, August 1993

12   Expert Advisory Group on AIDS. AIDS/HIV-infected health care workers: guidance on the management of infected health care workers. London. UK Health Department, March 1994

Further reading

•   AIDS/TB Committee of the Society for Healthcare Epidemiology of America. Management of healthcare workers infected with hepatitis B virus, hepatitis C virus, human immunodeficiency virus, or other bloodborne pathogens. Infect Control Hosp Epidemiol 1997;18:349-363

Occupational Health for Health Care Workers - A Practical Guide
H.-M. Hasselhorn, A. Toomingas and M. Lagerström (Editors)

Gastrointestinal infectious diseases

Friedrich Hofmann

Gastro-enteritis in health care institutions may pose a time consuming problem for the occupational health service (OHS). Prevention of patient to personnel transmission of gastroenteritic pathogens is usually a matter of hospital hygiene standards. Prevention of transmission from infectious personnel to patients may be a role for the OHS.

Gastrointestinal infectious diseases (GID) are caused by a variety of bacteria and viruses. The most serious of these are salmonellae (e.g. *S. typhi/paratyphi, S. enteritidis, S. typhimurium*), shigellae, *Campylobacter jejuni/coli, Yersinia enterocolitica*, enteropathogenic *Escherichia coli* (EPEC), enterohaemorrhagic *E. coli* (EHEC), rotaviruses, *Clostridium difficile* and *Vibrio cholerae*. GID caused by adenoviruses, astroviruses and Norwalk virus are less common.

Transmission

GI-pathogens are predominantly transmitted by contaminated food and water. Infection through contaminated hands, instruments etc. is also possible [1, 2]. Hands are probably the most important means of occupational transmission of enteric viruses in hospitals.

Epidemiology

GID are among the most frequent diseases worldwide. The incidence of the various causative agents is different in different regions. While the majority of them are important for patients all over the world and in all age groups, severe EPEC and EHEC are mostly diagnosed in infants. Rotavirus disease is predominantly observed in infants aged 6-24 months [3] but recently a major outbreak was observed in a community of adults [4]. The seventh pandemic of cholera continues today. With the spread of cholera through South and Central America in the beginning of the 1990's all developing countries have been affected [5].

Occupational risk

The occupational risk depends on the standard of hygiene and the development of the health care system. In the course of a German study, 8634 health care workers (HCW) were tested for bacteria causing GID during routine occupational health check-ups [6].

130 (2%) stool specimens were positive. 53% of the infectious persons were symptomatic, the rest had no symptoms whatsoever. The majority (75%) of all cases had no history of a recent visit to endemic countries. The analysis of the microorganisms involved, showed salmonellae (74%), followed by *Campylobacter jejuni/coli* (12%), shigellae (7%) and *Yersinia enterocolitica* (7%).

Symptoms and signs

The incubation period of most GID is a few days, except for EHEC and enteric fevers which may be up to 10–21 days. The case to infection ratio (symptomatic cases per infected persons) varies between 1:2 to 1:100. Symptoms of GID can range from mild diarrhoea to acutely dehydrating watery diarrhoea disease or dysentery with mucoid-bloody evacuations. Case-fatality rates depend on the age of infected persons, the extent of the loss of fluid volume and electrolytes, the availability of treatment, volume replacement and general hygienic and medical conditions. Chronic carriage (> 1 year) of salmonellae (especially *S. typhi)* occurs in up to 1-5% of all cases.

Diagnosis

The diagnosis of GID in general is clinical. Confirmation of the diagnosis is made by culturing the organism from faeces. Determination of antibodies is less important.

Prevention

Prevention of infection in HCW coming in contact with cholera patients is enhanced by using live vaccine. This is not licensed in all countries but inactivated vaccine is not very effective [7]. The first rotavirus vaccine was licensed in the USA in summer 1998. At the moment its high price prevents wide use [8]. Vaccination against *S. typhi* is compulsory for all HCW in France. However, most of the pathogens causing GID are not vaccine-preventable. Therefore, the most important measures against GID in HCW are hygienic ones, especially disinfection of the hands. Gloves and overalls or aprons should be worn when exposed to urine or faeces. Disposable plastic gloves should be used when in direct contact with ill patients. Separate toilets for infectious patients and special disposal facilities for contaminated materials are recommended.

When it becomes known that a patient has been/is infectious with *S. typhi, S. paratyphi,* or shigella, it may be advisable to inform all personnel, who had direct close physical contact with the patient, about the risk of transmission and symptoms of the disease. Those with symptoms should immediately seek medical advice. Legal regulations may require stool samples to be obtained from those with close contact even when no symptoms are present. In a case of *S. typhi,* or *S. paratyphi,* the sample should be taken not less than 5 weeks after the *last* contact with the *infectious* patient, and in a case of shigella, 4 days.

Stool examination should be performed in a HCW presenting with symptoms regardless of their occupation.

Restrictions for infected HCW

GID-related work restrictions for infected (or possibly infected) hospital personnel depend on characteristics of the work place and the pathogen involved. The following measures may be proposed if no other official regulations exist:
- Nursing staff infected (or suspected to be infected) with *S. typhi, S. paratyphi,* shigellae or *V. cholerae* must be put off duty.
- Kitchen staff infected (or suspected to be infected) with any salmonellae, with shigellae, *V. cholerae, Campylobacter jejuni/coli, Yersinia enterocolitica* must be put off duty.
- Nursing staff infected (or suspected to be infected) with *Campylobacter jejuni/coli, Yersinia enterocolitica* or Salmonellae other than *S. typhi/paratyphi*
  - must not work in intensive care units, oncology or neonatology wards or transplantation units.
  - They may, however, work in other areas (including operating theatres), but should use a separate toilet,
  - should disinfect hands with alcoholic disinfectant following a visit to the toilet and
  - must not handle food and medicine.
- Nursing staff infected (or suspected to be infected) with enteric viruses should be excluded from contact with potentially susceptible persons (e.g. neonates, infants, immunocompromised, elderly) and from work with food until at least 2 days after resolution of symptoms.

Hospital staff with severe GID symptoms (e.g. blood tinged diarrhoea or ongoing diarrhoea >4 days) must be put off duty and should hand in a stool specimen as soon as possible. Further restrictions then depend on the result of the stool investigation (see 1–4).

GID can be assumed to have resolved and work restrictions lifted when 5 (*Salmonella typhi, S. paratyphi,* shigellae) or 3 (all other bacterial pathogens) negative stool cultures have been obtained. Specimens should be taken ≥48 hours apart, and not during the intake of antibiotics or within 3 days after the last dose.

References

1   Jarvis WR, Hughes M. Nosocomial gastrointestinal infections. In: Wenzel RP (Ed). Prevention and control of nosocomial infections. Baltimore: Williams&Wilkins, 1993:708-745
2   Mitchell DK, Pickering LK. Nosocomial gastrointestinal tract infections in paediatric patients. In: Mayhall CG (Ed). Hospital epidemiology and infection control. Baltimore: Williams&Wilkins, 1996:506-523
3   Matson DO, Estes MK. Impact of rotavirus infection at a large paediatric hospital. J Infect Dis 1990;162:598-604

4   Hung T, Chen GM, Wang CG, Yao HL, Fang ZY, Chao TX, Chou ZY, Ye W, Chang XJ, Den SS, et al. Waterborne outbreak of rotavirus diarrhoea in adults in China caused by a novel rotavirus. Lancet 1984;1:1139-1142

5   Anonymous. Cholera in the Americas, Wkly Epidemiol Rec 1992;67:33-40

6   Mlangeni D, Hofmann F, Grundmann HJ, Daschner F, Kist M. Gastroenteritis as a problem among health care workers. In: Hagberg M, Hofmann F, Stößel U, Westlander G (Eds). Occupational health for health care workers. Landsberg: ecomed publishers, 1993:204-206

7   Peltola H, Siitonen A, Kyronseppa H, Simula I, Mattila L, Oksanen P, Kataja MJ, Cadoz M. Prevention of travellers' diarrhoea by oral B-subunit/whole cell cholera vaccine. Lancet 1991;338:1285-1289

8   Keusch GT, Cash RA. A vaccine against rotavirus - when is too much too much? N Engl J Med 1997;337:1228-1229

Occupational Health for Health Care Workers - A Practical Guide
H.-M. Hasselhorn, A. Toomingas and M. Lagerström (Editors)

Cytomegalovirus

Antoon De Schryver, Philippe Kiss

Cytomegalovirus (CMV) is currently the major infectious agent associated with congenital brain damage and deafness. CMV is ubiquitous and can be acquired sexually and by blood transfusion, but is more commonly transmitted via breast milk, saliva and urine. CMV can survive and remains infectious outside the body for several hours, but is very sensitive to detergents and it does not appear to be highly contagious. Asymptomatic infants, young children and infected immunocompromised patients (e.g. AIDS patients) may shed the virus for months or even years in urine and saliva. Up to 60% of all children in day care centres were found to be shedding the virus and about 30-50% of all women of childbearing age in Western Europe are CMV seropositive [1]. Infection does not give complete life-long immunity and re-infection is possible, especially in immunocompromised patients.

Symptoms and signs

Infection is usually asymptomatic, but may cause a mononucleosis like disease in adults. In immunocompromised people, the infection can lead to interstitial pneumonia, hepatitis, encephalitis, nephritis and additional problems.

Foetuses may be infected by their mothers, both as a consequence of primary and reactivated infection. The infection affects approximately 1-2% of all new-born babies in the United States and Western Europe and about 10-15% of those will suffer mental retardation and/or deafness. Maternal antibodies to CMV do not prevent foetal infection, but symptomatic manifestations are rare among infants of women with CMV reactivation and/or re-infection during pregnancy. Studies suggest that rates of acquisition of the virus in hospital staff are similar to those found in the general population (2% per annum) [2, 3]. This probably reflects the effectiveness of normal infection control procedures within the health care setting as higher rates (8% per annum) were found among day care workers [4], who are less likely to be as aware of infection control issues.

Diagnosis

A primary CMV infection is diagnosed serologically by measuring IgG and IgM antibodies; one acute and one convalescent sample are recommended. The CMV-IgM titre following re-infection or reactivation is usually less elevated than in primary infection. PCR antigen detection and virus isolation are normally used for diagnosis of active CMV infection in immuno-compromised persons.

Prevention

Prevention must be particularly focused on pregnant health care workers (HCW), and more generally so, on HCW of childbearing age, especially those caring for children or the immunocompromised. They should be educated about the risks and the protective measures required. If strictly adhered to, standard precautions in relation to blood and body fluids will protect personnel. Pregnant HCW should assume that all body fluids are potentially infectious and should practice frequent hand washing after patient contact. When they perceive that they are likely to be exposed to body fluids and when they are handling urine or respiratory secretions, they should wear gowns and gloves.

Serological CMV screening before conception (e.g. at pre-employment examination or routine health monitoring) should be limited to women at high risk of acquiring infection so that appropriate counselling can be offered. At present there is no consensus as to whether susceptible pregnant women should be excluded from work with children or infants. If a seronegative pregnant women has had close contact with a patient shedding CMV and is concerned about this, counselling and information about the relatively low risk of acquiring the disease and even lower risk of foetal damage is one of the major tasks of the occupational health unit. Vaccines against CMV are not yet available but are under development.

Restrictions for infected or exposed HCW

There are no restrictions for infected or exposed HCW since they will not transmit the disease when observing good personal hygiene.

References

1   De Schryver A, De Backer G, Van Renterghem L. Cytomegalovirus infection: epidemiology and association with congenital malformations. Arch Public Health 1998;56:233-250
2   Balcarek KB, Bagley R, Cloud GA, Pass RF. Cytomegalovirus infection among employees of a children's hospital. JAMA 1990;263:840-844
3   Balfour CL, Balfour HH. Cytomegalovirus is not an occupational risk for nurses in renal transplant and neonatal units. JAMA 1986;256:1909-1914
4   Murph JR, Baron JC, Kice Brown C, Ebelhack CL, Bale JF. The occupational risk for CMV infection among day-care providers. JAMA 1991;265:603-608

Occupational Health for Health Care Workers - A Practical Guide
H.-M. Hasselhorn, A. Toomingas and M. Lagerström (Editors)

Hepatitis A

Friedrich Hofmann

Immunity to hepatitis A virus (HAV) has decreased significantly in industrialised countries since the end of World War II [1]. In the course of epidemiological studies an increased occupational risk for health care workers (HCW) in psychiatry [2], nursing and paediatrics [3] and for kitchen workers in hospitals [4] has been demonstrated. Transmission is by the faecal-oral route. Infection leads to lifelong immunity.

Symptoms and signs

After an incubation period of 15-45 days a variety of symptoms of sudden onset often occur: jaundice (80%), dark urine (94%), fatigue (91%), loss of appetite (90%), abdominal pain (65%), light coloured stool (58%), nausea or vomiting (87%), fever (73%) [5]. In 90% hepatitis A is self-limiting after 4-6 weeks. In 10% remission for about 8-12 weeks is followed by a second phase of several weeks duration. In children, disease is mostly asymptomatic. Chronic cases have not been reported. Overall lethality is 0.25% and is higher among the elderly and those with chronic liver disease.

Diagnosis

Clinical diagnosis is accompanied by serological demonstration of the presence of anti-HAV IgM, using the ELISA technique.

Prevention

HCW below 50 years of age from Europe, North America and Australia should be vaccinated without screening. Other persons should be screened for anti-HAV IgG. Inactivated vaccine should be inoculated twice, the second dose after 6-12 months. Vaccine efficacy is >98% within 4 weeks of the first vaccination. Protection lasts at least 5 years and is possibly lifelong. Vaccination is also effective as post exposure prophylaxis when given up to 14 days after the probable date of infection. Those with severe chronic liver disease should be given standard immunoglobulin as post exposure prophylaxis in order rapidly to obtain protective levels of anti-HAV.

Restrictions for exposed or infected HCW

As infectivity ends 2 weeks after onset of symptoms, HCW are able to return to work following resolution of clinical hepatitis. Potentially infected HCW without prophylaxis should follow universal hygiene precautions, especially after urinating and defecating and before handling of food.

References

1   Gust ID. Epidemiological patterns of hepatitis A in different parts of the world. Vaccine 1992;10(Suppl.1):56S-58S
2   Steinert G, Hofmann F, Ahrens K, Berthold H, Bock HL, Clemens R, Hess G. The frequency of hepatitis A, B and C among mentally retarded residents of an institution for the mentally handicapped. In: Hagberg M, Hofmann F, Stössel U, Westlander G (Eds). Occupational Health for Health Care Workers. Landsberg: Ecomed publishers, 1993:161-171
3   Hofmann F, Berthold H, Wehrle G. Immunity to Hepatitis A in Hospital Personnel. Eur J Clin Microbiol Infect Dis 1993;12:1195
4   Köster D, Hofmann F, Berthold H. Hepatitis A-Immunity of food handling staff. Eur J Clin Microbiol Infect Dis 1990;9:304-305
5   Koff RS. Features and diagnosis of hepatitis A, Vaccine (Suppl.1)1992;10:S15-S17

Occupational Health for Health Care Workers - A Practical Guide
H.-M. Hasselhorn, A. Toomingas and M. Lagerström (Editors)

Hepatitis B and D

Hans-Martin Hasselhorn

Hepatitis B (HB) has been the most common severe infectious occupational disease for health care workers (HCW). Since a safe and effective vaccine became available in 1981, vaccination and verification of immunity have become major tasks within occupational health care for HCW. Hepatitis D (HD) is caused by an "incomplete" virus which is dependent on the presence of the hepatitis B virus (HBV). Since the mode of transmission as well as prevention are identical to HB both diseases are discussed in one chapter.

Symptoms and signs

Infection with HBV may lead to severe viral liver disease. Transmission occurs mainly by sexual and percutaneous contacts as well as during birth from an infectious mother to her child. Infection in adults results in acute symptomatic liver disease in about 50% of cases, in fulminant and fatal liver disease in about 1% and in chronic liver disease in about 5-10%. The World Health Organization estimates that world-wide, 350 million people are chronic HBV carriers (HB surface antigen [HBsAg] positive) [1]. Blood from patients with acute or chronic HB can be highly infectious. Following a needle stick injury with a HBV-contaminated needle the risk of transmission to a non-immune HCW ranges from 2% (source patient HBsAg positive but HB e antigen [HBeAg] negative) up to 40% (source patient HBsAg positive and HBeAg positive) [2]. The prevalence of serological HB markers shows regional differences. Whereas about 5-10% of the population in industrialised countries show serologic evidence of past (or active) HBV infection (anti-HBc), up to 100% of the population in developing countries are anti-HBc positive.

Hepatitis D shows the same symptoms as for HB and can occur:
- as "coinfection" with HBV. This often leads to a more severe disease (fulminant hepatitis in up to 20%) than HBV infection alone. The risk for chronic infection, however, is low.
- as superinfection, i.e. when a chronic HBV carrier is being infected. In this case chronic HDV infection almost always occurs and the risk of developing liver cirrhosis later is high (about 75%).

For HDV, the percutaneous route is the most common mode of transmission. Sexual transmission is less common. The main risk groups are injecting drug users and persons with haemophilia. The prevalence of HD varies. In most industrialised countries, it is below 10% among asymptomatic HBV carriers and below 25% among those with chronic HB liver disease. In certain areas with higher HB prevalence, like Southern Europe, higher rates are found with maximum HD prevalences of >20% among asymptomatic HBV carriers and >60% among people with chronic HB liver disease. In Asia, the prevalence of HD is low.

Diagnosis

HB is diagnosed serologically. HBsAg is the first parameter to be found, followed by the HBeAg. Anti-HBc indicates contact with the virus and usually persists lifelong. Anti-HBs indicates post infection, whereas chronic disease is indicated by persistence of HBsAg, HBeAg and anti-HBe. Following HBV/HDV coinfection IgM and/or IgG antibodies against HDV (anti-HDV) can be found first after the appearance of HBV surface antigen (HBsAg). Anti-HDV IgM and IgG disappear when the infection resolves and no serological marker indicates previous infection. Throughout chronic infection IgG and sometimes IgM remain detectable. Commercial tests are available for testing of anti-HDV IgG.

Occupational risk

Hepatitis B is a major infectious hazard for HCW in industrialised countries (relative risk in relation to general population is 2-10) [1]. In Germany the number of occupationally acquired hepatitis B infections among health care personnel has decreased after introduction of HB vaccine from an estimated 2000 cases/year in 1980 to an estimated 400 cases in 1990. Since then the numbers are increasing again indicating insufficient vaccination coverage among HCW especially within the private sector. Occupational transmissions of HDV by needlesticks have also been reported. Only HCW who are susceptible to HBV or HBV carriers are at risk for acquiring HDV.

Prevention

Hepatitis B vaccination

Within health care all non-immune personnel with potential contact to blood or other body fluids are at risk of HB and should be vaccinated against HBV. This includes all HCW, physiotherapists, cleaning and janitorial staff and other personnel working in the health care system. The available vaccines (recombinant or plasma derived) are safe, effective and well tolerated. However, side effects such as flu-like symptoms may occasionally occur. More extensive reactions are extremely rare. HB vaccination should be administered in the deltoid muscle. Basic vaccination comprises of 3 doses, the 2nd 4 weeks and the 3rd 6-12 months after the 1st. About four weeks to three months after the third vaccination serologic testing for anti-HBs should be done. An alternative, rapid course, involving doses at 0,1 and 2 months and a booster at 12 months gets antibody levels up quicker and may have better success in overall conversion rates.

Approaches to HB vaccination
In practice there are two possible approaches to HB vaccination in health care:

a) Pre-vaccine serological screening
In some countries (e.g. Germany) the HCW is tested for anti-HBc prior to basic vaccination.
- If anti-HBc is negative, vaccination is necessary.
- If anti-HBc is positive, the respective person has been infected earlier with HBV and no vaccination is necessary. Further testing will reveal whether chronic infection exists (if HBsAg- and/or HBeAg positive) or not (anti-HBs positive).
- In rare instances anti-HBc is positive and both HBsAg and anti-HBs are negative. In this case vaccination may be advisable.

At least 4 weeks after the basic vaccination, testing for anti-HBs needs to be performed for verification of vaccine induced protection.

b) No pre-vaccine serological screening
In the UK serological tests are not performed before basic vaccination of HCW and all unvaccinated HCW are offered vaccination. About 3 months after the third vaccine dose serological testing of anti-HBs is performed.
- If anti-HBs is positive and ≥10 IU/l, the HCW is protected (either by vaccination or by previous infection).
- If anti-HBs is negative, testing for anti-HBc and possibly HBsAg and HBeAg is recommended, to distinguish between non-responders and chronically infected persons.

This procedure may be cost-effective in countries with low HBV prevalence and low vaccine costs. The disadvantage is that this procedure takes at least 9 months until the first serological examination is being performed and during this time, HBV infectious HCW may have put patients at risk for HB. Consequently, HCW performing invasive procedures with risk for HCW-to-patient transmissions must be checked for HBV carrier status unless they are HB immune, before performing such "exposure prone procedures".

Immunity levels, non-responders
Anti-HBs ≥10 IU/l confers immunity. Present data indicate that immunocompetent people with post vaccination anti-HBs levels above 100 IU/l (or even less, possibly above 10 IU/l) may remain protected for at least 5-10 years (maybe even lifelong) even when anti-HBs drops below detectable levels. Therefore in some countries no further booster vaccination is given for those with post vaccination anti-HBs levels above 10 IU/l whereas in other countries a serological check of immunity is performed every 5 years.

Vaccinees with anti-HBs values below 10 IU/l after the third vaccination are called "*non-responders*". Obesity, smoking, increasing age, male sex and immunosuppression are risk factors for low post vaccination immunity. Those who remain non-responders even after several booster attempts (e.g. up to 4 further attempts) have to be regarded as susceptible to HBV. In cases of contact to HBV infectious material they have to be treated as described below. Regular testing for anti-HBs and HBsAg every 6 months may be considered for non-responders working in areas with high risk for HBV infection (e.g. dialysis centres).

Postexposure measures

When a person reports a percutaneous or mucocutaneous contact with blood or blood contaminated material, immediate investigation is necessary to determine whether the person is susceptible to HBV and the source patient is or might be HBV infectious. If the person is susceptible and the source person is unknown or HBV infectious, HB prophylaxis should be administered within 48 hours. This includes the simultaneous administration of (expensive) HB immunoglobulin and a regular hepatitis B vaccination. This task should be performed by staff in a unit with constant presence even on holidays, e.g. the accident and emergency unit. It is advisable to refresh the knowledge of the staff at this unit regularly (e.g. every three months) as staff turnover is often high. In case of HDV superinfection, no postexposure prophylaxis is known.

Chronic carriers and restrictions for exposed or infectious HCW

If a HCW is found to be chronically infected with HBV medical consultation for liver disease is advisable and evaluation of infection risk for others is necessary. This includes consideration of work restrictions to protect patients (see respective chapter in this book) and possibly vaccination of partners. Since chronic HBV carriers are susceptible to HDV, they should not work at places where HD patients are more prevalent (e.g. infectious disease wards), and not perform procedures carrying a risk of infection on patients known to be infected with HDV. There are no restrictions for susceptible HCW with known recent exposure to HBV.

References

1   Van Damme P, Tormans G, Van Doorslaer E, Kane M, Roure C, Meheus A. A European risk model for hepatits B among health care workers. Eur J Publ Health 1995;5:245-252
2   Gerberding JL. Management of Occupational Exposures to Blood-Borne Viruses. N Engl J Med 1995;332:144-151 (Survey information)

Occupational Health for Health Care Workers - A Practical Guide
H.-M. Hasselhorn, A. Toomingas and M. Lagerström (Editors)

Hepatitis C

Monika A. Rieger

After discovery of hepatitis C virus (HCV) in 1988, parenteral non-A, non-B hepatitis could be identified as primarily caused by HCV infection. Surveys indicate that HCV infection is prevalent in many countries all over the world, but seroprevalence differs considerably: in the USA about 1.8% of the population is infected with HCV [1] whereas in countries like Egypt this can be ten times more. No data exist to determine the threshold viral dose required for transmission [1].

Transmission – occupational exposure

HCV is primarily transmitted through direct percutaneous exposure to blood. The highest prevalence of infection is found among injecting-drug users, haemophiliacs, and recipients of transfusions [1]. An estimated 2-4% of HCV infections occur among health care personnel who were occupationally exposed to blood [2]. Thus health care workers (HCW) and public safety workers (e.g. fire-service, law-enforcement, and correctional facility personnel) who are exposed to blood at their work place are at risk for being infected with HCV [1]. The average risk of being infected after accidental needle stick or sharps exposure from an HCV positive patient is about 2% (range: 0-7%) [1]. A study from Japan reported an incidence of HCV infection of 10% based on detection of HCV RNA. In one case, the transmission of HCV from blood splashes to the conjunctiva has been described, otherwise no transmissions associated with mucous membrane or non-intact skin exposures have been reported [1].

Symptoms and signs

Acute HCV infection is asymptomatic in about two thirds of cases, whilst others may present with a mild clinical illness characterised by symptoms such as jaundice, anorexia, malaise and abdominal pain. Fulminant hepatic failure following acute hepatitis C is rare. Elevations in serum ALT levels (alanine-amino-transferase) are the most characteristic feature of acute hepatitis C, often in a fluctuating pattern. Chronic HCV infection develops in about 80% of all infected persons. It should be noted that only about two thirds of chronically infected individuals show persistent or fluctuating ALT elevations (indicating active liver disease) whereas in one third ALT levels are normal. Cirrhosis develops in 10-20% of persons with chronic hepatitis C over a period of 20-30 years, and hepatocellular carcinoma in 1-5%. Extrahepatic manifestations of chronic HCV infection include cryoglobulinemia, membranoproliferative glomerulonephritis, and porphyria cutanea tarda.

HCV positive people should be evaluated for presence and severity of chronic liver disease. This evaluation should include multiple measurements of ALT at intervals because of fluctuating ALT activity.

Diagnosis

The diagnosis of HCV infection can be made within 1-2 weeks of exposure to the virus by detecting HCV RNA in serum or plasma by means of reverse transcription polymerase chain reaction. This test is expensive and the accuracy of the results are highly variable. Antibodies against HCV (anti-HCV) can be measured by enzyme immunoassay (EIA) at the earliest ten weeks and at the latest nine months after infection in immunocompetent individuals [1]. A positive test result needs to be confirmed by supplemental anti-HCV testing (e.g. immunoblot). It does not distinguish between acute, chronic, or resolved infection. Indeterminate anti-HCV results might indicate a false positive result, particularly in those persons at low risk for HCV infection. ALT elevations first appear 8-10 weeks after infection and are usually found before anti-HCV.

Prevention and postexposure measures

No vaccine against hepatitis C is available [4]. HCW should be educated about the risk for and prevention of bloodborne infections, including hepatitis C, in occupational settings, with the information routinely updated to ensure accuracy. Following a needlestick immediate measures should be taken as described in the chapter "Management of needlestick injuries". Postexposure prophylaxis by means of immunoglobulin is considered not to be effective. Postexposure use of antiviral agents (e.g. interferon) has not been shown to prevent HCV infection [3, 4].

The Centers for Disease Control and Prevention (CDC), recommend that health care institutions consider implementing procedures for follow-up of possible HCV infection after percutaneous or mucosal exposures to blood. At a minimum, such policies should include [4]:
- for the source (usually: patient): baseline testing for anti-HCV;
- for the person exposed to an anti-HCV positive source: baseline and follow-up (e.g. 6-month) testing for anti-HCV and ALT activity;
- a recommendation against the use of postexposure prophylaxis with immunoglobulin or antiviral agents (e.g. interferon).

It is of importance to detect a newly infected HCW as early as possible because interferon treatment begun early in the course of an acute HCV infection seems to be associated with a higher rate of resolved infections [4]. A cheap and practical way is to regularly measure ALT levels following an exposure, e.g. every 6 weeks up to 6 months. When finding an ALT increase during the follow-up period, specific tests can immediately clarify whether an HCV infection has occurred.

Routine HCV testing of HCW is implemented in some countries (e.g. Germany). Voluntary testing of HCW should be in their own interest as they may benefit from knowing their infection status so they can seek evaluation for chronic liver disease and treatment for early infection.

Restrictions for exposed and infected HCW

There are no restrictions for exposed or infected HCW except possibly for those who perform "exposure prone procedures". This is discussed in the chapter "The hepatitis B, hepatitis C or HIV infectious health care worker".

References

1   CDC. Recommendations for prevention and control of hepatitis C virus (HCV) infection and HCV-related chronic disease. MMWR 1998;47(RR-19):1-39 (http://www.cdcgov/epo/mmwr/preview/mmwrhtml1/00055154.htm)
2   Alter MJ. Epidemiology of Hepatitis C. N Engl J Med 1997; 26(Suppl 1): 62S-65S
3   CDC. Immunization of Health-Care Workers: Recommendations of the Advisory Committee on Immunization Practices (ACIP) and the Hospital Infection Control Practices Advisory Committee (HICPAC). MMWR 1997; 46(RR-18):1-42 (http://www.cdcgov/epo/mmwr/preview/mmwrhtml1/00050577.htm)
4   CDC. Recommendations for follow-up of health-care workers after occupational exposure to hepatitis C virus [Notice to Readers]. MMWR 1997; 46:603-606 (http://www.cdcgov/epo/mmwr/preview/mmwrhtml1/00048324.htm)

Occupational Health for Health Care Workers - A Practical Guide
H.-M. Hasselhorn, A. Toomingas and M. Lagerström (Editors)
© 1999 Elsevier Science B.V. All rights reserved.

Hepatitis E

Hans-Martin Hasselhorn, Lars Olof Magnius

Hepatitis E virus (HEV) is the major cause of acute enterically acquired non-A hepatitis in India, neighbouring Asian countries, and Africa [1]. Outbreaks occur primarily in areas with low hygienic standard. Sporadic cases occurring in non endemic areas are mostly travel associated. Infection is transmitted by the faecal-oral route. In endemic areas large water borne outbreaks are reported. Transmission by contaminated food such as shellfish, and person to person spread may occur.

In countries with a high living standard such as the USA and Germany, antibodies to HEV (anti-HEV) are found in about 1% of the population. This can often be attributed to previous visits to endemic areas.

There are only a few reports of transmissions to child care and health care workers (HCW) [2] and overall person to person transmission seems to be uncommon. Although there is little evidence of an occupational risk for HCW in countries with high hygienic standard, an occupational risk of infection can be assumed to exist in endemic areas.

Symptoms and signs

Clinical disease mainly affects young and middle aged adults. Asymptomatic infection is less common than in hepatitis A. The incubation period may vary from 15 to 60 days, and is generally longer than for hepatitis A. The disease is often more severe with a prolonged icteric phase as compared to hepatitis A. Viral shedding in faeces occurs for at least 2 weeks after the onset of illness. Hepatitis E infection usually resolves without sequelae and does not become chronic. Fulminant hepatitis occurs in 5% of cases and in 20% of affected pregnant women (30% may die if affected in the third trimester).

Diagnosis

IgM and IgG antibodies appear about 3-4 weeks after onset. IgG antibodies persist and may possibly provide at least short term protection. Commercial tests for anti-HEV are now available.

Prevention

Vaccination against HEV is not yet available. Postexposure prophylaxis with immunoglobulin from non-endemic areas does not seem to be effective. Whether immunoglobulin from endemic areas may be effective is not known. Standard hygienic measures in a health care setting should prevent occupational transmission of HEV.

References

1   Purcell R. Hepatitis E. In: Fields BN, Knipe DM, Howley PM (Eds). Fields Virology. Philadelphia: Lippincot-Raven Publishers, 1995:2831-2844
2   Robson SC, Adams S, Brink N, Woodruff B, Bradley D. Hospital outbreak of hepatitis E [letter]. Lancet 1992;339:1424-1425

Occupational Health for Health Care Workers - A Practical Guide
H.-M. Hasselhorn, A. Toomingas and M. Lagerström (Editors)
© 1999 Elsevier Science B.V. All rights reserved.

Herpes simplex infection

Jacob Amir

Health care workers (HCW) are at occupational risk of contracting herpes simplex virus (HSV-1 and HSV-2) from infected patients. Susceptibility to primary infection on exposure is rendered by a lack of pre-existing antibodies to HSV-1 and HSV-2 [1]. Research has shown that by the third decade of life, approximately 50% of individuals are seronegative to HSV-1 and approximately 90% to HSV-2. After primary infection, HSV becomes latent within the sensory nerve ganglion sites and may be reactivated under certain circumstances resulting in orofacial/genital herpes or asymptomatic carriage. The mechanisms by which various stimuli cause reactivation of HSV are under intense investigation. Ultraviolet light, immuno-suppression, trauma, emotional stress and menstruation are associated with reactivation. Serological techniques are helpful in diagnosing past HSV-infection but type-specific assays (HSV-1 or HSV-2) are still not used extensively. Reinfection with either type of HSV is possible despite the presence of neutralising antibodies. The route of infection is direct inoculation of HSV from lesions or oropharyngeal/genital secretions from an infected patient to the abraded skin or mucosal surface of a health care provider. The incubation period for primary infection ranges from 2-12 days. The major known risk groups are dentists [2], dental hygienists, anaesthesiologists, respiratory technicians [3], intensive care unit (ICU) physicians and nurses [4] and paediatric personnel [5]. Most suffer from herpetic whitlow, an HSV-infection of the distal segment of the fingers.

Symptoms and signs

Whereas mucosal primary infection either remains asymptomatic (>90%) or causes stomatitis aphthosa and vulvo-vaginitis, respectively, the earliest signs of herpetic whitlow infection are tenderness and erythema consisting of small, extremely painful fluid-containing vesicles. Fever and axillary lymphadenopathy are seen in some patients. Healing is usually complete after approximately three weeks, but recurrence is possible.

Other clinical manifestations in medical personnel are gingivo-stomatitis and pharyngitis with multiple oral vesicles, later replaced by shallow ulcers; symptoms include sore throat, fever, cervical lymphadenopathy and eating difficulties. The course of the disease lasts from 10-14 days.

Diagnosis

The typical clinical manifestation of HSV-infection makes the diagnosis straightforward in most cases. Viral isolation in cell cultures remains the definitive diagnostic method rendering positive results with in 2-3 days.

Treatment

Acyclovir 200-400 mg x 5 per day for 5-7 days is recommended upon diagnosis. Treatment shortens the duration of the clinical manifestations and the infectivity [6]. Topical acyclovir has a minor effect on symptoms and on duration of viral shedding.

Prevention

An effective vaccine against HSV-1 or HSV-2 is not available in spite of continued investigation in the field. Adherence to universal precautions should minimise the risk of contracting HSV. Glove wearing will prevent herpetic whitlow in personnel handling patients with extensive oral, genital or cutaneous disease and hand-washing/disinfection practices and use of a facemask will protect them from oral infection. The latter is particularly important for HCW in frequent contact with the oropharynx (dentists, ICU workers, etc.) since asymptomatic carriers commonly shed HSV in oral secretions.

Restrictions for exposed or infected HCW

Since HSV-infection can be transmitted to patients [7] and since under certain clinical conditions it can cause unusually severe infections, HCW with active HSV-infection should not be in contact with high risk patients including those with premature and newborn infants, immunocompromised patients and patients with extensive imperfections in skin integrity (burns, atopic eczema, etc). Infected medical personnel working with these patients, should cover their hand lesions with double gloves and their orolabial lesions with a face mask, until all lesions are entirely crusted and dry. In some countries HCW with orofacial HSV-infections are excluded from work with risk patients.

References

1   Whitley RJ, Kimberlin DW, Roizman B. Herpes simplex viruses. Clin Infect Dis 1988;26:541-553
2   Brooks S, Roe N, Drach J. Prevalence of herpes simplex virus disease in a professional population. J Am Dent Assoc 1981;102:31-34
3   Gill MJ, Arlette J, Buchan K. Herpes simplex virus infection of the hand. A profile of 79 cases. Am J Med 1988; 84:89-93

4   Adams G, Stover BH, Kennlyside RA, Hooton TM, Buchman TG, Roizman B, Stewart JA. Nosocomial herpetic infections in a pediatric intensive care unit. Am J Epidemiol 1981;113:126-132

5   Amir J, Nussinovitch M, Kleper R, Cohen HA, Varsano I. Primary herpes simplex virus type 1 gingivostomatitis in pediatric personnel. Infection 1997;25:310-312

6   Amir J, Harel L, Smetana Z, Varsano I. Treatment of herpes simplex gingivostomatitis with acyclovir in children: a randomized double blind placebo controlled study. Br Med J 1997;314:1800-1803

7   Manzella JP, McConville JH, Valenti W, Menegus MA, Swierkosz EM, Arens M. An outbreak of herpes simplex virus type I gingivostomatitis in a dental hygiene practice. JAMA 1984;252:2019-2020

Further reading

*   Bolyard E, Tablan O, Williams W, Pearson M, Shapiro C, Deitchman S, the Hospital Infection Control Advisory Committee. Guideline for infection control in health care personnel, 1998 (CDC personnel Health Guideline). AJIC;23(3):332-333

Occupational Health for Health Care Workers - A Practical Guide
H.-M. Hasselhorn, A. Toomingas and M. Lagerström (Editors)

HIV / AIDS

Dominique Abiteboul

HIV is a retrovirus that infects specific target cells such as CD4 lymphocytes or macrophages. With time, it damages the immune system and is responsible for progressive immune dysfunction with the latest stage of the disease being AIDS. HIV-1 is responsible for the majority of HIV infections world-wide, but a second less aggressive virus, HIV2, has been found mainly in West Africa. The main routes of transmission are through sexual contact, percutaneous or muco-cutaneous exposure to blood and vertical infection from mother to infant.

Since 1981 when the first cases of AIDS were described in the United States, 10.7 million adults and 3.2 million children throughout the world have died from AIDS and more than 33 million people, including 1.2 million children are living with HIV/AIDS at the end of 1998. 5.8 million were newly infected during 1998; that is to say 16.000 new cases per day [1]. Two thirds of the total number of HIV infected people are living in sub-Saharan Africa where heterosexual contacts are the main route of transmission. At the same time, AIDS is declining sharply in the industrialised world, except in Eastern Europe where rates of HIV infection have recently dramatically risen [1]. The decrease is mainly due to combined antiretroviral treatment, which delays disease progression.

Occupational risk

As is the case for the other blood-borne viruses (HBV and HCV), health care workers (HCW) are particularly at risk of exposure to HIV. To date, 95 documented cases and 191 possible cases of occupationally acquired HIV infections have been reported world-wide [2]. Over 94% have been notified by countries with well implemented surveillance systems. In developing countries with a higher prevalence of HIV, there is major under-notification with only 5 cases being reported from Africa and none from South East Asia. Although HIV has been detected in various body fluids, seroconversions have been documented only for blood, visibly bloody fluids and concentrated HIV in the laboratory. Most cases (89%) occurred following a percutaneous exposure (mainly needle stick injuries with hollow needles among nurses and phlebotomists) and eight cases were from mucocutaneous exposure. 95% of seroconversions occurred within 6 months of the exposure and most of them by 2-3 months. Symptoms of primary HIV infection were frequent (70%), generally within 6 weeks [2]. Three seroconversions have also been published in non-hospital settings: two workers in France handling wastes were wounded by a needle incorrectly discarded and one prison officer was stabbed by an inmate in the US.

The risk of transmission after a single *percutaneous* exposure to HIV infected blood is around 0.32%, ten times less than the HCV risk and at least a hundred times less than that for HBV [2]. This rate is an average of different types of exposure with different patients at different stages of the disease. In some cases, the risk is probably higher. A recent case control study showed an increased risk associated with four factors: 1) a deep injury; 2) a device visibly contaminated with blood; 3) a procedure involving a needle placed in an artery or a vein, and 4) a source patient in the terminal stage of AIDS [3]. Post exposure prophylaxis (PEP) with zidovudine (ZDV) appeared to be protective with a 79% risk reduction, although 18 cases of ZDV failure have been reported [4]. The first three factors show the importance of the quantity of blood transferred following an injury. The risk after a less well defined mucocutaneous exposure is estimated at around 0.03% [2].

For an exposed HCW, the risk also depends on
- the *incidence of blood exposures*. The frequency of blood exposures (BEs) is difficult to evaluate considering the frequent under-reporting, estimated at 10 to 60%. Nevertheless, estimates of the annual incidence of BEs based on prospective studies show that the frequency of percutaneous BEs per HCW per year ranges from 0.3-2 for nurses, phlebotomists and doctors on medical wards, whereas rates are higher for surgeons (6-13) [3, 5]. These average rates, calculated on selected studies, must not be generalised to apply to every worker. The procedures which different categories of HCW undertake vary according to the country.
- the *prevalence of HIV infection among patients.*

Prevention

Since the 1980's, the Centers for Disease Control and Prevention (CDC) in the USA, followed by other countries, has issued guidelines to prevent the transmission of HIV and other blood-borne pathogens, based on the concept of Universal Precautions which emphasise the use of standard precautions with blood and body fluids from all patients (see list below). A prevention strategy should also include the use of safer devices, modification of techniques and practices, information and training for HCW.

Main general protective measures

- Cover cuts and abrasions with water proof dressings and/or gloves.
- Wash hands before and after all procedures and when contaminated with body fluids.
- Take particular care in handling and disposal of all sharps; do not re-sheath needles.
- Wear appropriate protective equipment:
  - gloves when direct contact with body fluids on non-intact skin or mucous membranes is possible.
  - protective eyewear and mask when splashing is a possibility.
  - impermeable gowns, plastic aprons when contamination of clothing is possible.
- Dispose of all contaminated waste safely; use conveniently placed disposal containers.

Appropriate post-exposure management must be offered to each HCW after exposure to possible HIV infection, in consultation with people having an expertise in the HIV field. This should include:

- first aid care (clean and decontaminate any exposure as soon as possible, but do not cut into wounds);
- reporting of the incident;
- rapid assessment of the risk based on the type of exposure (see risk factors above) and the source patient status: likelihood of HIV infection (if possible; in case of unknown status, test blood of the source patient with informed consent), viral load, resistance to treatments;
- recommendation of anti-retroviral therapy depending on the careful assessment of the risk (combination of 2 or 3 drugs chosen on a case by case basis) within the first hours after the exposure with full information for the HCW about the limited relevant data on PEP and the potential side-effects [6];
- appropriate counselling and follow-up: medical and serological surveillance (minimum is a base line blood specimen and a test 6 months later).

Restrictions for exposed or infected HCW

There are no restrictions for exposed or infected HCW except for HIV-positive physicians who perform „exposure prone procedures" as described in chapter "The hepatitis B, hepatitis C or HIV infectious health care worker ".

References

1   UNAIDS. Global summary of the HIV/AIDS epidemic, December 1998. AIDS epidemic update - December 1998,1-17 (http://www.unaids.org/unaids/document/epidemio/index.html)
2   PHLS AIDS & STD Centre at the CDSC and Collaborators. Occupational transmission of HIV. Summary of Published Reports - December 1997 Edition. Internal PHLS report
3   Bell D. Occupational risk of HIV infection in health care workers: an overview. Am J Med 1997;102(5B):9-15
4   Cardo D, Culver D, Ciesielski C, Srivasta P, Marcus R, Abiteboul D, Heptonstall J, Ippolito G, Lot F, Mc Kibben P, Bell D and the CDC needlestick surveillance group. A case-control study of HIV seroconversion in health care workers after percutaneous exposure. N Engl J Med 1997;337:1485-1490
5   Abiteboul D. Blood exposure data in Europe. In: Collins C, Kennedy D (Eds). Occupational Blood-borne Infections: risk and management. Oxon, Cab International, UK 1997:59-74
6   CDC. Public Health Service Guidelines for the Management of Health-Care Worker Exposures to HIV and Recommendations for Postexposure Prophylaxis. MMWR 1998;47(RR-7):1-28 (http://www.cdc.gov/epo/mmwr/preview/mmwrhtml/00052722.htm)

Further reading

- http://www.cdc.gov/ncidod/hip/blood/expose.htm
- http://www.unaids.org

Ocupational Health for Health Care Workers - A Practical Guide
H.-M. Hasselhorn, A. Toomingas and M. Lagerström (Editors)
1999 Elsevier Science B.V.

Influenza

Feroza Daroowalla

The influenza virus continues to infect humans and to cause epidemics because the virus strains have the ability to mutate resulting in frequent changes in the antigenic profile (called antigenic drift). Less often, a novel virus subtype, to which humans are not immune, appears due to antigenic shift and can result in worldwide pandemics.

The influenza virus is spread through infected aerosol or secretions generated during sneezing, coughing or talking. Incubation time ranges from 18-36 hours and even persons with mild symptoms or sub-clinical infection may transmit virus.

Health care workers (HCW) who have close and prolonged exposure to infected secretions and droplets released during talking, coughing or sneezing by infected persons are at highest risk for becoming infected. HCW can serve as vectors for the person-to-person transmission of influenza virus in the workplace. Furthermore, HCW who are not vaccinated are likely to transmit virus to patients who may be susceptible to severe infection and even fatal outcomes after nosocomial transmission of influenza.

Symptoms and signs

Illness is characterized by an abrupt onset of fever, myalgias, sore throat, non-productive cough and severe malaise for several days. More severe illness results if primary influenza pneumonia or secondary bacterial pneumonia occur or if there are other lower respiratory tract complications.

Diagnosis

Rapid "point-of-care" diagnostic tests (available within one hour on throat swab or naso-pharyngeal aspirate specimens) for virus antigen of types A and B are available and should be used for identification of infected patients. These tests should be used in conjunction with confirmatory viral cultures.

Prevention

Existing strategies for prevention and treatment include immunization with inactivated vaccine, and treatment and chemo-prophylaxis with anti-viral drugs. In addition, the spread of virus in health care settings can be prevented by isolating infected patients, restricting visitors with respiratory illness, limiting elective surgery during community outbreaks and limiting contact with secretions of infected persons with the use of masks and hand-washing.

Vaccination

Vaccination is recommended to reduce staff illness and absenteeism as well as to reduce nosocomial spread. HCW, including nurses, physicians, aides, and home care workers, who have direct prolonged contact with "high-risk patients", should receive annual vaccine to reduce the chance of transmission to those in their care. Patients who are at high-risk for complications and increased morbidity due to influenza include those in medical/surgical units and chronic care facilities; persons with pulmonary, cardiovascular, metabolic or immune system disorders; persons on aspirin therapy; women in the last two trimesters of pregnancy during the influenza season; and persons aged 65 and older. In addition, HCW who fit into any of the above categories are themselves at increased risk for morbidity due to influenza and should receive the vaccine regardless of their contact with patients. These recommendations are based primarily on those distributed in the USA and recommendations in different countries vary.

Type of vaccine
The vaccine is made of purified, egg-grown inactivated virus and is usually configured to contain the virus strains that match the circulating viruses for that season. The vaccine recipient develops antibody titers that will prevent influenza.

Effectiveness and impact of vaccine in HCW
The effectiveness of the vaccine depends on the age and immuno-competence of the recipient. In addition, when a good match exists between vaccine and circulating virus, the vaccine has been shown to prevent illness in 70-90% of healthy recipients less than 65 years of age. Although the vaccine is less effective in preventing illness in older individuals (50% of recipients), it does reduce the severity of illness in this group. The optimal time for vaccination is October to mid-November in the Northern Hemisphere and from May to June in the Southern Hemisphere. HCW should continue to get vaccinated even after disease activity has occurred in the community. If illness due to influenza does develop, the vaccine may still be effective in preventing lower respiratory tract involvement and other secondary complications.

Vaccination of HCW employed in geriatric long-term care facilities has been associated with a reduced rate of mortality and influenza-like illness among patients [3, 4].

Contraindications and adverse reactions to the vaccine
Contra-indications to vaccine include allergy to egg or egg products, allergy to other vaccine components, or acute febrile illness. The vaccine is considered safe in pregnancy and should be given in the first trimester (this refers to USA recommendations; third trimester vaccination is listed in British documents [6]). The vaccine cannot cause

influenza and serious side effects are rare. Most often, the recipient experiences soreness at the vaccination site. Systemic reactions include: fever, malaise, myalgia in persons who have had no prior exposure to the virus antigens (usually occurs in young children) and immediate, allergic reactions (hives, angioedema, asthma, anaphylaxis) on rare occasions in persons with hypersensitivity to some vaccine component or residual egg protein. Development of Guillain-Barré syndrome (GBS) may be associated with the vaccine and studies have shown an excess of 1-2 cases of GBS per million persons vaccinated. Persons who have developed GBS within six weeks of influenza vaccine may consider avoiding subsequent influenza vaccine.

Use of anti-viral drugs

Amantadine and rimantadine interfere with the replication of type A virus and can be used for prophylaxis of healthy persons to prevent illness. They do not prevent sub-clinical infection and the accompanying immune response. Prophylaxis with these drugs is not a feasible or recommended substitute for vaccination. These antivirals can also be used within two days of onset of illness to reduce the severity and duration of the illness. New antiviral drugs include neuraminidase inhibitors which stop viral replication of both influenza A and B and can be used as a prophylactic agent as well as treatment to decrease severity of illness.

Restrictions for infected HCW

A high index of suspicion for influenza infection should be maintained for upper respiratory symptoms during influenza season. In some countries it is recommended that HCW with acute symptoms of influenza should not have contact with patients or others at the workplace who have not received vaccination prophylaxis, especially those over the age of 65 or under the age of two years and immuno-compromised individuals, until acute symptoms resolve. Because workers with sub-clinical or unrecognized infection may not take the appropriate precautions, the best strategy for preventing outbreaks in a health care setting is to achieve high rates of vaccination among staff. The vaccination campaign should include education about the rarity of severe adverse effects and should make the vaccination easily available on-site and at convenient hours.

References

1   World Health Organization Page: http://www.who.int/emc/diseases/flu/index.html (contains general information and surveillance results)
2   Centers for Disease Control and Prevention Page: http://wonder.cdc.gov (contains the gateway to search CDC guidelines and Morbidity and Mortality Weekly Reports as well as other CDC reports pertaining to influenza)
3   Potter J, Stott DJ, Roberts MA, Elder AG, O'Donnell B, Knight PV, Carman WF. Influenza vaccination of health care workers in long-term-care hospitals reduces the mortality of elderly patients. J Infect Dis. 1997 Jan;175:1-6

4   Wilde JA, McMillan JA, Serwint J, Butta J, O'Riordan MA, Steinhoff MC. Effectiveness of Influenza Vaccine in health care professionals: A Randomized Trial. JAMA .1999;281:908-913
5   Sepkowitz KA. Occupationally acquired Infections in Health Care Workers. Ann Intern Med. 1996; 125: 826-834
6   UK Department of Health page: http://www.doh.gov.uk/publich.htm (contains influenza pandemic document)

Occupational Health for Health Care Workers - A Practical Guide
H.-M. Hasselhorn, A. Toomingas and M. Lagerström (Editors)
© 1999 Elsevier Science B.V. All rights reserved.

Measles

Friedrich Hofmann

Seroepidemiological studies have demonstrated worldwide occurrence of measles with a shift to adulthood infection in recent decades [1]. Non-immune health care workers (HCW) are at increased risk of acquiring measles at work [2]. In countries with limited childhood vaccination coverage the highest occupational risk for HCW exists for those working with children.

The measles virus is highly contagious and transmitted by droplets. Transmission is possible from the beginning of prodromal symptoms up to 7 days after appearance of the rash. Infection leads to lifelong immunity.

Symptoms and signs

Prodromal symptoms with onset of fever, malaise, conjunctivitis and tracheobronchitis are observed 10-12 days after infection, clinical disease 3 days later. The typical enanthem (Koplik's spots) is observed on the buccal mucosa, followed by a maculopapular erythematous eruption two days later. Complications are much more common among adults. These can be otitis media (7-9/100), pneumonia (1-6/100), encephalitis (1/1000-1/2000) and encephalomyelitis (1/1000 with a 10% lethality rate). Death due to measles is observed in one out of ten thousand cases [3]. Causal therapy is not possible.

Diagnosis

The diagnosis of measles is usually performed clinically. Diagnosis can be serologically confirmed by an increase of antibodies between acute and convalescent specimens (ELISA technique).

Prevention

Prevention of measles is performed using live vaccine (normally combined with mumps and rubella vaccine, MMR-vaccine, no vaccination in pregnancy). HCW without a history of measles or with no or only one measles vaccination in childhood should be given one dose of MMR (most cost-effective method). Vaccination is even effective when given up to 72 hours after exposure to the virus.

Restrictions for exposed or infected HCW

Up to 72 hours after first contact with an infected person, non-immune HCW should be vaccinated and allowed to work without restrictions. If the exposure occurred more than three days ago, the HCW should be vaccinated and be restricted from patient care from day 5 after the first to day 21 after the last exposure. If infection occurs, the infected HCW should not work with patients for at least 7 days after onset of the rash.

References

1   Black FL. Measles. In: Evans AS (Ed). Viral Infections of Humans, Epidemiology and Control. 3rd ed. New York: Plenum, 1989:451-465
2   Hofmann F, Wehrle G, Bitzenhofer W, Weilandt R. Measles-epidemiology in German health care workers. In: Hagberg M, Hofmann F, Stössel U, Westlander G (Eds). Occupational Health for Health Care Workers. Landsberg: Ecomed publishers, 1993:201-203
3   Babbott FL Jr, Gordon JE. Modern measles. Am J Med Sci. 1954;228:334-361

Occupational Health for Health Care Workers - A Practical Guide
H.-M. Hasselhorn, A. Toomingas and M. Lagerström (Editors)
© 1999 Elsevier Science B.V. All rights reserved.

Mumps

Friedrich Hofmann

Seroepidemiological studies have demonstrated world-wide occurrence of mumps with a shift to adulthood infection in recent decades [1]. Non-immune health care workers (HCW) can be at risk of contracting mumps from patients. In Germany, higher immunity rates in paediatric personnel compared to adult care and the general population indicate a higher risk for HCW working with children [2]. Infectivity is high from the second week after infection until four days after onset of parotitis. Infection leads to lifelong immunity.

Symptoms and signs

The mumps virus is transmitted by droplets leading to viral shedding at two weeks and clinical disease (parotitis) three weeks after infection. Complications are common among adults and include orchitis (in 60% of infections in men, half of them bilateral – leading to infertility in 25-50%), pancreatitis (50%), mastitis (24% of infections in women) and (rarely) abortion [3]. Causal therapy is not possible.

Diagnosis

The diagnosis of mumps is usually performed clinically. For serological confirmation ELISA technique is used.

Prevention

Prevention of mumps is performed using live vaccine (normally combined with measles and rubella vaccine, MMR-vaccine, no vaccination in pregnancy). HCW without a history of mumps or with no or only one mumps vaccination in childhood should be given one dose of MMR vaccine (most cost-effective method).

Restrictions for exposed and infected HCW

Non-immune HCW should not work with patients from day 12 after first exposure until day 26 after last exposure to mumps. Diseased HCW should be excluded from work with patients until 9 days after onset of parotitis.

References

1   Anonymous. Seroepidemiology of measles, mumps and rubella. Wkly Epidemiol Rec 1992;67:231-233
2   Hofmann F, Bitzenhofer W, Wehrle G, Weilandt R. Mumps epidemiology in health care workers and efficiency of vaccination. In: Hagberg M, Hofmann F, Stössel U, Westlander G (Eds). Occupational Health for Health Care Workers. Landsberg: Ecomed publishers, 1993:222-224
3   Philip RN, Reinhard KR, Lackman DB. Observations on a mumps epidemic in a "virgin" population. Am J Hyg 1959;69:91-111

Occupational Health for Health Care Workers - A Practical Guide
H.-M. Hasselhorn, A. Toomingas and M. Lagerström (Editors)
© 1999 Elsevier Science B.V. All rights reserved.

Parvovirus B19

Friedrich Hofmann

Parvovirus B19 infection (erythema infectiosum) is a mild illness that may lead to severe complications in risk subjects. Parvovirus B19 is transmitted by droplet infection after close contact exposures. The incubation period is usually 4-14 days. Infectivity begins 5-10 days before and lasts until 1-5 days before onset of the rash. The transmission rate to susceptible household members is about 50%.

Infection occurs in outbreaks or as sporadic cases and probably leads to lifelong immunity. Sero-epidemiological studies have shown world-wide occurrence of parvovirus B19 with low seroprevalence rates in children. At least 40% of adults are susceptible [1]. Laboratory infections and nosocomial transmissions from patients to hospital staff or vice versa have been reported [2, 3]. Reports about outbreaks in hospitals and child care underline the occupational risk for health care workers (HCW). In Germany, high infection risks were observed in paediatric and nursing personnel below 30 years [4].

Symptoms and signs

The disease is asymptomatic in about 20%. In some cases a typical garland like erythema on the trunk and extremities is observed. Often, mild systemic symptoms have preceded the rash 1-4 days before. Erythema is often combined with malaise, moderate fever and arthralgia and sometimes with pruritus. Very often, arthropathy is the only clinical symptom of B19 infection in adults. Parvovirus B19 infection may lead to transient aplastic crisis (TAC) in people with chronic haemolytic anaemias and to chronic infection with severe chronic anaemia in people with congenital or acquired immuno-deficiency (e.g. chemotherapy, HIV infection). The virus can be transmitted transplacentally to the foetus, leading to hydrops foetalis and possibly to foetal loss. There is a risk during the whole pregnancy but it is highest within the gestation weeks 20-28. The risk of foetal loss due to infection is estimated to be less than 10% among pregnant women infected by B19 [5]. There are no indications that parvovirus B19 leads to congenital abnormalities. Causal treatment of parvovirus infection is not possible.

Diagnosis

Diagnosis of parvovirus B19 infection is clinically possible in typical cases. Confirmation should be made serologically (IgM).

82   F. Hofmann

Prevention

A vaccine is not available and the effectiveness of post-exposure prophylactics with immunoglobulin has not yet been evaluated. Routine infection control practices minimise the risk of transmission; this includes the wearing of masks, gloves and gowns when caring for patients with TAC or chronic B19 infection. The Centers for Disease Control and Prevention, USA, do not recommend a policy to routinely exclude members of high-risk groups from work, but proposes that an individual decision has to be made in each case [5]. It seems reasonable that pregnant women who are known to be seronegative should not work with suspected B19 infectious patients, and should be subject to special surveillance during outbreaks. Pregnant HCW worried about exposure to B19 should be tested for immunity.

Restrictions for exposed or infected HCW

HCW with typical rash symptoms of parvovirus B19 infection are no longer infectious and may work with patients. Possibly infected HCW should not work with at risk patients from day 5 to day 13 following their possible date of infection.

References

1   Schwarz TF, Hottenträger B, Roggendorf M. Prevalence of antibodies to parvovirus B19 in selected groups of patients and healthy individuals. Zbl Bakt 1992;276:437-442
2   Evans J, Rossiter M, Kumaran T, Marsh G. Human parvovirus aplasia: Case due to cross infection in a ward, Br Med J 1984;288:681
3   Pillay D, Patou G, Kibbler C, Griffiths P. Parvovirus B19 outbreak in a childrens ward. Lancet 1992;339:107-109
4   Schwarz TF, Hofmann F, Jäger G, Wehrle G, Bitzenhofer W, Weilandt R. Parvovirus B19 infections - occupational risk in the nursing profession? In: Hagberg M, Hofmann F, Stössel U, Westlander G (Eds). Occupational health for health care workers. Landsberg: Ecomed publishers, 1993:211-214
5   CDC. Current Trends Risks Associated with Human Parvovirus B19 Infection. (http://aepo-xdv-www.epo.cdc.gov/wonder/prevguid/m0001348/body0001.htm, survey information)

Rubella

Philippe Kiss

Rubella (German measles, 3-day measles) is caused by the rubella virus and is spread by droplet transmission. In many countries vaccination policies have drastically reduced the incidence of rubella. However, infection may be reintroduced through importation from countries that do not routinely promote rubella vaccination. Despite the vaccination campaigns, approximately 8-15% of women of childbearing age remain susceptible to rubella. In certain Asian countries (e.g. China and Korea) seronegativity rate among women even reaches 19-23%. Furthermore, the selective vaccination of girls in the past combined with the reduced circulation of the wild virus has created a pool of susceptible adult males. In the USA 75% of all rubella cases since 1994 were reported among persons 15-44 years of age [1]. Infection leads to lifelong immunity.

The disease poses an occupational risk for non-immune pregnant health care workers (HCW). In addition, there is a risk of rubella transmission from infected HCW to susceptible patients. The shifting age distribution of rubella susceptibility puts *every* non-immune HCW at risk of rubella infection, and does not restrict the risk to paediatric settings.

Symptoms and signs

Most cases of postnatal rubella are subclinical. If symptomatic, infection usually causes a mild self-limiting disease with rash and adenopathy in children, preceded by flu-like prodromal symptoms in adults. Complications include various forms of arthritis (1/3 of all cases among women, less frequent in children and men), haemorrhagic manifestations (1/3000 cases) and encephalitis (1/5000 cases) [2]. Maternal infection during pregnancy is serious and can induce spontaneous abortion, stillbirth and a variety of congenital defects, which are usually denoted as the congenital rubella syndrome (CRS). The risk of acquiring CRS after primary maternal infection ranges from 50-80% during the first trimester to virtually zero beyond the 20th week. In most cases (maternal) immunity prevents clinical disease as well as the occurrence of CRS. Causal therapy is not possible.

Diagnosis

Humoral immunity is routinely evaluated by assessing rubella IgG antibodies, of which a level of 10 IU/ml is considered to be protective [3].

Prevention

All personnel, both male and female, working in a health care setting, should be immune to rubella. If laboratory evidence of immunity or if reliable vaccination records are not available, IgG antibody levels should be assessed and subsequently HCW with negative or indeterminate levels should be (re)vaccinated. The vaccine of choice is the combined measles-mumps-rubella (MMR) vaccine. If there is an immunity or a contra-indication for one or two of the other components, the bi- or monovalent vaccine can be administered.

Single-dose vaccination results in ≥ 95% seroconversion [4]. Contra-indications in healthy persons are (a) history of anaphylactic reaction to neomycin and (b) pregnancy (however, up to now no CRS has been reported following accidental vaccination during pregnancy).

Restrictions for the exposed or infected HCW

There is no postexposure prophylactic treatment. However, for (future) outbreak control purposes, exposed susceptible HCW should be vaccinated and excluded from duty from the 7th day after the first exposure till the 21st day after last exposure or – in the case of disease – until 5 days after the rash appears [5].

References

1   CDC. Rubella and congenital rubella syndrome-United States 1994-1997. MMWR 1997;46(16):350-354
2   Gershon AA. Rubella virus (German measles). In: Mandell G, Bennet J, Dolin R (Eds). Principles and Practice of Infectious Diseases. 4th ed. New York: Churchill Livingstone, 1995:1459-1465
3   Skendzel LP. Rubella immunity. Defining the level of protective antibody. Am J Clin Pathol 1996;106:170-174
4   CDC. Rubella prevention. Recommendations of the Immunization Practices Advisory Committee (ACIP). MMWR 1990;39 (RR-15):1-13 (Survey information)
5   CDC. Immunization of health-care workers. Recommendations of the Advisory Committee on Immunization Practices (ACIP) and the Hospital Infection Control Practices Advisory Committee (HICPAC). MMWR 1997;46 (RR-18):1-44 (Survey information)

Occupational Health for Health Care Workers - A Practical Guide
H.-M. Hasselhorn, A. Toomingas and M. Lagerström (Editors)

Varicella Zoster infection

David Snashall

Varicella Zoster Virus (VZV) is a herpes virus that infects almost everyone eventually. Varicella (chicken pox) is the result of a first infection with VZV whereas Herpes Zoster (shingles) results from reactivation of latent VZV at a later date. There are no known occupational causes of reactivation. Individuals are infectious to non-immunes at various stages of both diseases. Chicken pox is highly infectious, spread by droplet infection up to 48 hours before the rash appears and by contact. The shingles rash is also infectious but is not spread by the respiratory route in immuno-competent individuals. Primary VZV infection confers almost 100% lifelong immunity to chicken pox. Nosocomial transmission of VZV has been well documented in the medical literature [1]. Those at risk are non-immune medical staff and those in childcare who are exposed more often.

Symptoms and signs

In childhood the primary infection is usually mild. Adults often suffer more. Those at risk of severe, possibly life-threatening complications are the immuno-compromised (transplant recipients, patients receiving chemotherapy, radiotherapy or substantial steroid treatment, HIV infected people), persons with skin lesions (burns, eczema), non immune pregnant women and their unborn babies and neonates, especially premature ones in whom perinatal chicken pox can be fatal. Congenital infection with the risk of foetal malformation or mental retardation is estimated to occur in 1-2% of cases when a primary infection occurs in a non-immune mother during the first twenty weeks of pregnancy. There is no risk of shingles affecting the foetus of a pregnant mother who is immune.

Prevention

Primary prevention could be achieved by reducing the community burden of VZV by vaccination. A live attenuated vaccine has been available for several years [2]. In many hospitals the VZV immune status of the newly employed is measured and non-immunes are thereby easily identified and could be vaccinated.

Before this strategy is universally implemented - there are issues of cost, efficacy and safety of the vaccine in adults and doubts as to the long-term immunity conferred - other methods have to be used to prevent nosocomial infection.

Secondary prevention can be achieved by giving VZV immunoglobulin (VZIG) to vulnerable individuals potentially exposed to the virus. This is expensive and VZIG is in short supply.

The treatment of clinical varicella with high dose acyclovir is well established but the drug is not licenced in all countries for use in pregnancy. Other antivirals have also been used.

Management of exposed or infected HCW

The Centers for Disease Control and Prevention (CDC) have issued guidelines designed to prevent VZV transmission to and from HCW [3]. When a case of VZV is imported into a hospital the following steps should be taken:

- The diagnosis is confirmed (clinical, serological or by electron microscopy).
- A list of potential staff contacts is drawn up and matched against a known history of clinical VZV. If an individual's VZV history is not known the immune status should be checked by VZV antibody estimation.
- Those non-immune staff who have been exposed to the index case are regarded as potentially infectious from ten to twenty one days after their contact with VZV.
- They are either given leave during this period or redeployed to areas of the hospital with no patient contact.

The time taken and expense of dealing with potential VZV outbreaks in this way can be significant. The most cost effective solution would seem to be to ask all newly employed staff about their past history of VZV, antibody test all those who have had no exposure or who are uncertain and then to vaccinate those deemed to be non immune [4].

References

1   Weber DJ, Rutala WA, Parham C. Impact and Costs of Varicella Prevention in a University Hospital. Am J Public Health, 1988;78:19-23
2   Asano Y, Suga S, Yoshikawa T, Kobayashi I, Yazaki T, Shibata M, Tsuzuki K, Ito S. Experience and reason: twenty-year follow-up of protective immunity of the OKA strain life varicella vaccine. Pediatrics, 1994;94:524-526
3   Williams WW. CDC Guidelines for Infection Control in Hospital Personnel. Infect Control, 1983;4:326-349
4   Gray AN, Fenn P, Weinberg J, Miller E, Maguire A. An Economic Analysis of Varicella Vaccination for Health Care Workers. Epidemiol Infect, 1997;119:209-220

Occupational Health for Health Care Workers - A Practical Guide
H.-M. Hasselhorn, A. Toomingas and M. Lagerström (Editors)
© 1999 Elsevier Science B.V. All rights reserved.

Diphtheria

Hans-Martin Hasselhorn

During the recent diphtheria epidemic in the new states of the former Soviet Union, health care workers (HCW) were reported to have been one of the major occupational risk groups [1]. Due to the rare occurrence of diphtheria nowadays in industrialised countries (up to nine cases annually in Germany), new cases are being diagnosed in a later stage of the disease, often more than a week after admission to a hospital. This situation puts the unaware HCW at increased risk. Since 50 years ago, a shift of diphtheria disease has been observed from children to those of adult age. Serological surveys indicate that especially young to middle aged adults often lack evidence of sufficient antibody protection.

Diphtheria is caused by toxinogenic *Corynebacterium diphtheriae*. The risk for transmission is high for unprotected people and transmission occurs mostly via *close* contact with an infectious person such as exposure to coughing. In a hospital there may be exposure to respiratory droplets during laryngeal inspection or direct contact with cutaneous lesions. However, even if the contact with the infectious patient was not *close* (as defined above), transmission cannot be excluded. Vaccination is highly effective but does not prevent nasopharyngeal carriage of the bacterium. Transmission is therefore possible via vaccinated people.

Signs and symptoms

Following an incubation period of 2-5 days, non-specific respiratory symptoms like sore throat (pseudo membraneous pharyngitis), low grade fever and swelling of the neck ("bull-neck") may occur. In the later stages, myocarditis and nerve paralysis may develop. Cutaneous diphtheria consists of non-distinctive sores and ulcers.

Diagnosis

The diagnosis of the disease is made by culture. Serological protection demonstrated by protective antibody levels is commonly confirmed by two techniques. The Cell Culture Neutralisation Assay is regarded as the gold standard with a diphtheria antitoxin (AT) level ≥ 0.1 IU/ml being considered protective. A more common technique is the Enzyme-Linked Immunosorbent Assay (ELISA) and here, levels ≥ 1 IU/ml may be considered protective because this technique is not exact in the low range.

Antitoxin levels do not always reflect immunity. Often, infected people with AT levels below 0.1 IU/ml and even below 0.01 IU/ml will not develop clinical disease. In rare cases, clinical disease may occur in spite of high AT levels ≥1.0 IU, especially in people with reduced physical conditions, such as alcohol abusers.

Prevention

Primary prevention of diphtheria should be achieved by regular vaccination of all health care personnel, including those with a history of diphtheria, every 10 years.

If it becomes known that a patient has been, or is currently infectious, all personnel involved in the care of this patient and other staff such as cleaners working in the patient's room need to be monitored [2]:

- All personnel should be informed about the disease and monitored daily for diphtheria-specific signs for at least seven days.
- Nasopharyngeal cultures should be obtained from all personnel.
- Unvaccinated or insufficiently vaccinated HCW *closely* exposed (as described above) as well as carriers should receive either a) a single intramuscular dose of benzathine penicillin (1.2 mU) or b) oral erythromycin for seven days (1gm/day). In addition one dose of diphtheria vaccine for adults (diphtheria or Tetanus/diphtheria) should be given.
- HCW with the last diphtheria vaccination dating back more than five years should receive a booster dose.

Restrictions for exposed or infected HCW

Insufficiently vaccinated personnel who have had *close* contact with the infectious patient must be treated as described above and may not work until two cultures obtained ≥24 hours apart and ≥24 hours after last intake of antibiotics, are negative. Personnel with positive cultures must not work until two cultures obtained ≥24 hours apart and ≥24 hours after completion of antimicrobiological therapy, are negative. Cultures should then be repeated on alternate days during a 14-day period. Personnel with clinical diphtheria may not work until the disease has resolved and two cultures obtained ≥ 24 hours after last intake of antibiotics and ≥24 hours apart, are negative [2, 3].

References

1   WHO. Expanded Programme on Immunization: Outbreak of diphtheria, update. Wkly Epidemiol Rec 1993;19:134-138
2   CDC. Guideline for infection control in health care personnel, 1998. AJIC 1998;26:289-354
3   CDC. Immunization of Health-Care Workers: Recommendations of the Advisory Committee on Immunization Practices (ACIP) and the Hospital Infection Control Practices Advisory Committee (HICPAC). MMWR 1997;46(RR-18):1-44

Helicobacter pylori

Antoon De Schryver, Myriam Van Winckel

Since 1983, *Helicobacter pylori* has been recognised as a major cause of gastric and duodenal ulcers. Infection with *H. pylori* has been associated with an increased risk of gastric cancer and gastric lymphoma. *H. pylori* can be eradicated with antibiotics.

Acquisition of *H. pylori* infection occurs mostly in early childhood and persists throughout life if not treated. Prevalence in childhood ranges from 5-10% in industrialised countries to 80-90% in developing countries. Humans are the only identified reservoirs of *H. pylori*. Although the exact mode of transmission remains uncertain, current knowledge favours person-to-person transmission early in life. *H. pylori* has been isolated both in faeces and saliva, so both faecal-oral as well as oral-oral transmission may occur and may be of different relevance in different populations.

Symptoms and signs

Primary infection is mostly asymptomatic or may present as gastritis. Eradication success is between 70-90% after appropriate therapy.

Occupational risk

With the close personal contact inherent in patient care, including handling of faecal and oral materials, health care workers (HCW) may be at an increased risk of acquiring *H. pylori* and subsequent development of associated conditions. There have been case-reports of *H. pylori* infection after mouth-to-mouth resuscitation; several studies have shown that *H. pylori* can be transmitted through upper gastrointestinal endoscopy [1]. However, detailed studies about the occupational risk in HCW are scarce, and the results remain controversial. An increased risk for infection by *H. pylori* has been shown in endoscopy staff, particularly in gastroenterologists [2]; in other HCW including dentists no clearly increased risk has been demonstrated, but this may reflect the protective nature of normal infection control procedures within the health care setting. Among inhabitants of institutions for the intellectually disabled the prevalence of *H. pylori* is high; in one study an increased risk was found in employees with prolonged close physical contact with the intellectually disabled [3].

Prevention

To prevent occupational transmission, HCW should practice good basic infection control techniques with all patients. Preventive measures are particularly important in upper gastrointestinal endoscopy units. Wearing gloves, masks and the appropriate use of disinfectants for hands and instruments are essential for staff in contact with patients in these units. In all other medical settings, gloves should be worn when handling gastric secretions, faecal material or articles contaminated with faeces. HCW should wash their hands after contact with patient saliva or faeces.

References

1   Langenberg W, Rauws EA, Oudbier JH, Tytgat GN. Patient-to-patient transmission of Campylobacter pylori infection by fiberoptic gastroduodenoscopy and biopsy. J Infect Dis 1990;161:507-511
2   Rudi J, Toeppe H, Marx N, Zuna I, Theilmann L, Stremmel W, Raedsch R. Risk of infection with Helicobacter pylori and Hepatitis A virus in different groups of hospital workers. Am J Gastroenterol 1997;92:258-262
3   Boehmer CJ, Klinkenberg-Knol EC, Kuipers EJ, Niezen-de Boer MC, Schreuder H, Schuckink-Kool F, Meuwissen SG. The prevalence of Helicobacter pylori infection among inhabitants and healthy employees of institutes for the intellectually disabled. Am J Gastroenterol 1997;92:1000-1004

Further reading

- http://www.helicobacter.org/

Meningococcal meningitis

Jean François Gehanno, Christophe Paris

Neisseria meningitidis causes both endemic and epidemic disease, and has become the leading cause of bacterial meningitis in children and young adults in the United States [1]. Transmission of *N. meningitidis* occurs via respiratory droplets from patients and 3% of the cases are considered secondary (defined as one that occurs among close contacts of a primary-case patient more than 24 hours after onset of illness in the primary-case patient). Only very few secondary cases among health care workers (HCW) have been reported in the literature. These are mostly laboratory-acquired infections but also several cases occurred following mouth to mouth resuscitation and one case when assisting in the evaluation of a patient with meningococcaemia and meningitis [2]. More recently, we reported one case of nosocomial meningococcaemia in a physician who had performed intubation on a child suffering from meningococcaemia. These cases highlight the important need for preventive strategies to avoid meningococcal disease among HCW.

Symptoms and signs

Bacterial meningitis can develop dramatically 2-5 days after infection. Symptoms of meningococcal disease include headache, nausea, vomiting, fever, altered mental status, with or without purpuric lesions. Meningococcaemia is lethal in 5-10% of treated and 50% of untreated cases.

Diagnosis

Diagnosis is made clinically and by culture of blood and cerebrospinal fluid (CSF) or PCR (CSF).

Prevention

First, it is necessary to eradicate nasopharyngeal carriage of *N. meningitidis* from the patient. Second, to prevent secondary cases among HCW, chemoprophylaxis is necessary for those who have been very closely exposed without a mask. Such exposure would include performing endotracheal intubation, undertaking respiratory physiotherapy, closely examining the oropharynx or taking throat samples. In these cases, rifampicin 600 mg orally twice a day for 2 days is suggested, ideally within 24 hours after the case is identified [1]. Alternative available drugs are ciprofloxacin (500 mg, single oral dose) or ceftriaxone (250 mg, single IM dose). Nevertheless, the risks of adverse effects and of increasing bacterial resistance are reasons for providing prophylaxis only to HCW who have been in close contact with the index patient. Knowledge about these procedures must be available in all medical areas of increased risk, such as accident and emergency and paediatrics. HCW with more remote contact with the infected patient should be given advice to seek medical care in case of early signs indicating an infection with *N. meningitidis* especially during the following 5 days.

The above measures should not overshadow the importance of promoting preventive behaviour including adherence to droplet precautions, designed to decrease the risk of being infected by *N. meningitidis*. Thus, the use of masks should be strongly promoted for HCW highly exposed to oropharyngeal secretions of patients who are known or suspected to suffer from meningococcaemia or meningococcal pneumonia. Preventive vaccination for HCW should be proposed in areas with very high endemicity or during community outbreaks when serogroups A, C, Y and W-135 are involved. In central Europe the B strain is most common.

Restrictions for exposed or infected HCW

The prevalence of asymptomatic nasopharyngeal carriers of *N. meningitidis* in the general population is high, ranging from 19-39% in adult men [3]. Therefore, there is no need to identify, to treat or to exclude HCW from duty who are found to be asymptomatic carriers.

References

1   Morbidity and Mortality Weekly Report (MMWR). Control and prevention of meningococcal disease. MMWR 1997;46:1-12
2   Centers for Disease Control and Prevention. Nosocomial meningococcemia - Wisconsin. MMWR 1978;27:358-363
3   Wenzel RP, Davies JA, Mitzel JR, Beam WE. Nonusefulness of meningococcal carriage rates. Lancet 1973;2:205

Occupational Health for Health Care Workers - A Practical Guide
H.-M. Hasselhorn, A. Toomingas and M. Lagerström (Editors)   93
© 1999 Elsevier Science B.V. All rights reserved.

Tuberculosis

Nenad Kralj

Tuberculosis (TB) is the leading cause of death associated with infectious diseases globally. Ten million new cases of active disease appear each year, with as many as 3 million deaths, primarily in developing countries. The incidence of TB is expected to increase substantially world wide during the next 10 years because of interaction between TB and human immunodeficiency virus (HIV), the development of multi-drug resistant TB (MDR-TB), the decline of public health services and the increase in immigration of people from countries with a high prevalence of TB [1].

Mycobacterium tuberculosis, the acid-fast, aerobic bacillus that causes TB, is carried in airborne particles, or droplet nuclei. The particles are an estimated 1-5µm in size, and normal air currents can keep them airborne for prolonged time periods, spreading them through rooms or buildings, where they can be inhaled. Once in the alveoli, bacilli are taken up by alveolar macrophages and spread through the body. Usually within 2-10 weeks after initial infection with *M. tuberculosis*, the immune response limits further multiplication of the tubercle bacilli. However some bacilli remain dormant and viable for many years. Active disease develops in only 5% of individuals within two years after infection. In another 5%, active disease develops sometime later, resulting in a total of 10% active cases amongst infected but otherwise healthy individuals over a lifetime. Immunocompromised persons have a greater risk of progression of latent TB infection to active TB disease; HIV infection is the strongest known risk for this progression.

Occupational risk

Transmission of *M. tuberculosis* is a recognised occupational risk for health care workers (HCW). Nosocomial transmission of *M. tuberculosis* is associated with close contact with persons who have infectious TB, especially during the performance of certain diagnostic and therapeutic procedures, including bronchoscopy, endotracheal intubation and suctioning, open abscess irrigation, autopsy and sputum induction. Transmission has also been reported following distant contact and even via ventilation. Besides departments such as respiratory medicine, infectious diseases, emergency care and areas involving care of immunocompromised patients, pathology departments seem to carry an increased risk of transmission to HCW.

Several TB outbreaks among persons in health-care facilities have been reported [2]. Many of these outbreaks involved transmission of MDR-TB to both patients and HCW. Most of the patients and some of the HCW were HIV-infected persons in whom TB progressed rapidly to active disease. Mortality associated with those outbreaks was high (range: 43%-93%). Furthermore, the interval between diagnosis and death was brief (range of median intervals: 4-16 weeks) [3].

Symptoms and signs

Primary pulmonary tuberculosis in adults is usually asymptomatic or associated with malaise, low grade fever and/or lymphadenopathy. When primary infection is not contained or reactivated, disease is manifest as bronchopneumonia with symptoms like fever, night sweats, weight loss, haemoptysis and productive cough. Advanced disease may even involve pleural, skeletal, CNS, and other sites. Immunocompromised people may develop severe miliary tuberculosis (abrupt onset of fever, malaise, weakness, anorexia, weight loss, lymphadenopathy, hepatosplenomegaly) always with bilateral pneumonitis and often with meningitis.

Diagnosis

The PPD skin test (Purified Protein Derivative) is the only screening method available for demonstrating infection with *M. tuberculosis*. The Mantoux test administration of a measured amount of PPD-tuberculin is currently the preferred method for doing the test. In PPD-testing usually 5 tuberculin units (TU) is injected just beneath the surface of the skin on the volar surface of the forearm. As the result of the injection a discrete, pale elevation of the skin, a weal or induration, that is 6-10 mm in diameter should be produced. According to the Centers for Disease Control and Prevention (CDC) multiple puncture tests (MPT) should not be used to screen high-risk populations because they are less specific than the Mantoux test. On the other hand studies in Europe have proved the efficacy of MPT in tuberculosis screening in occupational health units [4].

Interpretation of PPD skin test results

PPD test results should be read by designated, trained personnel between 48 and 72 hours after injection (Mantoux test) or 5-7 days after application of MPT. The transverse diameter of induration should be recorded in millimetres, erythema should not be measured. Patient or HCW self-reading of PPD test results should not be accepted. In MPT an induration ≥ 2 mm on the spot of application is classified as positive.

In case of the Mantoux skin test the classification of the test result is based on the size of induration at the injection site as well as other criteria as listed in table 1. Bacille Calmette-Guérin (BCG) vaccinated HCW will mostly show a PPD test reaction for up to 15 years or even longer. In these, a Mantoux test reaction ≥ 10 mm (in UK ≥ 15 mm) induration should be rated as possible TB infection, especially if the HCW has had contact with a TB infectious person or to populations with high prevalence of TB [5]. Mantoux testing methods vary between countries and operators, tuberculins used, methods, readings and interpretations therefore vary.

Table 1. Interpretation of PPD (Mantoux) skin test results (modified CDC recommendations [3])

Classified as positive if induration	among persons
<5 mm	• Never classified as positive
≥5 mm	• Who have had recent close contact with persons who have active TB; • Who have human immunodeficiency virus (HIV) infection or risk factors for HIV infection but unknown HIV status; • Who have fibrotic chest radiographs consistent with healed TB

≥10 mm	• Who do not meet any of the above criteria, but who belong to one or more of the following groups having high risk for TB:
	   – Injecting-drug users known to be HIV seronegative.
	   – Persons who have other medical conditions that have been reported to increase the risk for progressing from latent TB infection to active TB. These medical conditions include diabetes mellitus, conditions requiring prolonged high-dose corticosteroid therapy and other immunosuppressive therapy (including bone marrow and organ transplantation), chronic renal failure, some haematological disorders (e.g. leukaemia and lymphomas), other specific malignancies (e.g. carcinoma of the head or neck), weight loss of ≥10% below ideal body weight, silicosis, gastrectomy, jejunoileal bypass.
	   – Residents and employees of high-risk congregate settings: prisons and jails, nursing homes and other long-term facilities for the elderly, health-care facilities (including some residential mental health facilities), and homeless shelters.
	   – Foreign-born persons recently arrived (i.e., within the last 5 years) from countries having a high prevalence or incidence of TB.
	   – Some medically underserved, low-income populations, including migrant farm workers and homeless persons.
	   – High-risk racial or ethnic minority populations, as defined locally.
	   – Children < 4 years of age or infants, children, and adolescents exposed to adults in high-risk categories

≥15 mm	• Always classified as positive

PPD skin test conversion

PPD converters are those who show a positive PPD skin test reaction and whose previous test result has been recorded as negative. Further, an increase in induration of ≥10 mm in Mantoux test within a 2-year period is classified as a conversion to a positive test among persons < 35 years of age. An increase in induration of ≥15 mm within a 2-year period is classified as a conversion for persons ≥35 years of age. Regardless of age, for employees in facilities where a person who has TB poses a hazard to many susceptible persons (e.g. health-care facilities, schools, and child-care facilities), an increase of ≥10 mm induration should be considered positive. Although currently available PPD tests are <100% sensitive and specific for detection of infection with *M. tuberculosis*, no better diagnostic methods have yet been devised [6].

Tuberculin skin testing during pregnancy

Studies in which the same patients were tested during and after pregnancy have demonstrated that pregnancy has no effect on cutaneous tuberculin hypersensitivity. Tuberculin skin testing is considered valid and safe throughout pregnancy [7]. No teratogenic effects of testing during pregnancy have been documented.

Chest radiography

Tuberculin positive HCW should be screened using chest radiography at the *preemployment examination* if there are clinical or laboratory signs (e. g. enhanced white cell count, raised erythrocyte sedimentation rate) of possible tuberculosis and when former chest radiography during the last 6 months cannot be documented. *Follow-up* radiography should be performed using the same clinical and laboratory criteria. Immediate chest radiography is the preferred method when the objective is to exclude/verify acute disease after tuberculin skin test *conversion*. Another chest-X-ray should be done 6 months after tuberculin skin test conversion to exclude late onset of disease [4].

Bacteriology

Smear and culture examination of at least three sputum specimens collected on different days is the main diagnostic procedure for pulmonary TB. Sputum smears that fail to demonstrate acid-fast bacilli (AFB) do not exclude the diagnosis of TB. HIV-infected patients who have pulmonary TB may be less likely than immunocompetent patients to have AFB present on sputum smears, which is consistent with the lower frequency of cavitary pulmonary disease observed among HIV-infected persons. A culture of sputum or other clinical specimen that contains *M. tuberculosis* provides a definitive diagnosis of TB. Conventional laboratory methods may require 4-8 weeks for species identification; however, the use of radiometric culture techniques and nucleic acid probes facilitates more rapid detection and identification of mycobacteria.

Prevention

Often, transmission in health care is caused by incomplete or absent preventive measures. Prevention of tuberculosis among HCW is handled quite differently internationally and may be performed at different levels. Diagnostic skin tests and chest radiography as described above may be seen as part of tuberculosis prevention as well as the following measures in Table 2.

Table 2. Prevention of tuberculosis

Primary Prevention:
- negative airflow in areas where infectious patients are housed and use of negative pressure rooms
- using germicidal ultraviolet irradiation
- early identification of infected patients and provision of effective treatment
- using respiratory protection[1]
- reducing droplet nuclei generation by use of respiratory protection by the patient when coughing and sneezing

Secondary Prevention:
- early identification, isolation and effective treatment of HCW with active TB
- monitoring of occupational risk using PPD skin test (purified protein derivative) and/or chest X-ray
- systematic TB screening by periodic retesting of employees with negative PPD skin test
- in case of PPD test conversion immediate chest radiography examination; another chest radiography after 6 months and/or possibly isoniazid prophylaxis

Tertiary Prevention:
- prompt treatment of symptomatic individuals, with follow up to insure that chemotherapy is continued throughout the recommended period

---

[1] The minimal acceptable level of respirator protection for TB is the Type 95 Respirator (US), FFP 2-class mask (EU), respectively. Use of surgical mask is insufficient [8].

Isoniazid (INH)

In the USA, it is recommend that HCW with positive PPD test results should be evaluated for preventive therapy regardless of their ages if they a) are recent converters, b) are close contacts of persons who have active TB, c) have a medical condition that increases risk for TB, d) have HIV infection, or e) are injecting drugs. HCW with positive PPD test results who do not have these risk factors should be evaluated for preventive therapy if they are <35 years of age. Preventive therapy should be considered for *anergic* persons (those who do not react to skin tests in spite of sensitisation) who have known contacts with infectious TB patients and for persons from populations in which the prevalence of TB infection is very high (e.g. a prevalence of >10%). The usual preventive therapy regimen is oral isoniazid (INH) 300 mg daily for adults. The recommended duration of therapy is 12 months for persons with HIV infection and 9 months for children. Other persons should receive INH therapy for 6-12 months [3]. In contrast to the USA, preventive INH therapy in HCW with skin test conversion is not being performed in most European countries.

Bacille Calmette-Guérin (BCG) vaccine

Whereas BCG is administered in developing countries, its use has been discontinued or diminished in many countries in Europe and North America. In a recent and large study performed in India, with more than 200.000 participants, BCG showed no protective effects among adults [9]. In two meta-analyses the efficacy of the vaccine was found to be 50% in adults, however [5]. The BCG vaccine is more likely to prevent disseminated forms of tuberculosis in children than pulmonary tuberculosis in adolescents or adults [10]. Most often, intradermal injection of the BCG vaccine causes a local superficial ulcer, or pustule. Severe or prolonged ulceration, regional cervical, or axillary lymphadenitis may occur in a small percentage of patients. BCG vaccination for HCW is controversial. Whereas it is compulsory in France and also widely used in the UK it is not performed at all in some other countries, e.g. Germany. BCG vaccinated people will show a positive PPD skin test reaction for about 10-15 years. Consequently the skin test becomes difficult to interpret and diagnostic chest X-ray exposure to may HCW increase.

Measures for exposed or infected HCW

HCW with active TB have to be excluded from duty until the HCW has become non-infectious. This may be the case when the HCW is being treated adequately, the cough has resolved and TB cultures of three consecutive sputum samples taken on different days are negative [5].

There are no work restrictions for HCW exposed to patients with open pulmonary tuberculosis. There is a need however, for verification that no infection has occurred or that possible infection will be diagnosed at an early stage. When it becomes known that a patient (or HCW) has or has had unknown pulmonary tuberculosis and may have spread the bacilli, all persons who have worked in the same area (HCW, cleaning staff etc) need to be monitored for possible infection. All personnel involved need to be informed about the symptoms of primary infection. Personnel with previously positive PPD skin test should have a chest radiograph taken at the earliest 2 months after the last contact with the infectious patient. Personnel with known negative PPD skin test should be re-tested at the earliest 8 weeks after the last contact with the infectious patient. Where there is tuberculin test conversion the procedure described above should be followed.

References

1   Global Tuberculosis Control WHO Report 1997; Geneva 1997
2   Menzies D, Fanning A, Yuan L, Fitgerald M. Tuberculosis among health care workers. N Engl J Med 1995; 332: 92-98
3   Guidelines for Preventing the Transmission of Mycobacterium tuberculosis in Health-Care Facilities, 1994. CDC Morbidity and Mortality Weekly Report (MMWR) 1994;43: RR13
4   Kralj N, Hofmann F, Michaelis M. Zur Methodik der Tuberkulosefrüherkennung bei arbeitsmedizinischen Vorsorgeuntersuchungen im Gesundheitsdienst. Sozialmed. Umweltmed 1997;32:50-54 (in German, abstract in English)
5   CDC. Guideline for infection control in health care personnel, 1998. AJIC 1998;26:289-354
6   Evans DJ, Barker RJ, Geddes DM. Tuberculosis skin tests [letter]. Lancet 1996;348:1512-1513
7   Snider D. Pregnancy and tuberculosis. Chest 1984; 86(suppl.):S10-S13
8   Willeke K, Qian Y. Tuberculosis control through respirator wear: performance of National Institute of Occupational Safety and Health-regulated respirators. Am J Inf Control 1998;26:139-142
9   Baily GV. Tuberculosis Prevention Trial, Madras. Trial of BCG vaccines in south India for tuberculosis prevention. Indian J Med Res 1980;72(suppl.):1-74
10 Cohn DL. Use of Bacille Calmette-Guérin vaccination for the prevention of tuberculosis. Am J Med Sci 1997;313:372-376

Further reading

- http://www.osha.gov/safelinks.html
- http://www.cdc.com
- http://www.who.ch
- http://hna.ffh.vic.gov.au/phb/hprot/tb/tbm/tbindex.html

Occupational Health for Health Care Workers - A Practical Guide
H.-M. Hasselhorn, A. Toomingas and M. Lagerström (Editors)

Occupational infections – briefing notes

Hans-Martin Hasselhorn

Specific infectious diseases with major occupational health relevance due to high prevalence and/or severe outcome have been described in separate chapters in this book. Brief information on other selected infectious diseases with possible relevance for the occupational health of health care workers (HCW) are presented in this chapter.

Haemorrhagic fevers

Haemorrhagic fevers in humans are rare but severe diseases which often lead to death or disability. twelve viral pathogens are known to lead to diseases such as Ebola haemorrhagic fever, Yellow fever, Dengue fever, Rift Valley fever, Crimean Congo haemorrhagic fever, Marburg haemorrhagic fever, and Lassa fever. These diseases are found in temperate and tropical climates, especially Africa. Most haemorrhagic fevers are zoonoses (with an animal reservoir) and may thus be acquired by contact with infected animals, by vectors (ticks, mosquitoes) or by aerosols and may be spread to non-endemic regions by import of animals (e.g. monkeys). Rift valley fever has been acquired by the aerosol mode of transmission in laboratory workers. Person to person transmission may occur by direct contact with blood or secretions from an infected person. Blood may be highly infectious (e.g. Ebola virus). The risk from sharps injuries must be reduced as much as possible. Infection may be prevented by adhering to hygienic and isolation procedures and barrier nursing techniques according to the universal and standard precaution measures presented in the chapter "Hygienic infection control". Direct contact, also with dead patients, must be prevented.

Legionellosis

Case reports indicate an increased occupational risk for HCW exposed to legionella (mostly: *Legionella pneumophila*). The organism is spread by aerosols. Patient to HCW transmission has not been reported. Occupational exposure is possible when showering patients and via infected air conditioning. Dental personnel are at special risk. Non-specific symptoms occurring among infected personnel are likely to be misdiagnosed as influenza. Severe symptoms occur mainly among immuno-compromised subjects. Constant exposure to a legionella species (e.g. by air conditioning) may induce a transient immunity which wanes when away from exposure (e.g. during vacation). Water pipes should regularly be flushed with water over 60°C, which will kill the bacteria. Regular microbiological surveillance of water supplies is also necessary.

Pertussis

Vaccine induced immunity wanes 5-10 years after the last pertussis vaccination and many become susceptible in adulthood. Occupational acquisition of pertussis occurs far more often in health care than commonly believed, especially among those who work in child care and also in laboratories. Symptoms are non-specific in the early stage of disease. Therefore, it is difficult to limit occupational exposure to HCW by placing patients and their families under droplet precautions alone.

Since disease may be severe in adults, vaccination of staff is advisable at least in child care work, once the acellular vaccine will be licensed for adults. Although its efficacy is questionable, post exposure prophylaxis may be provided for personnel who have had direct contact with respiratory secretions or aerosol from infected patients. Treatment regimens include erythromycin 500mg 4 times per day for 14 days or trimethoprim-sulphamethoxazole 1 tablet twice per day for 14 days. HCW with pertussis may not work from the early catarrhal stage up to the third week from the onset of paroxysms or until the fifth day after beginning of medication. No work restrictions exist for exposed, but not diseased, personnel [1].

Poliomyelitis

The World Health Organization puts much effort into the eradication of poliomyelitis. Exposure to wild poliomyelitis has become extremely rare in most parts of the world and vaccine associated polio may be more common in countries where the oral polio vaccine (OPV) is being used. In Germany, HCW are immunised against polio with inactivated polio vaccine (IPV) instead of OPV to prevent vaccine associated spread to patients. Booster doses may be necessary. In case of exposure to wild-virus, it may be advisable to boost exposed HCW with oral vaccine to induce immediate protection [1].

Rabies

All animal care workers and associated laboratory personnel should be vaccinated against rabies. In addition, the availability of postexposure prophylaxis should be made known to personnel working with animals. Transmission of rabies from infected patients to HCW has not been reported and standard precautions will minimise the risk. Whether or not postexposure prophylaxis should be offered to HCW caring for a rabies patient should be decided on an individual basis [1].

Respiratory Syncytial Virus (RSV) infection

Patients and HCW may acquire and transmit RSV in a health care environment. Transmission occurs via aerosols and contaminated hands. Those infected may be contagious for 3-8 days. Nosocomial transmissions have most commonly been reported from new-born babies and children. Patients most at risk for severe RSV infection are new-born babies, the chronically ill, the immuno-compromised and the elderly. Adherence to standard precautions effectively reduces risk of transmission. It is unrealistic to exclude all personnel with acute viral respiratory illness from patient care. This, however, might be necessary when caring for high-risk patients [1].

Scabies and pediculosis

Nosocomial outbreaks of scabies affecting both patients and personnel are numerous, especially in geriatric care. Transmission occurs via skin to skin contact but possibly even through infested clothes and bed linens. Preventive measures include wearing a long sleeve gown and gloves when working with infested patients, cleaning the environment of an infested patient, thorough follow-up of treated patients and HCW, and a precautionary check of all other patients at the ward. During treatment, adverse effects of lindane have been reported. Among the scabicides, benzylbenzoate and crotamiton are better tolerated. Ivermectin is being successfully used in several countries (single oral dose: 200 µg/kg body-weight) but is not approved of for this purpose in others. HCW infested with scabies may return to work with patients after successful treatment has been confirmed.

Transmission of lice (pediculosis) from infested patients to HCW is less probable since close contact with infested hair is necessary.

Staphylococcus aureus infections

HCW with suppurative skin lesions infected with *staphylococcus aureus* should not work with or near patients nor handle food. For those who are nasopharyngeal carriers of *staphylococcus aureus* no working restrictions should be set up unless the HCW could be linked to transmission in the course of epidemiological investigations.

Streptococcal infections

Streptococcus group A (GAS) can be transmitted from infected patients to HCW and infected HCW have been linked to outbreaks of wound or surgical site infections and food-borne transmission. HCW with GAS infections (mostly pharyngitis) may not work with patients or handle food until 24 hours after the start of antibiotic treatment. HCW found to be a-symptomatic carrier may continue to work unless they have been epidemiologically linked to infections. Whether GAS carrying HCW should receive antibiotic treatment is a matter for individual consideration. Recurrent carriage may occur [1].

Reference

1   CDC. Guideline for infection control in health care personnel, 1998. AJIC 1998;26:289-354
     (http://www.cdc.gov/ncidod/hip/Guide/infectcont98.htm)

Occupational dermatoses among health care workers

Birgitta Meding, Karin Wrangsjö, Hans-Martin Hasselhorn

Dermatoses

Skin disease is one of the major occupational health problems in the health care environment. Wet work, extensive glove use and exposure to hazardous substances are frequently encountered and act as potent risk factors for skin disease among hospital personnel. Consequently, dermatoses are more common among health care workers (HCW) than in the general population. Between a quarter and one third of all HCW suffer from skin symptoms which most often present as eczema or as dryness of the hands, with cleaning and kitchen staff at special risk. The consequences may be severe and sick leave due to skin problems is often of long duration.

In severe cases it may be necessary to alter the working environment or even change professional duties; loss of employment on health grounds may be a reality. Even private life is affected and in one Swedish investigation, sleep disturbances, change of mood and reduction of social contacts were reported by one third of subjects with hand eczema.

Skin disease in HCW leads to high costs for hospitals and increased insurance premiums. In Germany, for example, half of all reported and approved occupational diseases among HCW are skin diseases, with annual costs to the occupational health insurance systems of estimated 100 million US dollars.

Risk factors for skin diseases

The development of skin disease depends not only on constitutional factors in the individual, but also on the type of work and the extent of precautions taken. Recognised constitutional risk factors for hand eczema include atopic status (in particular a history of childhood eczema) and having dry skin. Wet work is also an important risk factor that damages the protective skin barrier by exposure to water and detergents. This doubles the risk of developing hand eczema and also increases the risk of sensitisation to different contact allergens. The risk will increase further when there is significant exposure to wet work at home. Occupational exposure to substances containing sensitising agents is an important risk factor for allergic contact dermatitis. While wearing gloves can effectively protect the skin barrier, this is also associated with a risk of developing skin problems. The combination of several risk factors leads to a synergistic increase in the overall risk.

Irritant contact dermatitis

Irritant contact dermatitis is the most common type of hand eczema among hospital personnel. This type of dermatitis is caused by an imbalance of irritant factors in relation to the repairing capacity of the skin. The most common cause of irritant contact dermatitis is wet work, i.e. skin contact with water and detergents. Slight erythema with scaling may be the first sign of damage and this may turn into a contact dermatitis with redness, oedema, pronounced scaling and sometimes fissures. Dermatitis located to the finger webs is often seen in wet work. In mild cases the dermatitis is predominantly seen on the back of the hands but a variety of presentations are encountered.

Allergic contact dermatitis

Allergic contact dermatitis occurs on contact with certain substances and is mostly seen on the hands. The immunological background is a delayed type of hypersensitivity in the skin that is cell-mediated. Contact allergy develops through exposure to a relevant allergen and currently over 3700 different contact allergens have been identified. These are often chemicals with a low molecular weight. Some potent contact allergens can sensitise at the first contact while others tend to sensitise after years of exposure. Usually, the dermatitis is restricted to contact sites, but can in some cases become more widespread. When the exposure is airborne facial dermatitis may develop. The symptoms are variable, with erythema, itching and vesicular eczema occurring in the acute stage; in the later stages dry crusty skin with fissures may be found.

Exposure to common contact allergens such as nickel, preservatives, and perfumes is the cause of the majority of cases of contact allergic dermatitis diagnosed among hospital personnel. Nickel allergy is common among young women and many develop this through contact with jewellery and metal clothing features. A high percentage of nickel sensitised individuals develop hand eczema and in wet work, only small amounts of nickel are required to evoke or aggravate hand eczema in such subjects. Examples of occupationally used objects which may release nickel include keys, handles and metal components of hospital furniture. Perfumes in soaps and detergents used for hand washing constitute a risk of contact allergy. In addition, the handling of a large variety of remedies and pharmaceuticals may induce allergic skin reactions in HCW and some of these substances may penetrate protective gloves. Additives to rubber in gloves can cause allergic contact dermatitis in HCW.

Pharmaceuticals

Several antibiotics (penicillin, streptomycin, gentamycin, neomycin, sulphonamide), local anaesthetics (benzocaine, procaine, tetracaine), antihistamines for local use and neuroleptics (chlorpromazine) are known sensitisers. During the last decade there have been several reports of contact allergy to topical corticosteroids. In addition to the substances described above, a large number of other pharmaceuticals may also lead to sensitisation.

Germicides / preservatives

Formaldehyde is a known contact-sensitiser incorporated into a large variety of products including medicaments, detergents and cosmetics. Many preservatives used in such products are formaldehyde "releasers" or "donors". Glutaraldehyde is irritant to the skin and airways but may also induce contact sensitisation. Other examples of irritating and sensitising agents used for sterilisation and disinfection are ethylene oxide, chlorhexidine, chloramine and benzalconium chloride.

Others

Acrylate monomers used in orthopaedic surgery and dentistry are contact allergens which can easily penetrate protective gloves.

Contact urticaria

Contact urticaria is an immediate wheal-and-flare reaction following skin exposure to certain substances. Examples such as natural rubber latex (NRL) and some food substances act through an immunological mechanism mediated by IgE-antibodies. Others such as benzoic acid or aromatics act through non-immunological mechanisms. Allergen contact with skin or mucous membranes may result in generalised allergic reactions in highly sensitised individuals.

Skin infections

The probability of skin infections is higher when skin is already damaged or if the hygiene routines are insufficient. Bacterial super-infections on hand eczema, by staphylococci or streptococci is a real risk and multi-drug resistant strains may pose serious problems. Damaged skin may also make the HCW more susceptible to blood-borne infective agents. Herpes simplex infection of the distal segment of fingers has been a problem especially for dental workers. Use of gloves, however, effectively prevents transmission. Paronychia, often infected with candida, may be seen among HCW performing wet work. Persistent skin infection is an obstacle for several tasks in medical care and it may be necessary for the HCW to withdraw from certain duties until the infection is dealt with.

Nosocomial outbreaks of scabies affecting both patients and personnel may occur, especially in geriatric care. Transmission occurs mainly via skin to skin contact.

Diagnosis

HCW suffering from skin problems, which do not resolve after a few weeks, need specialist examination if possible by a dermatologist with special knowledge of occupational exposures and risks. Patch testing is undertaken to verify contact allergy and should only be performed by experienced dermatologists. The internationally used standard patch tests include about 30 common allergens such as nickel, perfumes, topical drugs and rubber chemicals. In addition, further products used by the HCW might need to be patch tested. Latex allergy is diagnosed by a history of NRL-provoked allergic symptoms in combination with demonstration of NRL-specific antibodies. This could be done by blood tests such as CAP-RAST test to NRL or by skin prick testing. It should be emphasised that a test exposure of patients to NRL-allergens may involve a risk of eliciting generalised symptoms in highly sensitised individuals.

When dealing with HCW with skin problems, occupational health service (OHS) personnel should carefully examine the working conditions and evaluate whether further personnel working in the area show similar symptoms.

Protective gloves

Protective gloves have been used in medical care for the past 100 years. They are used mainly to protect HCW from transmission of infections but in some cases they also serve as protection from toxic or sensitising chemical substances. This must be taken into consideration to ensure that gloves with adequate chemical resistance are chosen. Other factors such as duration of work, risk of allergy and economic issues should also be considered.

Glove intolerance reactions

In the last two decades the frequency of skin reactions related to protective gloves has increased dramatically due to their more frequent use in health care. Intolerance reactions from gloves are reported by about one third of HCW. Irritant reactions are the most frequent but two different types of allergic reaction (contact allergy to rubber additives and IgE-mediated allergy to NRL) are also recognised. Allergic reactions are however seldom provoked by synthetic glove materials.

Irritant reactions
When working with tight gloves, mild local symptoms of skin irritation are common. There is an increased penetration of irritant substances from soap residues, ointments and glove materials. The glove donning powder is usually corn starch and may by its mechanical properties and high pH, contribute to skin irritation.

Allergic contact dermatitis from rubber chemicals
Most cases of allergic contact dermatitis following exposure to gloves are due to reactions to chemicals used in the rubber manufacturing process, especially thiurames and carbamates.

Latex allergy
The IgE-mediated allergy to NRL is characterised by contact urticaria as well as generalised symptoms. The allergen derives from the sap (latex) from the rubber tree, *Hevea brasiliensis* and consists of several allergenic proteins. The prevalence of latex allergy in glove-using HCW has in several studies been estimated to be around 10%. The symptoms when exposed to products made from NRL are very variable. Most cases show mild or moderate symptoms at NRL-exposure. A small group of sensitised individuals,

however, is extremely allergic to NRL and is at risk of anaphylaxis when operated on or when mucous membranes are exposed. NRL-sensitised HCW may often experience not only localised contact urticaria from gloves but also facial itching and rhino-conjunctivitis from airborne exposure to the NRL-allergens which stick to the glove powder. Due to this exposure, latex allergy is currently recognised as a relevant cause of occupational asthma among HCW.

All those sensitised should be advised to avoid domestic and occupational exposure to products containing NRL, although this is difficult due to the large range of articles made from this material. In medical care the use of non-latex gloves is recommended for sensitised personnel and patients.

Which type of glove should be used and when?

Since allergic reactions are seldom provoked by synthetic materials, these are preferable from an allergic perspective. When latex gloves continue to be used these should be "low-allergenic". Non-latex alternatives should also be easily accessible, but synthetic rubber gloves may however also cause contact allergic reactions due to thiurames and carbamates.

When considering gloves made from NRL it should be noted that several different qualities are on the market. Due to problems connected with latex allergy and inflammatory reactions in surgical areas from glove powder, several manufacturers have developed non-powdered latex-gloves. These are mainly obtained by chlorination that may make the gloves more fragile. Intense development work is proceeding in this area and currently there are different international standards for the physical properties and integrity of medical gloves. Standards regarding biocompatibility are also approaching.

Surgical gloves
Due to the elastic properties necessary for gloves used in surgery, the majority of surgical gloves are still made of NRL, but the proportion of non-latex surgical gloves is increasing. NRL-gloves should contain low levels of latex allergens and should be free from powder. A thin sterile inner-glove made from a co-polymer, polyeten, may serve as protection from allergens and also facilitate detection of leakage through the outer glove.

Non-sterile examination gloves
This group includes several alternative materials, including NRL-gloves, synthetic rubber gloves and gloves made from polyvinyl chloride (PVC). From an allergy perspective the PVC-gloves are preferable, but these gloves are less elastic.

Gloves used in laboratory work and dentistry
The same alternatives as for medical examination gloves are available for work in laboratories and in dentistry. When handling chemicals the permeability of the glove material must be considered. Some chemicals such as acrylates used in orthopaedic surgery and dentistry penetrate medical gloves made from commonly used materials in a few minutes. Wearing double gloves made from two different materials usually increases the protective effect.

Gloves used in wet work

Common types of household gloves made from PVC are suitable for wet work such as cleaning or kitchen work. An inner cotton glove may reduce skin irritation.

Occupational health skin programme

The aim of a skin disease prevention programme is to reduce the frequency of skin diseases among personnel by preventing the development of hand dermatoses and supporting those with existing dermatoses. The programme should be developed by a group consisting of the administrative manager, the supervisor of the health care personnel, representatives of employees, and occupational health staff. All hospital working areas should be covered by the programme and the responsibilities for each part of it should be clear to everyone involved.

Evaluation of risk

Professional activities with the potential to cause occupational skin disease should be identified and receive special attention when delivering the programme.

Information for managers

Providing high quality information for managers will increase their willingness to support skin protective measures. The administration has to approve the purchase of non-sensitising skin care products and gloves and the replacement of materials harmful to the skin with suitable alternatives. In addition, rehabilitation and redeployment need to be negotiated in co-operation with managers.

Information for employees

All employees (including kitchen and cleaning staff) should be informed about the size of the problem, the risk factors and what preventive measures are available. They should be encouraged to seek advice from the OHS when suffering from skin problems on the hands or other occupationally related allergy symptoms.

Purchase, distribution and evaluation of products

All employees should have easy access to hygienic washing devices and skin care products. The range of soaps, disinfectants and skin creams necessary for daily use in the hospital should be limited to carefully selected products for which all constituents are known. The objective should be to select products that are the least sensitising and irritating to the skin as possible. Clear and distinct instructions on how to use the products should be accessible. Employees should have the option to choose from a range of selected products in order to reduce the need to bring their own sometimes hazardous alternatives. At regular intervals, the skin disease prevention programme team should evaluate the products in use.

Special attention should be paid to the possibility of offering staff and patients a hospital environment free from exposure to NRL. All products or gloves made from or containing components made from NRL should be labelled. To prevent new cases of latex allergy among HCW, it is important to reduce the total NRL-exposure. As gloves constitute the main source of NRL-exposure the use of latex-free gloves should be encouraged. The choice of latex-free glove alternatives may also prevent the development of contact allergy to rubber chemicals. When latex gloves are selected, the manufacturer should be asked for gloves with as low a content of sensitising latex proteins and rubber chemicals, as possible. Since powder on latex gloves may contribute to sensitisation to NRL, some hospitals have chosen to work entirely without powdered latex gloves. Manufacturers of medical devices and gloves, and standardising committees are working hard to set standards for NRL-containing products in medical care.

Managing employees with skin problems

When hospital staff with skin problems seek advice, the OHS should thoroughly evaluate the working conditions in relation to risk factors and the potential for improvement. Severe and longstanding cases should be referred to dermatologists with experience in this field. HCW with skin problems need to be informed about the preventive measures available, the health risks and the prognosis. It may be necessary for the OHS to act as an advocate for the employee because the necessary measures may be perceived as inconvenient and expensive for the employer. On-going follow up of the HCW's health and working conditions by the OHS is essential. Compensation from relevant occupational insurance systems may be claimed by HCW with occupational skin diseases and information should be given by the OHS.

When skin disease has resolved after treatment and avoidance of exposure, reappearance of the symptoms is likely to occur if the working conditions are not improved. Such improvements may include reduction of hazardous working procedures and replacement of irritant and allergenic substances and materials. Stepwise re-integration into work may be useful. This is often only possible in co-operation with several responsibility levels. Rehabilitation and re-introduction to work after long term absence requires substantial support from the OHS and those directly responsible for the workplace.

Redeployment to other workplaces may become inevitable in the course of caring for a diseased HCW. This procedure may be one of the tasks of the skin disease prevention programme team in co-operation with others involved. Again, the OHS has a central role in this process.

Pre-employment screening

Pre-employment examination may present an opportunity to counsel those at risk of skin disease. Since an atopic status is common in the population and many atopics manage to perform health care work without having skin problems it is not justifiable to generally exclude atopics from hospital work. However they may need special precautions and preventive measures. HCW with known allergies e.g. to NRL or acrylates need special help to avoid occupational exposure to these materials. There is no reason to perform pre-employment patch testing in symptom-free individuals.

Basic rules for prevention of hand eczema

- Wash your hands as often as the work demands – but not more.
- Use appropriate hand hygiene products.
- Do not apply soap on dry skin and do not use too much.
- Rinse off the soap and dry the hands thoroughly.
- Use emollients frequently but not immediately before use of gloves.
- Glove use protects the skin. Chose gloves of appropriate materials for the intended work.
- Non-latex gloves reduce the risk of allergy.
- Only use gloves on dry hands free from irritating or sensitising substances.
- Avoid skin contact with substances that may cause contact allergy.

Further reading

- Toxicological database: Keith LH, Walters DB (Eds). The National Chemical Data Compendium. Volume VI. Boca Raton, Florida: Lewis publishers, 1992
- Palosuo T, Mäkinen-Kiljunen S, Alenius H, Reunala T, Turjanmaa K. Measurement of natural rubber latex allergen levels in medical gloves by allergen-specific IgE-ELISA inhibition, RAST inhibition and skin prick test. Allergy 1998;53:59-67
- Nilsson E. Eczema. In: Brune DK, Edling C (Eds). Occupational Hazards in Health Professionals. Boca Raton, Florida: CRC press, 1989:271-289
- Von Hintzenstern J, Heese A, Koch HU, Peters K-P, Hornstein OP. Frequency, spectrum and occupational relevance of type IV allergies to rubber chemicals. Contact Dermatitis 1991;24:244-252
- Tarlo S, Sussman GL, Holness L. Latex sensitivity in dental students and staff: a cross-sectional study. J Allergy Clin Immunol 1997;3:396-401
- Warshaw EM. Latex allergy. J Am Acad Dermatol 1998;39:1-24
- Wrangsjö K, Meding B. Hospital workers. Clinics in Dermatology 1997;15:573-578
- Mellström GA, Wahlberg JE, Maibach HI (Eds). Protective Gloves for Occupational Use. Boca Raton, Florida: CRC Press, 1994
- Adams RM. Occupational Skin Disease, 2nd ed. Philadelphia: W.B. Saunders Company, 1990

Occupational Health for Health Care Workers - A Practical Guide
H.-M. Hasselhorn, A. Toomingas and M. Lagerström (Editors)
© 1999 Elsevier Science B.V. All rights reserved.

Chemical disinfectants

Hans-Martin Hasselhorn, Markus Dettenkofer

Chemical disinfection or sterilisation (high-level disinfection) involves substances which pose health hazards to health care workers (HCW) and others coming into contact with them. Therefore, whenever possible and feasible, other methods of disinfection or sterilisation, such as the use of hot water or steam, should be chosen. Yet, chemical disinfection is commonly used in the health care setting and different procedures require different disinfectants.

Most of the disinfecting substances used in health care may be hazardous if not handled properly. The main factors to consider when assessing the potential health risk are the intensity and duration of contact as well as the route of exposure [1].

General precautions

The basic principle when using disinfectants should be to use them only where it is necessary for infection control purposes [2, 3]. If possible, substances with a low hazard potential should be chosen. For example, an alcohol-based disinfectant is preferable to chlorine compounds for the decontamination of a small spillage of blood or pus. The agent chosen, however, has to be proven to be effective against the pathogens expected.

It is the employer's responsibility to inform and educate all HCW who have possible exposure to disinfectants, about the health risks associated with their use. This should cover how to implement adequate measures of control and prevention including emergency procedures and extend to appropriate systems for decontamination and waste disposal.

In general, good ventilation is necessary at workplaces where disinfectants are in use. Most disinfectants have an odour level below the permissible exposure limit. However, smell is not a good indicator of exposure, as many individuals cannot detect odours precisely and the odour sense may adapt to the smell [4].

Appropriate personal protective equipment must be provided to protect the eyes, skin and airways from contact (such as gloves, gowns/non-impervious clothing, goggles, face shields, and respiratory protection) and workers should be required to use the protective devices in a proper manner. Eating, drinking and smoking are not allowed in areas where disinfectants are in use or stored. Hands need to be washed with a mild soap or detergent following the use of disinfectants, especially before eating, drinking or smoking.

Those handling disinfectants must understand that following an accidental exposure, they are required to wash those parts of the skin affected, with mild soap or a detergent. If the eyes are contaminated they should be flushed immediately with large amounts of water for approximately 15 minutes and it is advisable to seek medical advice. In cases of whole body exposure a shower must be taken. Contaminated clothing needs to be removed immediately and stored in air tight containers until cleaning takes place. Laundry personnel handling contaminated clothing must be informed about its nature and the health risks involved.

Hazards of commonly used chemical disinfectants

Alcohols

Ethanol and isopropyl alcohol (conc. 70%) are convenient and often used as skin antiseptics or for disinfection of instruments and small surfaces. Exposure may occur by ingestion, inhalation or absorption via the skin, but these substances are of relatively low toxicity. In addition to narcotic effects, however, they may cause irritation to skin and mucous membranes including the eyes, and the risk of explosion needs to be considered, especially when disinfecting larger surfaces.

Chlorine compounds and hypochlorites

Solutions of sodium hypochlorite (chlorine) are widely used to disinfect environmental surfaces (floors), patient equipment, water distribution systems, and (as bleach) in laundry systems. Exposure to chlorine leads to irritation of mucous membranes and general discomfort. Accidentally mixing bleach with acids or ammonia, forms chlorine gas or chloramine, which may lead to severe respiratory symptoms. The odour sense adapts quickly to chlorine leading to underestimation of exposure.

It may be necessary to enclose the process to prevent exposure. In addition to health hazards there are also environmental reasons for limiting the use of chlorine compounds and hypochlorites.

Iodine

Iodine is widely used as skin antiseptic and iodophor germicidal detergent solution is used to disinfect surfaces. Iodine vapour irritates mucous membranes and leads to headache and feelings of tightness in the chest. Skin contact to strong solutions may induce severe irritation and burns. The widely used *povidone* iodine is well tolerated.

Phenolics

Phenolics are used for disinfection of surfaces but also for instruments. However, they are not the preferred agents in terms of efficacy, toxicity, and environmental aspects. Exposure to phenolics such as para-tertiary butylphenol and para-tertiary amylphenol may occur via skin absorption, inhalation or ingestion. Local effects include tissue irritation, burns and necrosis. In addition, arrythmias, abnormal breathing, convulsions, collapse and death may occur. Phenol is known to lead to contact sensitisation and persistent depigmentation of the skin.

Careful precautions should be taken not only where phenolics are in use but also where they are handled and stored. Enclosure of the process should be initiated where possible.

Quaternary ammonium compounds

These disinfectants are widely used in the health care setting, and also in housekeeping and kitchens. However, their efficacy against some gram-negative pathogens is limited. Benzalkonium chloride is the most commonly used quaternary ammonium compound and is found in many products. Quaternary ammonium compounds are less irritant to skin and mucous membranes than other disinfectants but may cause contact dermatitis.

Glutaraldehyde

As a highly active agent, glutaraldehyde is widely used for high-level disinfection and so called chemical sterilisation, mainly for instruments such as endoscopes. Disinfecting solutions containing glutaraldehyde need to be prepared regularly. At room temperatures glutaraldehyde has a high vapour pressure and may easily lead to air concentrations with hazardous potential. Inhalation, skin contact and ingestion may be hazardous. Glutaraldehyde is highly irritant to the skin, mucous membranes and airways and may also induce contact sensitisation. Headache has been reported among those exposed. The frequency of symptoms among staff exposed to glutaraldehyde is high, and the severity of symptoms may make redeployment necessary.

   Consequently, exposure to air containing glutaraldehyde should be avoided by using closed containers and well maintained ventilation. Skin contact should be completely prevented.

Formaldehyde

Formaldehyde is used for disinfection of surfaces, instruments, dialysis equipment, and in the laboratory and embalming process. By means of a special process it can also be used for sterilisation. In combination with methanol and water it becomes formalin.

   At low concentrations (0.1-5 ppm) formalin is irritant to skin, eyes and upper airway. Splashes in the eye may result in severe corneal damage. At higher concentrations (up to 20 ppm) coughing and an increased heart rate are observed and above 50 ppm, pulmonary oedema and pneumonitis can occur. Death may take place above 100 ppm. Concentrations up to about 8 ppm have been found in autopsy rooms. Repeated exposure may result in sensitisation within days or months following the first exposure. In sensitised individuals exposure to low levels is sufficient to provoke eye and upper respiratory tract reactions and even asthma. Dermatitis may commonly develop in the course of repeated skin contact with formalin. The National Institute for Occupational Safety and Health in the USA regards formaldehyde as a potential occupational carcinogen for nasal cancer [4]. The sense of smell is dulled by ongoing exposure.

   Substitution of formalin should be considered whenever possible. Good ventilation is essential and environmental air monitoring may be performed when occupational exposure to workers is suspected. Personal protection (including boots, positive-pressure air-line respirators) should be of high standard when spills are likely to occur. Latex gloves are too fragile to withstand the chemical effects of formaldehyde [4].

Hospital staff should be examined for risk factors prior to working in areas with exposure to formaldehyde for skin and respiratory risk and periodic occupational health monitoring is essential.

Peroxygens

Hydrogen peroxide and peracetic acid are oxidising agents with a broad spectrum of activity. Their final decomposition products (oxygen and water) are innocuous. Inhalation of high concentrations of hydrogen peroxide vapour leads to irritations and inflammation of skin and mucous membranes. Toxic irritation of skin following repeated exposure with 0.1% solutions of peracetic acid may occur.

In summary, chemical disinfectants are widely used in the health care environment. The processes involving these substances should be regularly monitored using risk assessment techniques to ensure that effective control measures are in place and hospital staff are appropriately trained in the relevant health and safety issues.

References

1   Weber DJ, Rutala WA. Occupational risks associated with the use of selected disinfectants and steriliants. In: Rutala WA (Ed). Disinfection, sterilization and antisepsis in health care. APIC and Polyscience Publications. Washington: Champlain, 1998:211-226
2   Rutala WA, Weber DJ. Principles of disinfecting patient-care items. In: Rutala WA (Ed). Disinfection, sterilization and antisepsis in health care. APIC and Polyscience Publications. Washington: Champlain, 1998:133-150
3   Russell AD, Hugo WB, Ayliffe GAJ (Eds). Principles and practice of disinfection, preservation and sterilization. 3rd ed. Oxford: Blackwell Science, 1999
4   National Institute for Occupational Safety and Health. Guidelines for Protecting the Safety and Health of Health Care Workers. DHHS (NIOSH) Publication No. 88-119, Washington US Government Printing Office, September 1988 (http://www.cdc.gov/niosh/hcwold0.html)

Cytotoxic drugs

Olle Nygren

The traditional techniques used for drug preparation and administration are designed to ensure aseptic handling of the drugs, but do not necessarily consider the work environment for the health care workers (HCW). Therefore, safety precautions employing preparation work inside a Biological Safety Cabinet (BSC) and protective clothing for handling cytotoxic drugs have been described and have also been introduced to varying extent in many countries [1-3]. However, regulations, especially regarding the use of protective clothing, are often not adhered to. One major objection is consideration for the patients, since extensive protective clothing may disturb the patients [3].

Exposure

There has been an increasing concern about exposure to cytotoxic drugs [4]. Cytotoxic drugs are usually characterised depending on their anti-tumour action, e.g. alkylating, DNA-cross binding, inhibition of mitosis etc. All these actions will also affect normal cells and explain the adverse effects after exposure to cytotoxic drugs, e.g. irritations of lungs, skin, mucous membranes and eyes. Many cytotoxic drugs are also known to be carcinogens [5-7].

Many groups of HWC may be exposed to cytotoxic drugs, e.g.
* pharmacist preparing drugs,
* nurses preparing and administrating drugs,
* staff nurses caring for treated patients,
* cleaning staff in wards with treated patients,
* technical staff transporting and handling waste and laundry,
* laundry staff cleaning contaminated bedclothes, linen, beddings etc.

The exposure can be either direct to the drugs or indirect to contaminated excretions, e.g. urine, faeces, vomit, sweat etc, from the patients and contaminated laundry and waste. In several studies abnormalities in various biological markers, e.g. hair loss, chromosome aberration, sister chromatide exchange, have been reported among nurses, pharmacists and other HCW working with cancer patients and cytotoxic drugs [8-10]. Increased spontaneous abortions and foetal abnormalities are other reported effects of exposure to cytotoxic drugs [11]. Non of these studies have been correlated with exposure to specific drugs.

Recently, however, different studies have shown that cyclophosphamide can be found in urine from occupationally exposed HCW [12]. Cyclophosphamide, methotrexate and 5-fluorouracil have also been found inside BSC and, furthermore, on the floor and workbenches in drug preparation rooms, although the preparations had been carried out inside BSC [12-13]. Increased levels of platinum have been found in blood samples from HCW, who nursed patients treated with Cisplatin [14].

An unpublished investigation of different preparation and administration systems has shown considerable difference in the spill that occurs with different techniques. The traditional pump technique (also called the milking technique) is frequently used inside BSC and was compared with a closed system (PhaSeal, Carmel Pharma AB, Gothenburg, Sweden). With the pump technique, the enclosed air is manually pumped with the syringe plunger between the vial and the syringe to equilibrate the possible pressure build-up in the closed drug vial. With the closed system, the air in the sealed vial is transferred into the flexible expansion bulb during injection of liquid and back into the vial during withdrawal of liquid to avoid any pressure build-up. After this procedure, the needle is moved back into its sleeve and then the two parts can be disconnected and all parts, which have been in contact with the drug, are in closed compartments and no air from the vial or syringe has to be expelled outside the system. The pump technique resulted in significant spill, while the closed system resulted in a 1000-fold less spill, and, thus, eliminated several of the possible emissions sources during preparation and administration of drugs.

These reported findings show that exposure to cytotoxic drugs occurs during preparation and administration using traditional techniques, even when preparation is carried out inside BSC. The routes of exposure, however, are not always evident. Both exposure to airborne drugs and skin exposure due to leakage must be considered. Contamination on the outside of the vials has also to be considered as a possible source of skin exposure. In another recent report the vapour pressure of a number of cytotoxic substances have been investigated. The possibility of evaporation and sublimation of these substances were discussed and vapour emission of cytotoxic drugs cannot be excluded as a source of exposure.

In most developed countries, regulations for handling cytotoxic drugs are based on preparation in a BSC and use of protective clothing, e.g. extra gown, double gloves and face mask. This has been assumed to be satisfactory protection. Recent reports [12-14] and unpublished work, however, indicate that these precautions may not be fully adequate and may need to be complemented by control measures to verify that no leakage from the BSC or closed systems occur. These recent reports have just been reviewed and it is evident that current guidelines for handling cytostatics do not provide effective protection for HCW. The Swedish National Board of Occupational Safety and Health (NBOSH) has initiated a revision of the Ordinance for handling cytotoxic and similar drugs. A more strict regulation for the use and control of BSC and closed systems for preparation and administration will be implemented.

Practical measures to prevent exposure

Exposure can be expected to occur during preparation, administration, nursing patients and handling contaminated material both in the ward and during waste and laundry work. Each of these work situations require specific considerations to avoid unnecessary drug exposure. In many countries pregnant women are not allowed to work with cytotoxic drugs, due to the reports of the effects on the foetus [11]. There is also a growing concern that the fertility of males may be affected from exposure to cytotoxic drugs. This possibility, however, has not been investigated so far. It is therefore recommended that HCW, who feel uncomfortable working with cytotoxic drugs, shall be allowed to have other work tasks.

Education

It is important that all categories of staff receive adequate information of the possible risk of exposure and education on how to perform their work in such way that the risk for exposure is minimised. Standard operating procedures (SOP) including written handling instructions are important tools to maintain a good and healthy work environment.

Drug preparation

Today, in the developed world, all preparations of cytotoxic drugs shall be performed using a BSC or a closed preparation system. In developing countries this may not always be the case. Possible exposure during drug preparation will be minimised by using a leak tested preparation system (see below). It can be a closed preparation system or a BSC. The use of a centralised preparation unit with adequate protective facilities and routines based on SOP will minimise the risk for exposure.

A closed system can usually be used on an open bench. It is therefore important that the work surface, in case of an accidental spill of the whole drug volume, can absorb the complete spill in a confined absorbing unit. This unit can be, e.g. a tray with an absorbing material under a hard and perforated surface, which can be easily gas tight sealed and placed in a hazardous waste container. If such an absorbing unit is not available, it is recommended to use the closed system inside a BSC to minimise the spread of a large accidental leak.

If a BSC is used, it is important to consider the performance of the box and work organisation. The more things placed in a BSC, the more disturbance of the laminar flow will occur and decrease the performance of the BSC. Consequently, the number of items inside the box shall be kept to a minimum. A modern BSC has a possibility to adjust the exhaust ratio and a ventilation system with air circulating through a High Efficiency Particulate Air (HEPA) filter in order to create a laminar flow of particle free air over the work area in the box. It also has an HEPA-filter in the exhaust, which goes to the outside, preferably (but not always being the case), via a separate ventilation duct. By constantly running the air circulation system in the BSC at highest exhaust ratio, emission of drug vapours (see below) will be evacuated as effectively as possible. The use of a fume cupboard with separate exhaust will further decrease the risk for exposure to drug vapours. It is not recommended to use a BSC with an air circulation system that, after filtration through an HEPA-filter, returns the exhaust air into the workroom due to the possibility of drug vapours being emitted. It is also important to have a scheduled maintenance program for the BSC. The maintenance program shall include regularly leak and air flow tests and change of the HEPA-filters according to the manufacturers recommendations, which normally suggests tests every 6 month and filter change when the total pressure drop in the box has increased to a specified level. The maintenance program shall be part of a SOP, which also shall include information on who is responsible for the maintenance program and its schedule.

Cytotoxic drugs may be emitted both as aerosol and vapour during preparation. A closed preparation system or a leak tested BSC shall be utilised. If necessary and under special circumstances, preparations can be made on an open bench using full covering protective clothing, gloves, goggles and appropriate protective breathing equipment.

A preparation system can be tested regarding possible leakage of drug substances to the work environment employing 99m-technetium as a tracer. This test can be performed using a method recommended by NBOSH [15], which also can be used to compare different techniques. Leak tests can also be made by wipe sampling on surfaces in the workroom and qualitative analysis of residues of the drugs in use according to the method presented by Sessink et al [13].

Drug administration

In the administration situation drug spills occur using traditional techniques. It is therefore important to use adequate precautions, i.e., protective clothing, gloves etc. With a closed system spills can be minimised and the need for a full protective garment is not necessary. This will facilitate and improve the contacts with the patients. The use of protective gloves, however, is recommended. There are special gloves available for preparation of cytotoxic drugs, which can withstand penetration for up to thirty minutes. If any work task is longer than thirty minutes it is recommended to change the gloves after each thirty-minute period. If a spill occurs it is important to immediately clean up the spill and place the contaminated material in a sealed container to avoid possible vaporisation of the drug. It is recommended to change gloves after cleaning up a spill.

Nursing patients

The most difficult work task to assess for possible exposure risk is nursing duties. Emissions from the patient are diffuse and therefore difficult to avoid unless full protective garment is worn, which may affect the patients. Many tasks, e.g. collection and volume measurement of urine, cleaning up patient excretions, also involve handling body-warm materials, which, in the light of new reports, can be expected to emit drug vapours. Consequently, a SOP shall exist, which includes instructions to immediately collect and remove these materials and all other contaminated material to avoid unnecessary exposure, e.g. place body-warm material in gas tight containers to cool before further treatment. To avoid emission from bed linen, towels etc, it may be useful to change these on a more frequent basis during days with cytostatic treatment.

Waste and laundry handling

There are two major concerns regarding occupational exposure for handling of waste and laundry contaminated with cytotoxic drugs. First, the staff do not always know what kind of material they are handling and may therefore become unnecessarily exposed because normal handling of the material may be inappropriate, e.g. how to handle broken or damaged laundry and waste bags. Second, the staff has not received adequate information on possible exposure risks and education on how to handle waste and laundry contaminated with cytotoxic drugs. It is therefore essential to establish a SOP, that includes relevant routines for this handling to ensure that the staff gets appropriate information and education on how to handle these materials in such way that the exposure can be minimised.

All excess drugs, which cannot be used, shall be put in the hazardous waste and handled accordingly, e.g. transported and handled separately and destroyed by burning. Recent studies indicate that excess of antibiotics and cytotoxic drugs in the sewer may affect microbial system in sewage-treatment plants.

Control measures

Biological monitoring is a useful tool for assessment of the exposure situation. However, biological monitoring of HCW's exposure to cytotoxic drugs can only be done for a few drugs (cyclophosphamide, i-phosphamide, methotrexate, 5-fluorouracil and drugs containing platinum) and may therefore not give relevant information to assess the exposure situation in all cases. If not appropriate, the efforts shall be made on minimising the risk for exposure by having a relevant SOP and routines for different work tasks and control measures, e.g. leak tests, wipe-sampling etc.

Accidental spill

In case of accidental spill, immediately wipe up all visible spills and place the contaminated materials in an airtight bag or waste container. In case of spill on persons, immediately remove all cloth and take a shower. If the spill gets in contact with mucous membranes, immediately flush with luke-warm water, or in the eyes, immediately flush with luke-warm water and then immediately consult an ophthalmologist.

References

1   Harrison R B. Developing guidelines for working with antineoplastic drugs. Am J Hosp Pharm 1981; 38:1686-1693
2   Valanis B, Vollmer WM, Labuhn K, Glass A, Corelle C. Antineoplastic drug handling protection after OSHA guidelines. Comparison by profession, handling activity, and work site. J Occup Med 1992;34:149-155
3   Barhamond BA. Difficulties encountered with implementing guidelines for handling antineoplastic in the physician's office. Cancer Nurs 1986; 9:138-143
4   Zellmer W A. Fear of anticancer drugs. Am J Hosp Pharm 1984; 41:665

5   Kolmodin-Hedman B, Hartvig P, Sorsa M, Falck K. Occupational handling of cytostatic drugs. Arch Toxicol 1983; 54:25-33.

6   Bingham E. Hazards to health workers from antineoplastic drugs. N Engl J Med 1985; 313:1173-1178

7   Sorsa M, Hemminki K, Vainio H. Occupational exposure to antineoplastic drugs. Potential and real hazards. Mutat Res 1985;154:135-149

8   Nikula E, Kiviniitty K, Leisti J, Taskinen PJ. Chromosome aberrations in lymphocytes of nurses handling cytostatic agents. Scand J Work Environ Health 1984;10:71-74

9   Stucker I, Hirsch A, Doloy T, Bastie-Sigeac I, Hemon D. Urine mutagenicity, chromosomal abnormalities and sister chromatide exchanges in lymphocytes of nurses handling cytostatic drugs. Int Arch Occup Environ Health 1986;57:195-205

10   Waksvik H, Klepp O, Brögger A. Chromosome analyses of nurses handling cytostatic agents. Cancer Treat Rep 1981;65:607-610

11   Hemminki K, Kyyrönen P, Lindbohm M-L. Spontaneous abortions and malformations in offspring of nurses exposed to anaesthetic gases, cytostatic drugs, and other potential hazards in hospitals based on registered information of outcome. J Epidemiol Community Health 1985;39:141-147

12   Sessink PJM, Cerná M, Rössner P, Pastorkova A, Bavarova H, Frankova K, Anzion RB, Bos RP. Urinary cyclophosphamide excretion and chromosomal aberrations in peripheral blood lymphocytes after occupational exposure to antineoplastic agents. Mutat Res 1994; 309:193-199

13   Sessink PJ, Van de Kerkhof MC, Anzion RB, Noordhoek J, Bos RP. Environmental contamination and assessment of exposure to anti-neoplastic agents by determination of cyclophosphamide in urine of exposed pharmacy technicians: Is skin absorption an important exposure route? Arch Environ Health 1994;49:165-169

14   Nygren O, Lundgren C. Determination of platinum in workroom air and in blood and urine from nursing staff working with patients receiving cisplatin chemotherapy. Int Arch Occup Environ Health 1997;70:209-214

15   Nygren O, Gustavsson B, Eriksson R. Testmetod för läckage vid läkemedelsberedning. Arbetslivsrapport 1999:3, Solna: Arbetslivsinstitutet 1999 (in Swedish with English summary: "Test method for drug preparation systems")

Occupational Health for Health Care Workers - A Practical Guide
H.-M. Hasselhorn, A. Toomingas and M. Lagerström (Editors)
© 1999 Elsevier Science B.V. All rights reserved.

Anaesthetic gases

Roberto Lucchini

Anaesthetic agents that are currently used in operating rooms are nitrous oxide (N_2O) and halogenated vapours (enflurane or ethrane, isoflurane or forane, sevoflurane).

About 30 years ago leaking anaesthetic gases (*waste anaesthetic gases*) were identified as a potential hazard for health care workers, when reports of adverse effects on anaesthetists emerged. Anaesthetic gases are highly volatile compounds and the pollution of closed and relatively small environments such as operating rooms can rapidly occur. Inhalation results in a high uptake among exposed persons. Occupational exposure to anaesthetic gases has subsequently been substantially reduced and epidemiological reports of adverse effects on operating room workers have become less frequent.

Occupational risk

Pollution by anaesthetic gases can be caused by leakage from the wall valve, the hoses that connect the central supplying system with the anaesthetic apparatus, and the anaesthetic machine, especially the on-demand valve. Leakage from this source can quickly cause pollution in the operating room, given the high pressure of gases at this level. More frequently leakage occurs from the low-pressure connections between the anaesthetic flowmeter and the scavenging mask. This leakage is due to loose-fitting connections, loosely assembled or deformed slip joints and threaded connections, and defective or worn seals, gaskets, breathing bags, and hoses. This is due to the daily use of these disposable parts that deteriorate after time. The rubber and plastic components of the anaesthetic equipment are potential sources of N_2O leakage because they may be degraded by the N_2O and the oxygen as well as by repeated sterilisation. Anaesthetists can contribute to anaesthetic-gases pollution by using excessive flows and not respecting safety procedures.

Occupational exposure to anaesthetic gases can take place in operating rooms, delivery wards and dental offices. The exposed groups include anaesthesiologists, surgeons, dentists, operating room nurses and dental assistants. Anaesthetists are generally the most exposed professionals, while surgeons are more exposed during intraocular or otolaryngological surgery, when the working area is closer to the potential main source of leakage, the "patient's mouth" [1]. Given the difficulty of using scavenging masks, the pollution levels in dental offices are generally high.

Exposure to waste anaesthetic gases, in addition to transmission of blood-borne and respiratory pathogens, is also the most important air safety hazard in post anaesthesia care unit [2]. Paediatric mask anaesthesia causes generally higher exposure levels than in adult intubated patients anaesthesia [3, 4].

The main target organ of occupational exposure to anaesthetic gases is the Central Nervous System. Headache, loss of attention and concentration are often reported by operating room personnel at high exposure levels. The use of neurobehavioral test batteries has allowed a more precise assessment of this phenomenon so that a reduction of vigilance and response speed has been observed at atmospheric concentrations of N_2O as low as 50 ppm [5]. However these neurobehavioral effects seem to be reversible and when the exposure levels are kept below 25 ppm of N_2O, they are not detectable [6].

Another group of effects from occupational exposure to anaesthetic gases which has been widely studied since the 1970s concerns reproductive toxicity, including spontaneous abortion and congenital defects. In addition, a reduction of fertility has been observed considering the time necessary to become pregnant. It must be emphasised that after preventive measures have been generally undertaken in the past 20 years, the epidemiological evidence for these type of effects is currently inadequate and the effects can actually be better related to night work and high work load [7]. Besides the reproductive effects, mutagenic and carcinogenic effects have also been suspected, but the existing data are inadequate [8].

The hepatological effects of waste anaesthetic gases have been also questioned, given the observation of hepatotoxicity of these substances for patients under certain conditions. An induction of the liver microsomal enzyme system has been currently observed [9]. Adverse health effects are likely to be avoided by the low exposure levels currently existing in the majority of operating rooms.

Prevention

Occupational exposure to anaesthetic gases can be detected by measuring atmospheric and biological concentration of N_2O and halogenated gases. Exposure limit values have been established by the US and most European countries for air concentrations of waste anaesthetic gases (table 1). Unfortunately, the halogenated gases considered are at present no longer frequently used, and no limit values are available for those currently utilised. In addition, some discrepancy exists between ACGIH and the other agencies, since the documentation on halogenated agents used by this organisation has not been updated.

Table 1. International threshold values as time-weighted averages of air concentrations in parts per million (ppm)

Country	N₂O	Halothane (fluothane) ppm	Enflurane (ethrane) ppm	Isoflurane (forane) ppm
Denmark	100	5	2	-
France	-	2	-	-
Germany	100	5	20	-
Italy	100/50*	-	-	-
Norway	100	5	2	2
Sweden	100	5	10	10
Switzerland	-	5	-	-
USA-NIOSH	25	2	2	2
USA-ACGIH	50	50/1#	75	-

*   for newly constructed operating rooms
#   if mixed with N₂O at 50 ppm

A precise assessment of exposure conditions can be obtained by periodical monitoring of airborne concentrations. Biological monitoring can also be programmed to obtain individual exposure levels. The leakage sources can be detected by means of environmental detectors.

In addition to exposure limit values, other preventive measures have to be undertaken and they include the connection of the anaesthesia apparatus to a central high-flow scavenging system; room ventilation should guarantee at least 15 air changes per hour. The post anaesthesia care units should be equipped with ventilatory system to reduce waste anaesthetic gases.

The use of double-masks and laryngeal masks can further reduce the pollution. The anaesthetic gas flow should also start after endotracheal intubation and intermittent mask ventilation avoided. In general, medium- and low-flow anaesthesia should be preferred to high-flow anaesthesia.

Health surveillance programs should be added and pregnant women should avoid exposure.

Overall, educational programs for operating room personnel are recommended, since a good knowledge of health risks and safety procedure can further facilitate a better control of anaesthetic-gases pollution. NIOSH has recently published guidelines for minimising workers exposures, through several steps including exposure monitoring, engineering controls and maintenance procedures, scavenging systems, room ventilation, work practices and respiratory protection in operating rooms [11], and during cryosurgery [12].

References

1   Tran N, Elias J, Rosenberg T, Wylie D, Gaborieau D, Yassi A. Evaluation of waste anesthetic gases, monitoring strategies, and correlations between nitrous oxide levels and health symptoms. Am Ind Hyg Assoc J 1994;55:36-41

2   Badgwell JM. An evaluation of air safety source-control technology for the post anesthesia care unit. J Perianesth Nurs 1996;11:207-222

3   Schuyt HC, Verberk MM. Measurement and reduction of nitrous oxide in operating rooms. J Occup Environ Med 1996;38:1036-1040

4   Hoerauf K, Funk W, Harth M, Hobbhahn J. Occupational exposure to sevoflurane, halothane and nitrous oxide during paediatric anaesthesia. Waste gas exposure during paediatric anaesthesia. Anaesthesia 1997;52:215-219

5   Lucchini R, Placidi D, Toffoletto F, Alessio L. Neurotoxicity in operating room personnel working with gaseous and non-gaseous anesthesia. Int Arch Occup Environ Health 1996;68:188-192

6   Lucchini R, Belotti L, Cassitto MG, Faillace A, Margonari M, Micheloni G, Scapellato ML, Somenzi V, Spada T, Toffoletto F, Gilioli R. Neurobehavioral functions in operating room personnel: a multicenter study. Med Lav 1997;88(5):396-405

7   Axelsson G, Ahlborg G, Bodin L. Shift work, nitrous oxide exposure, and spontaneous abortion among Swedish midwives. Occup Environ Med 1996;53:374-378.

8   IARC monographs on the evaluation of carcinogenic risk to humans. Suppl 7. Overall evaluation of carcinogenicity: an updating of IARC monographs volumes 1 to 42. International Agency for the Research on Cancer, Lion, 1987;93-95.

9   Franco G, Lorena M, Ghittori S. Occupational exposure of operating-theatre personnel to isoflurane and nitrous oxide. Appl Occup Environ Hyg 1992;82:527-532.

10   Hoerauf KH, Koller C, Taeger K, Hobbhalm J. Occupational exposure to sevoflurane and nitrous oxide in operating room personnel. Int Arch Occup Environ Health 1997;69:134-138

11   NIOSH ALERT. Controlling exposures to nitrous oxide during anesthetic administration. DHHS Publication, 1996;No.94-100

12   NIOSH HAZARD CONTROLS. Control of nitrous oxide during cryosurgery. DHHS Publication, 1999;No.99-105

Further reading

- http://www.cdc.gov/niosh/noxidalr.html
- http://www.cdc.gov/niosh/nitoxide.html
- http://www.cdc.gov/niosh/hc29.html
- Ahlborg G., Hemminki K. Reproductive effects of chemical exposures in health professions. J Occup Environ Med 1995;37:957-961

Occupational Health for Health Care Workers - A Practical Guide
H.-M. Hasselhorn, A. Toomingas and M. Lagerström (Editors)
© 1999 Elsevier Science B.V. All rights reserved.

Ethylene oxide

Kazuya Yahata, Toshiaki Higashi

Ethylene oxide (EO) is a gas that is widely used to sterilise medical equipment and supplies, especially those that can not be sterilised by steam or high temperature. EO polymerises easily and, therefore, is characterised by high reactivity including explosion on contact with various substances.

Health hazards

Symptoms of acute exposure to EO include irritation of the eyes, mucous membranes and upper respiratory tract, nausea, vomiting and headache and in high concentrations, pulmonary oedema and loss of consciousness. Symptoms of chronic exposure to EO in low concentrations include dermatitis, allergic dermatitis, cataract, and peripheral sensory neuropathy [1, 2]. EO is anticipated to increase the rate of spontaneous abortions. It has been shown to induce cancer in animals and is classified as a Group 1 substance (Carcinogenicity in humans) by the International Agency for Research on Cancer.

Exposure

Sterilisation with EO does not lead to an increased exposure to workers when correctly performed with today's generation sterilisation chambers. With older sterilisation chambers or in case of incorrect performance, occupational exposure to EO mainly occurs in two ways. When opening sterilisation chambers workers may be exposed to short-term concentrations of about 50-200 parts per million (ppm), if the exhaust procedures are inadequate. Furthermore, all hospital workers may be exposed to EO residues when opening sterilised medical equipment and supplies. In this case, the level of EO tends to be low, and sufficient aeration can reduce the concentration of residual EO [2].

Accidents

EO is highly reactive. Air containing 2.7% (volume) of EO is explosive. For sterilisation purposes, highly explosive 100% EO is being used in the USA and Europe. In Japan and Asia, EO diluted with carbon dioxide is used to prevent explosions. Accidental exposure of hospital workers to high concentration of EO can occur in case of leakage from the gas cylinder during loading and unloading of sterilisation chambers. Spilled EO from storage vessels or due to malfunctioning exhaust processes can lead to an exposure of several hundred ppm.

Exposure limits

Permissible exposure limits have been set in most countries. The American Conference of Governmental Industrial Hygienists sets an EO threshold limit value (time weighted average) of 1 ppm [3].

Exposure measurements

EO levels in the environment and the individual exposure can be continuously measured by an EO gas monitor, whereby the samples are evaluated quantitatively by gas chromatography. Haemoglobin adducts can be useful markers in biological monitoring [4]. The odour threshold is high, and only concentrations above 430 ppm can be smelled.

Screening / medical examination

EO does not induce specific effects on blood chemical or blood cell composition. Subjective symptoms are the most important indicators for an increased exposure to EO [1, 2].

Prevention

EO sterilisation should only be performed using modern sterilises with adjacent aeration chambers. Respiratory protective equipment, protective spectacles and adequate gloves should be used while working with the sterilising equipment. The sterilise should be adequately exhausted before its opening and the sterilised goods should be placed in an aeration chamber for at least one day. The sterilisation facility should be well-ventilated. Local exhaustion should exist at the site of EO release. An indicator of EO hazards should be installed at and near the storage vessel and its function examined periodically (at least once per year).

References

1   IPCS International Programme on Chemical Safety, Health and Safety Guide No.16 ethylene oxide health and safety guide, World Health Organization, Geneva 1988
2   IPCS International Programme on Chemical Safety, Environmental Health Criteria 55: ethylene oxide, World Health Organization, Geneva 1985

3   ACGIH World Wide Guide to Occupational Exposure Values - 1995, Compiled by the American Conference of Governmental Industrial Hygienists 1996;147-149
4   Sittert NJ. Monitoring Occupational Exposure to Ethylene oxide by the Determination of Hemoglobin Adducts, Environmental Health Perspectives 1993;99:217-220

Further reading

- ISO 11135, Medical devices - Validation and routine control of ethylene oxide sterilization, International Organization for Standardization, Geneva 1994
- ISO 10993-7, Biological evaluation of medical devices - Part 7: Ethylene oxide sterilization residuals, International Organization for Standardization, Geneva 1995
- ISO 11138-2, Sterilization of health care products - Biological indicators - Part 2: Biological indicators for ethylene oxide sterilization, International Organization for Standardization, Geneva 1994

Occupational Health for Health Care Workers - A Practical Guide
H.-M. Hasselhorn, A. Toomingas and M. Lagerström (Editors)

Prevention and rehabilitation of musculoskeletal disorders in nursing work

Monica Lagerström, Mats Hagberg

Epidemiological and scientific studies of hospital workers have considered a range of possible problems as representing work-related risk factors for musculoskeletal problems in nursing work. These factors which are considered below, can be divided into physical, psychosocial, and work-organisational as well as individual and life-style factors.

In several respects nursing work is not comparable with other types of work. The most significant factor is the close contact with another human being in need of help and support, which is considered rewarding but also mentally demanding for the nurse. The work may be physically strenuous, with frequent lifting and awkward working postures and it is not, for example, unusual that nurses stand and walk for more than 6 hours per day [1].

Nursing personnel in general have a high prevalence of musculoskeletal problems but not very much higher than the general population. Data from an English study show that nurses have an annual prevalence of self-reported back pain of 59% which was almost the same as the 58% reported in the general population [2]. There are, however, differences in the prevalence of musculoskeletal problems between the different grades of nurses. Auxiliary nurses (AN) and state enrolled nurses (SEN) have a more strenuous work load compared to registered nurses (RN) with the consequence of a higher prevalence of musculoskeletal problems. The professional education of SEN is 1-2 years and for AN less than one year (Table 1). It can also be seen from a Swedish study that most nurses report problems in the lower back but that many nurses also report neck and shoulder problems, irrespective of work category (Table 1).

Table 1. Prevalence (%) ongoing self-reported musculoskeletal problems among nurses (n=688) [3]

Body region	Registered nurses (%)	State enrolled nurses (%)	Auxiliary nurses (%)
Neck	44	46	59
Shoulder	48	54	60
Lower back	52	55	65
Hands	17	22	30
Knees	27	31	35

Physical hazards

There is a relationship between patient lifting frequency and low-back pain [4]. In geriatric, orthopaedic and rehabilitation wards nursing staff are at higher risk for musculoskeletal problems than in wards where there are fewer patient transfers [2, 6]. Each stressful patient-handling task involves some risk of a back injury for the nurse. If lifting aids are used and/or the patient behaves as predicted, everything goes smoothly, and the risk of injury is minimal. If anything unusual happens, for example, the legs of the patient give way or the patient slides out of the bed or off a chair, and a "save the patient" situation occurs, the risks of back problems for the nurse increase dramatically. It has been shown that the prevalence of lower back problems among nursing staff who more frequently handle patients is about 3.7 times that of nursing personnel who infrequently do so [5].

Work organisation and psychosocial hazards

Hospitals are high-stress work places. High work demands, limited possibilities to influence work (i.e. high job strain) and low social support at work has been related to lower back problems among nurses. Work satisfaction has been seen to predict lower back health especially among those who smoked and had earlier severe lower back problems [22].

The importance of work satisfaction and attitudes was shown in nurses from hospitals in Belgium and the Netherlands. Despite their heavier work load, Dutch nurses experienced higher work satisfaction, had more positive attitudes to pain, to their work, to physical activity, used more positive coping strategies and reported lower life-time prevalence of back problems than the Belgian nurses [7].

Staff density has been related to low-back pain [8]. When the staff density is low the nurses have to work alone for long periods and unassisted lifts can be a risk factor for back injuries. In two Italian hospitals with a nurse/ patient ratio of 0.57 or 1.27 patient per nurse, respectively, the prevalence of lower back problems among nurses were 48.2% or 32.8%, respectively [8].

Individual and life-style factors

Surveys in either the general population or vocational groups have in general shown that lower back problems increase with age up to 50-60 years, after which there is a decline. This is especially true for women. At 40-44 years the risk of lumbar pain was twice as high compared to below 35 years of age among French nurses [9]. For men, however, lower back problems usually are more common at a younger age.

Cigarette smoking as a risk factor for lower back problems has been postulated. Possible explanations for this are that a) severe and chronic coughing can lead to increased intradiscal pressure, thus resulting in low-back pain, b) cigarette smoke has a direct adverse effect on the spine in that blood flow is restricted thereby making the disc more susceptible to trauma, and c) a diminished mineral content of bone renders the spine more vulnerable [10].

In the general population there is usually no evidence for a relationship between lower back problems and physical fitness. In a Swedish study on nurses, however, those who regarded their physical fitness as low in comparison with others of their own age, had severe lower back problems [3]. It is not unusual for nurses to possess low physical fitness. Among French nurses as many as 27% did not reach the level of physical fitness required for their tasks [1].

A consensus emerges that a previous history of back problems is considered to be a risk for subsequent episodes, as shown in several studies [1, 10]. It might be supposed that when employing nursing staff those physically strong and without previous back problems would be preferentially hired. However, at present there is no scientific evidence of an effective screening test for pre-placement or pre-employment testing in order to reduce work-related or other non-specific musculoskeletal disorders [11].

Health promotion and prevention

Health promotion focuses on maintaining or improving general health. Interventions, mainly training programme by, for example, occupational physiotherapists are directed towards developing the resources of employees to maintain or enhance well-being. Primary prevention in nursing work is of importance to prevent new episodes of musculoskeletal problems as well as secondary and tertiary prevention to prevent deterioration of symptoms.

Some health promoting activities focus on the individual and some on the work environment and the work organisation. It should be stressed that interventions only focusing on the individual have not been successful in decreasing musculoskeletal problems. Such problems also need an organisational solution to be successful in leading to a change not only in behaviour and attitudes but also - focusing on the organisation - to changes in the work environment [12, 13].

It has been suggested that when nursing staff fail to benefit from training programmes this might because: a) the interventions lack sufficient intensity to bring about the desired change, b) of an inadequate recommended work technique or c) because of lack of support for the intervention programme from top management. It is believed that if nurses use a gentle work technique, musculoskeletal problems might not develop. However, there have been several studies published that have indicated little, if any, decrease in such problems among well-trained nurses as compared to other nurses. A British review of ten intervention programmes consisting of training and education in patient transfer technique of the staff to reduce lower back problems from 1976-1992 showed negligible long-term benefit [6].

Thus, musculoskeletal problems in nursing should be targeted at three levels [14]:
- New comprehensive, functional, and ergonomic planning should cover the entire hospital environment, architecture, and organisation of work.
- Wards must be equipped with lifting devices, and

- nurses should be given training, including recommendations for patient transfer techniques and body posture (see chapter Physical ergonomic risk factors).

Rehabilitation

Physical activity

It has been well documented that rest is not the best treatment for back problems [15]. Wadell noted in 1987 how experimental studies showed that controlled exercises did not only restore function, reduce distress and illness behaviour, and promote return to work, but also reduced pain. Thus, the cornerstone of management of lower back problems should now be not rest but rehabilitation and restoration of function [15]. A Swedish intervention study of nurses and auxiliary nurses both with and without back problems showed that light physical exercise during working hours leading to increased back muscle strength lowered sickness absence due to lower back problems [16].

Back schools

Back schools originated in Sweden in the early 1980s and have since become popular particularly in the treatment of chronic back pain [17]. The aims of back schools are to teach the worker with back problems how to handle his problematic back at work and at home. Patients receive theoretical information and take part in practical exercises. The training is mostly given in groups and lead by a physiotherapist. However, Banerjee summarised some reviews of back schools and found only one controlled trial that demonstrated short-term positive effects in a group of workers with acute or sub-acute back pain. Although it has been stated that the efficacy of the back schools is yet to be established, given the negligible potential harm and low cost, back schools may be helpful as an integral part of a comprehensive treatment programme [17]. Also, it is as yet unclear if the back school programmes per se or failing compliance by participants are the most important factors for inability to demonstrate clearly success in terms of the health status of nurses.

Vocational focus

To be effective rehabilitation must include removing factors that caused the problem leading to sickness absence. Rehabilitation is a process in which the individual will get stronger medically *and* vocationally. The process of rehabilitation should therefore aim at strengthening behaviour, attitudes, and social, vocational, and physical ability. Work-organisational, psychosocial factors and patient attitudes can affect pain perception and injury experience and as such also be of importance for the success or not of a return to work after injury. To prevent a permanent inability to work, a rehabilitation process must start early. The motivation to work decreases with time and the anxiety for work increases. Already after three months of sick leave it is difficult for the patient to return to work. After six to eight months of sick leave only 30-40% of all patients return to work and after two years almost no one returns to work. It is crucial to secure the supervisors´ active interest in returning a person to work after an attack of back pain [18], a factor that seems frequently to be neglected in the workplace. Support from fellow workers can be regarded as an important contributing factor for early return to work.

The importance of focusing on the organisation, the working environment, and the individual in the rehabilitation process cannot be over stressed. Of several programmes it is mainly those who have this broad focus that prove to be successful in reducing musculoskeletal disorders among nurses [19, 20]. An example of a successful approach is an ergonomic intervention programme of nursing assistants in a nursing home in USA. Training in the use of devices, modification of toilets and shower rooms, and application of technical aids in patient care proved efficient strategies to reduce lower back problems [19]. Another programme also resulted in a decrease in back injuries and in time loss, and was therefore considered cost-beneficial. This intervention consisted of prompt assessment, treatment, rehabilitation, and where necessary modified working conditions for injured nurses [20].

Interdisciplinary rehabilitation of Swedish hospital employees with musculoskeletal problems has been reported as successful. After a six-week programme, 77% of nursing staff on sick-leave were able to return to work. The programme consisted of a weekly four days of group training and education with a physiotherapist, an occupational therapist, a social worker, and a physician. The fifth day consisted of a visit to the work place. Ergonomic and appropriate work techniques as well as psychosocial factors at work were discussed and where necessary controlled [21]. During the whole rehabilitation process, close contact was maintained between the Occupational Health Service unit (OHS) and the Rehabilitation Clinic.

This programme is an example of the key role of OHS. One main ability of OHS is to give early vocational rehabilitation. As OHS knows both the individual and the workplace and work process it can see possibilities for change in all three. Thus, the OHS should be an important resource in the management of musculoskeletal problems and of the rehabilitation process and a co-ordinator facilitating the contacts between those who are in need of rehabilitation, rehabilitation clinics and other social institutions, and last but not least, their workplaces.

Suggestions for health promotion

Some suggestions of change to promote health and to prevent musculoskeletal problems, and facilitate the rehabilitation process are given below. Certain of these might be implemented by the OHS.

Both individual and organisational approaches to health promotion should originate from participatory action by the workforce if implementation is to be successful. You cannot use a standardised programme package at different work sites. All workers should have an opportunity to influence the health promotion programme at their work places.

For the individual:
- The employer should provide programmes for smoking cessation.
- The employer should provide possibilities for regular physical exercise during working hours.
- The employer should implement education programs aimed at prevention of musculoskeletal problems, including information on gentle patient transfer techniques.
- The employer should provide possibilities for skills development and career development of nurses by using a variety of strategies, a "competence ladder" or "clinical ladders", or other models of career development.
- There is wide range of skill and competence among nursing personnel, which should be acknowledged
- The employer should empower the injured persons and support them in playing an active role in the rehabilitation process.
- The employer should facilitate close contacts between the injured person, the rehabilitation clinic, the OHS, other (social) institutions, and the workplace.

For the work environment:
- Use of technical aids: transfer aids, mechanical hoists, adjustable beds and tables, toilet and bathroom aids (see chapter Physical ergonomic risk factors).
- Provide sufficient space around the bed of the patient and in the toilets.

For the work organisation:
- Formulate common goals for the work place to make the work more meaningful and to decrease role ambiguity.
- Provide possibilities for nurses to talk about vocational problems, also emotional problems both individually and in groups with work mates and supervisors.
- Facilitate social support for work mates and supervisors by for example team-work.
- Encourage team care or primary care with full responsibility for a small number of patients instead of traditional nursing care with shared responsibility for many patients.
- Support the supervisors so that the charge nurse may be given opportunities to learn management theories and practices.
- Encourage supervisors´ active interest in safety questions and develop a systematic accident reporting system.
- Provide support for nurses´ increased influence over their work and work environment.
- Ascertain there is sufficient staffing to reduce overload and stress when transferring patients.
- Use flexible working hours.
- Develop a prompt implementation of secondary preventive measures for the avoidance of long term sickness absence.
- Initiate effective rehabilitation measures for women with physically demanding work, perhaps through modified work.

References

1   Estryn-Behar M, Kaminski M, Peigne E, Maillard MF, Pelletier A, Berthier C, Delaporte MF, Paoli MC, Leroux JM. Strenuous working conditions and musculoskeletal disorders among female hospital workers. Int Arch Occup Environ Health 1990;62:47-57
2   Leighton D, Reilly T. Epidemiological aspects of back pain: the incidence and prevalence of back pain in nurses compared to the general population. Occup Med 1995;45(5):263-267
3   Lagerström M, Wenemark M, Hagberg M, Wigaeus Hjelm E. Occupational and individual factors related to musculoskeletal symptoms in five body regions among Swedish nursing personnel. Int Arch Occup Envir Health 1995;68(1):27-35
4   Lagerström M, Hansson T, Hagberg M. Work-related low-back problems in nursing. Scand J Work Environ Health 1998;24(6):449-464
5   Jensen R. Back injuries among nursing personnel related to exposure. Appl Occup Environ Hyg 1990;5:38-45
6   Hignett S. Work-related back pain in nurses. J Adv Nurs 1996;23:1238-1246
7   Burton A, Symonds T, Zinzen E, et al. Is ergonomic intervention alone sufficient to limit musculokeletal problems in nurses? Occup Med 1997;47(1):25-32
8   Larese F, Fiorito A. Musculoskeletal disorders in hospital nurses: a comparison between two hospitals. Ergonomics 1994;37(7):1205-1211
9   Niedhammer I, Lert F, Marne M. Back pain and associated factors in French nurses. Int Arch Occup Environ Health 1994;66:349-357
10   Rydén L, Molgaard C, Bobitt S, Conway C, Conway J. Occupational Low-back Injury in A Hospital Employee Population: an Epidemiologic Analysis of multiple Risk Factors of a High-Risk Occupational group. Spine 1989;14(3):315-320
11   Hagberg M, Silverstein B, Wells R, Smith MJ, Hendrick HW, Carayon P, Pérusse M. Work Related Musculoskeletal Disorders: a Reference Book for Prevention. London: Taylor & Francis, 1995
12   Kemmlert K, Lundholm L. Factors influencing ergonomic conditions and employment rate after an occupational musculoskeletal injury. J Occup Rehab 1994;4(1):11-20
13   Ekberg K, Wildhagen I. Long-term sickness absence due to musculoskeletal disorders: the necessary intervention of work condition. Scand J Rehab Med 1996;28:39-47
14   Takala E-P, Kukkonen R. The handling of patients on geriatric wards. Appl Ergon 1987;18(1):17-22
15   Wadell G. A new clinical model for the treatment of low-back pain. Spine 1987;12(7):623-644
16   Gundewall B, Liljeqvist M, Hansson T. Primary prevention of back symptoms and absence from work. Spine 1993;18(5):587-594
17   Banerjee SN. Nonsurgical treatment of acute low back pain. In: Basmajian JV, Benerjee N, (Eds). Clinical decision making in rehabilitation. New York: Churchill Livingstone, 1996
18   Wood D. Design and evaluation of a back injury prevention program within a geriatric hospital. Spine 1987;12(2):77-82
19   Garg A, Owen B. Reducing back stress to nursing personnel: an ergonomic intervention in a nursing home. Ergonomics 1992;35(11):1353-1375
20   Yassi A, Tate R, Cooper J, Snow C, Vallentyne S, Khokhar J. Early intervention for back-injured nurses at a large Canadian tertiary care hospital: An evaluation of the effectiveness and cost benefits for a two-year pilot project. Occup Med 1995;45(4):209-214
21   Nordström-Björverud G, Mortiz U. Interdisciplinary rehabilitation of hospital employees with musculoskeletal disorders. Scand J Rehab Med 1998;30:31-37
22   Ready AE, Boreskie SL, Law SA, Russel R. Fitness and lifestyle parameters fail to predict back injuries in nurses. Can J Appl Phys 1993;18(1): 80-90

Occupational Health for Health Care Workers - A Practical Guide
H.-M. Hasselhorn, A. Toomingas and M. Lagerström (Editors)
© 1999 Elsevier Science B.V. All rights reserved.

Physical ergonomic risk factors

Madeleine Estryn-Behar

Extensive research has been conducted into the ergonomics of hospitalisation, as it is of obvious benefit to understand the effects which particular factors in the patient's environment have on behaviours that are hazardous for patients or staff. Many studies have attempted to identify the extent to which the hospital organisation allows personnel to develop different strategies to reconcile acceptable workload with good quality of care [1].

Physical strain is one of the primary determinants of hospital workers' health and the quality of care they dispense. Albeit, the frequent interruptions that hinder care giving and the effect of psychological factors associated with confrontations with serious illness, ageing, and death, must also be addressed. Accounting for all these factors is a complex task, but approaches, which focus only on individual factors, will fail to improve either working conditions or quality of care. Similarly, patients' perception of the quality of their hospital stay is determined by the effectiveness of the care they receive, their relationship with physicians and other personnel, and the environment.

Work postures and distance walked

The effect of physical strain on health-care workers has been demonstrated through continuous observation of workdays. Research in Belgium, France, and Czechoslovakia [2-4] has shown that health-care workers spend 60 to 80% of their workday standing up. Belgian nurses were observed to spend approximately 10% of their workday bent over, Czechoslovakian nurses spent 11% of their workday positioning patients, and French nurses spent 16-24% of their workday in uncomfortable positions such as stooping, squatting, and positions in which their arms were raised or loaded. Nurses in these wards walked an average of 4-7 kilometres per day.

Detailed observation of entire workdays [4] is useful in revealing the interaction of the factors that determine quality of care and the manner in which work is performed. Continuous observation of Dutch nurses in long-term-stay wards revealed that they spent 60% of their time performing physically demanding work with no direct contact with their patients [5]. Housekeeping and preparation account for most of the 20% of time described as spent in "slightly hazardous" activities. Contact with patients was the type of activity most frequently associated with these hazardous postures.

Several epidemiological studies have indicated that inappropriate postures and handling techniques are associated with a doubling of the number of back problems, treatments, and work stoppages for musculoskeletal disorders.

Size of the rooms and equipment

The inadequacy of nursing equipment, particularly beds, in 40 Japanese hospitals was demonstrated by Shindo [6]. In addition, patients' rooms, both those for six to eight patients and single rooms reserved for the very ill, were poorly laid out and extremely small. Matsuda reported that these observations should lead to improvements in the comfort, safety and efficiency of nursing work [7]. Both authors are developing ergonomics programmes for Japanese nursing schools to enable future nurses to participate in these changes.

The size of patient rooms was a potential problem in 45 of 75 medium and long-term-stay wards in France. In table 1 the most common problems are shown.

Table 1. The most common ergonomical problems in 75 medium and long-term-stay wards in French hospitals

Ergonomical problem	Frequency (%)
Lack of space	40
Difficulty in manoeuvring patient-transfer hoists	23
Inadequate space for furniture	17
The need to take beds out of the room to transfer patients	16
Difficult access and poor furniture layout	13
Doors that were too small	11
Difficulty moving between beds	11

The mean available area per bed for patients and nurses is at the root of these problems. The French Department of Health prescribes a useful surface area of 16 m² for single rooms and 22 m² for double rooms (in this study they were 12.98 m², 19.68 m² respectively). The Quebec Department of Health recommends 17.8 m² and 36 m² respectively.

After noting that three-quarters of occupational accidents involving nurses occur in patient rooms, in Quebec, the Joint Sectoral Association, Social Affairs Sector (Association pour la santé et la sécurité du travail, secteur afffaires sociales, ASSTAS) initiated its "Prevention-Planning-Renovation-Construction" project in 1993. The association proposed new dimensions for patient's rooms. New rooms must now provide a minimum amount of free space around beds and accommodate patient-lifts. Measuring 4.05 m x 4.90 m the rooms are more square than the older, rectangular rooms. To improve performance, ceiling-mounted patient-lifts were installed, joining bed to toilet and shower, in collaboration with the manufacturer.

Evaluation of equipment that reduces physical strain

Proposals for improving beds and meal carts have been formulated but their impact is limited. Adjustable-height beds with electric trunk-lifts and mechanical mattress-lifts have been studied. The trunk-lifts were judged satisfactory by the staff and patients but the mattress-lifts were very unsatisfactory, since adjusting the beds required more than eight pedal-strokes, each of which exceeds appropriate ergonomic standards for foot force. Pushing a button located close to the patient's head while talking to her or him is clearly preferable to pumping a pedal eight times from the foot of the bed. Because of time constraints the mattress-lift was often simply not used.

Health-care workers were involved in the design of new hospital beds, testing 30 prototype beds over a six-week period [8]. Observations were made of workers' positions, the height of work surfaces, physical interactions between nurses and patients, and the size of the workspace. This was compared to data collected on the same ward over a seven-week period prior to the introduction of the prototype. Use of the prototype reduced the total time spent in uncomfortable positions while washing patients from 40% to 20%; for bed-making the figures were 35% and 5%. Patients also enjoyed greater autonomy and often changed positions on their own, raising their trunk or legs by means of electric control buttons. In Swedish hospitals, a double room is often equipped with ceiling-mounted patients-lifts [9]. It is also important to choose furniture which avoids people bending lower than 0.70 m and reaching higher than 1.40 m for those objects most frequently used. Many countries have established norms regarding this.

Personal equipment and physical activity

The adoption of better work postures is also conditioned by the possibility of wearing appropriate clothing. The quality of shoes is particularly important. Hard soles are to be avoided. Anti-slip soles prevent occupational accidents caused by slips and falls, which in many countries are the second highest cause of accidents leading to work absence in hospitals.

The female population in France is not very physically active. 0f 1505 nurses studied by Estryn-Behar et al. [10]. 68% participated in no athletic activity with inactivity more pronounced among mothers and unqualified personnel. In Sweden, fitness programmes for hospital personnel have proven useful [11] but are only feasible if potential participants do not end their workday too tired to participate.

Importance of anti lifting

Manual patient-handling techniques designed to prevent back injuries have been proposed in many countries. Given the poor results of these techniques [12, 13], other approaches seem necessary.

The application of European standard No. 90/269 of 1990.05.29 on back problems is an excellent starting point for this approach. Besides requiring employers to implement appropriate work organisation structures or other appropriate means, particularly mechanical equipment, to avoid manual handling of loads by workers, it also emphasises the importance of no-risk handling policies that incorporate training.

In 1996, the Danish working environment fund published a sector guide on the lifting of people [14]. This was aimed at management and safety organisations in hospitals, institutions for the elderly and handicapped, day-care and residential institutions, day-care for children below six years and in health care. It is a tool for management and safety organisations and gives recommendations on functional space requirements for technical aids and assistants.

Technical aids have been divided into 5 groups:
- Transfer aids: lifting cushions, turning carpets, sliding boards, sliding mats and turntables.
- Mechanical hoists: mobile or stationary hoists mounted on the ceiling, wall, floor or bathtub.
- Beds: adjustable beds, lateral tilting beds and turning sheets.
- Toilets aids: raise-able toilet seats, raised toilets seats and support grips.
- Bathroom aids: shower chairs, bath seats, and bath stools.

The need to act on multiple determinants

The Danish working environment fund's guide on the lifting of persons insists on the fact that prevention must be holistically approached and include work techniques, technical aids, work organisation, other working conditions, social relations and exposure to other factors in the working environment [14].

In Sweden, a training and education program consisted of advanced transfer and handling principles and techniques, physical fitness exercise and stress management [15]. The interaction of stress, support networks, work organisation and possibility to adopt good postures during work is apparent in different studies. In 1993 some of these factors were identified in 57 wards of a large hospital in the Paris region. In the three months preceding the study, only 35 wards had held meetings to discuss patients' prognoses, discharges and patients' understanding of and reaction to their illnesses. In the year preceding the study, dayshift workers in 18 wards had received no training, and only 16 wards had dispensed training to their night-shift workers. Nurses' complaints of frequent work interruptions and feelings of being overwhelmed by their work are no doubt attributable to this structure. The scarcity of seats (less than three in 42 of the 57 wards) and cramped quarters of the nursing stations, where over nine people must spend a good part of their day, don't allow team discussions nor preparation of care whilst in a sitting posture.

Analysis of the interaction of different factors influencing care - physical strain, cognitive strain, affective strain, scheduling ambience and hygiene protocols - is essential to reduce physical load (Table 2). It is important to adapt the schedules and the common work areas to the need of the work team when attempting to improve overall patient management. Participatory ergonomics is a way of using specific information to bring about wide-ranging and relevant improvements to the quality of care and to working life. Involving all categories of personnel in key stages of the search for solution helps to ensure that the modifications finally adopted will have their full support.

Table 2. Analysis of the interaction of different factors influencing care and physical load

Type of factor	Examples of factors
Physical strain	• working posture; lifting • physical load (heart rate) • distance walked
Space	• size of rooms, toilets and showers • distances between the main destinations • connections between clean and dirty circuits • number and types of elevators
Equipment	• characteristics of the furniture (height, width, depth) • number and characteristics of adjustable beds • number and characteristics of hoists, of adjustable trolleys
Cognitive strain	• presentation of information in a way that helps rapid decision making easier • written information: number of sources of information; number of different topics to memorise; kind of job aids; legibility; lighting • acoustic alarms: number of different types, frequency of false alarms • team work: co-operation or co-activity, interdependence between the different professions, ambiguities
Affective strain	• uncertainty about what and how to answer the patient's questions • conflicts among the team • frequency of ward meetings to discuss the psychological aspects of care; (who attends the meetings?)

to be continued on page 140

continued

Table 2. Analysis of the interaction of different factors influencing care and physical load

Type of factor	Examples of factors
Scheduling	• number of consecutive nights or days of work at a stretch and work schedules of colleagues • schedules of meals and pharmacy distribution, doctor's visits • hours of arrival of patients & hours of return from operating room • existence of overlapping between consecutive shifts; effective use of this time for discussion
Needs for prevention of infectious risks	• actual number of hand washing/number of entrances in a patient's room • place of containers, existence of double manipulation of needles • special clothing, masks and their actual use
Answer to patient's needs	• percentage of the working day in patient's room • possibilities for long stays beside the patient without interruption • quality of communication with patients

Architecture and working conditions

Construction of multi-purpose hospitals composed of identical modules is a design method that leads to the construction of facilities poorly suited to **any** speciality [16]. For example, the surface area needed to store machines, bottles, disposable equipment, and medication is different in surgical, cardiology and geriatric wards. Failure to recognise this will lead to rooms being used for purposes for which they were not designed, e.g. when bathrooms are used for bottle storage the HCW may be required to walk longer distances. Unfortunately, hospital architecture does not always reflect the needs of those who work there, and multifunctional design has been responsible for reported problems related to physical and cognitive strain.

Consider a 30-bed ward composed of one-and two-bed rooms, in which there is only one functional area of each type (nursing station, pantry, storage of disposable materials, linen or medication), all based on the same all-purpose design. In this ward, the management and allocation of care obliges nurses to change location extremely frequently, and work is greatly fragmented. A comparative study of ten wards has shown that the distance from the nurses' station to the farthest room is an important determinant of both nurses' fatigue (a function of the distance walked) and the quality of care (a function of the time spent in patients' rooms) [4].

The first mathematical model based on the Yale Traffic index, of the nature, purposes, and frequency of staff movements appeared in 1960 and was refined by Lippert in 1971. However, attention to one problem in isolation may in fact aggravate others. For example, locating a nurse's station in the centre of the building, in order to reduce the distances walked, may worsen working conditions if nurses must spend over 30% of their time in such windowless surroundings which are known to be a source of problems related to lighting, ventilation and psychological factors.

Research on the design of specific but flexible hospital units has been conducted over the last twenty years. Architectural design based on participatory ergonomics was recently developed as workers must be involved in the planning of the behavioural and organisational changes associated with the occupation of a new space [17].

Appropriate choices concerning the space and equipment of a workplace need to be considered along with those organisational elements that may require modification. A detailed report of the results of the renovation of the common areas of a medical ward and a cardiology ward of the same hospital was published [18]. The ergonomics of the work performed by the various professionals in each ward was observed over seven entire workdays and discussed over a two-day period with each group. The groups included representatives of all occupations (department heads, supervisors, interns, nurses, nurses' aides, and ancillary staff) from all the shifts. One entire day was spent developing architectural and organisational proposals for each problem noted. The whole group, in collaboration, spent two more days on the simulation of characteristic activities with an architect and the ergonomist, using modular cardboard mock-ups and scale models of objects and people. Through this simulation, representatives of the various occupations were able to agree on distances and the distribution of space within each ward. Only after this process was concluded was the design specification drawn up.

To evaluate the results, the observations of the same workers before and after the rearrangements were compared. The new space, with more chairs available so as not to disturb others, and the new organisation, allow the staff to sit down more. In the medical unit, the percentage of the working day spent sitting down is higher for morning and afternoon nurses, head nurses, resident and ancillary staff. The length of time seated is often higher and the period without the opportunity to sit down was reduced in three cases out of six. In cardiology, also, the trend is similar. The time interval without being able to sit was reduced in four cases out of six and no periods longer than three hours without sitting were observed.

References

1   Estryn-Behar M. Ergonomics and health care. In: ILO. Encyclopaedia of Occupational Health and Safety. IV Ed. Vol III. Geneva, 1998;97.26-97.33
2   Malchaire JB. Analysis of the work load of nurses. In: Estryn-Béhar M, Gadbois C, Pottier M. Ergonomie à l'hôpital- Hospital ergonomics. International Symposium Paris 1991. Toulouse, Octares Ed, 1992:217-221
3   Hubacova L, Borsky I, Strelka F. Work physiology problems of nurses working in patients departments. In: Estryn-Béhar M. Gadbois C. Pottier M. Ergonomie à l'hôpital- Hospital ergonomics. International Symposium Paris 1991. Toulouse, Octares Ed, 1992:411-414
4   Estryn-Behar M, Kaminski M, Peigne E, Maillard MF, Pelletier A, Berthier C, Delaporte MF, Paoli MC, Leroux JM. Strenuous working conditions and musculoskeletal disorders among

female hospital workers. Int Arch Occup Environ Health 1990;62:47-57

5   Engels J, Senden TH, Hertog K. Working postures of nurses in nursing homes. In: Hagberg M, Hofmann F, Stössel U, Westlander G (Eds). Occupational Health for Health Care Workers. Landsberg: Ecomed publishers, 1993:317-321

6   Shindo E. The present condition of nursing ergonomics in Japan. In: Estryn-Béhar M. Gadbois C. Pottier M. Ergonomie à l'hôpital- Hospital ergonomics. International Symposium Paris 1991. Toulouse, Octares Ed, 1992:205-208

7   Matsuda A. Ergonomics approach to nursing care in Japan. In: Estryn-Béhar M. Gadbois C. Pottier M. Ergonomie à l'hôpital- Hospital ergonomics. International Symposium Paris 1991. Toulouse, Octares Ed, 1992:215-216

8   Van der Star A, Voogd M. User participation in the design and evaluation of a new model hospital bed- Etude participative pour la conception et l'évaluation d'un nouveau lit d'hôpital. In: Estryn-Béhar M. Gadbois C. Pottier M. Ergonomie à l'hôpital- Hospital ergonomics. International Symposium Paris 1991. Toulouse, Octares Ed, 1992:273-278

9   Ljungberg AS, Kilbom Á, Hägg G. Occupational lifting by nursing aides and warehouse workers. Ergonomics 1989;32:59-78

10   Estryn-Behar M, Kapitaniak B, Paoli M, Peigne E, Masson A. Aptitude for physical exercise in a population of female hospital workers. Int Arch Occup Environ Health 1992;64:131-139

11   Wigaeus Hjelm E, Hagberg M, Hellström S, UPP-Study Group. Prevention of musculoskeletal disorders in nursing aides by physical training. In: Hagberg M, Hofmann F, Stössel U, Westlander G (Eds). Occupational Health for Health Care Workers. Landsberg: Ecomed publishers, 1993:364-366

12   Dehlin O, Berg S, Andersson G, Grimby G. Effect of physical training and ergonomic counselling on the psychological perception of work and on the subjective assessment of low back insufficiency. Scand J Rehab Med 1981;13:1-9

13   Stubbs D, Buckle P, Hudson M, Rivers P. Back pain in the nursing profession II. The effectiveness of training. Ergonomics 1983;26:767-779

14   Danish working environment fund. Sector guidance on the lifting of persons. Copenhagen: Sector safety council for health and social services (ssc 11), 1996

15   Lagerström M, Hagberg M, Wigaeus Hjelm E. Low back symptoms among female nursing personnel during a three-year intervention program, In: Hagberg M, Hofmann F, Stössel U, Westlander G (Eds). Occupational Health for Health Care Workers. Landsberg: Ecomed publishers, 1995:289-293

16   Games WP, Tatton-Braen W. Hospitals Design and Development. London, The Architectural Press, 1989

17   Estryn-Béhar M, Milanini G, Cantel MM, Poirier P, Abriou P, and the I.C.U.'s study group. Interest of participative ergonomic methodology to improve an intensive care unit. In: Hagberg M, Hofmann F, Stössel U, Westlander G (Eds). Occupational Health for Health Care Workers. Landsberg: Ecomed publishers, 1995:91-99

18   Estryn-Béhar M. Ergonomie hospitalière, Théorie et pratique. Paris, Editions ESTEM, 1996

Occupational Health for Health Care Workers - A Practical Guide
H.-M. Hasselhorn, A. Toomingas and M. Lagerström (Editors)
© 1999 Elsevier Science B.V. All rights reserved.

Radiation problems in the health care professions

Jean François Gehanno, Patrick Ledosseur

Ionising radiation has been used in medicine since the end of the 19th century. Deterministic effects, like skin burns and damage of fingers, as well as cancers induced by such radiation were observed very early, especially among radiologists. Therefore, the second International Congress of Radiology, in 1928, decided to create the International Commission on Radiological Protection (ICRP), which recommendations were then concerned solely with medical practice, but widened in the 1950s to deal with all situations in which humans are exposed to ionising radiation. Nowadays, the medical use of radiation accounts for a great part of the artificial radiation dose to which a population is exposed. Nevertheless, if radiation exposures in medicine are predominantly to the individuals undergoing diagnosis, screening or therapy, staff and other individuals helping to support and comfort patients can also be exposed.

Such exposure occurs mainly in radiodiagnostics, nuclear medicine and radiotherapy. In the first category, invasive and interventional radiology, and especially cardiology, are responsible for the higher amount of medical staff exposure [1].

Quantities and units

Ionising radiation is any electromagnetic or particulate energy capable of producing ions by interaction with matter and includes X-rays from X-ray producing equipment and gamma rays from radioactive material. The quantities and units used are:

- the *activity* of a radioactive substance is the number of disintegrations per unit time, and its unit per second is becquerel (Bq).
- the *absorbed dose* is the energy absorbed per unit mass of material, and its unit joule per kilogram is gray (Gy).
- the *equivalent dose* is the absorbed dose averaged over a tissue or organ and weighted for the radiation quality of interest by the radiation weighting factor. The unit of equivalent dose, joule per kilogram is sievert (Sv). Examples for the radiation weighting factor are 1 for all photons (X-rays or γ-radiation), 5 for protons and 20 for α-particles.
- The *effective dose* is the sum of the weighted equivalent doses in all tissues and organs of the body. The tissue weighting factors, by which the equivalent doses for the tissue or organ is multiplied, are in the range between 0.12 (e.g. for the lung) and 0.01 (e.g. for the skin). The unit in joule per kilogram is sievert (Sv).

These SI units have replaced former units like *rad, roentgen* and *rem*.

Negative health effects

The biological effects of radiation can be grouped into two kinds: deterministic and stochastic effects.

Deterministic effects occur when many cells in an organ and tissue are killed. Thus, they are observable only if the radiation dose is above a threshold, which depends on the dose rate (radiation dose per unit of time), the absorbed dose and the extent or part of the body exposed. Furthermore, the intensity of the effect increases with increasing dose. Such effects include the following: erythema, desquamation, cataracts, decreased white blood count, organ atrophy, fibrosis or sterility. The minimum amount in a single dose associated with the development of a progressive cataract is about 2 Gy, but much higher total doses can be tolerated when administered over longer time [1].

Stochastic effects are susceptible to occur when, in theory, the DNA in a single cell is damaged. This can lead to somatic effects (cancer) or hereditary effects (genetic risk), depending on the type of damage, the effectiveness of the body's defences, the specific responsiveness of the cellular system involved and association with exposure to other agents. The probability of biological effect, but not the intensity of this effect, increases with increasing dose. According to ICRP, there is sufficient evidence that stochastic effects attributable to radiation can occur, albeit at very low probability, even at very low doses, i.e. there will be no threshold of dose below which there will be no risk [2]. The shape of the dose-response relationship at intermediate to high dose levels appears to be linear-quadratic (at low doses, the effect is proportional to dose; at higher doses the probability of effects increases with dose more markedly than simple proportion and at even higher doses, close to the thresholds of deterministic effects, the probability increases more slowly and may begin to decrease) [2].

Extrapolations based on observation from Hiroshima and Nagasaki indicate that the risk of fatal cancer due to lifetime whole-body X-ray exposure is approximately 4% per Sv for levels encountered in medical settings for health personnel [3].

Concerning risks from prenatal exposure, it is necessary to distinguish between acute exposure in utero, chronic exposure during pregnancy, and exposure of the father or the mother before pregnancy. Following acute exposure during pregnancy, embryonic death may occur at a dose of 500 mGy. After lower acute exposure in utero mental retardation is the most probable outcome. Exposure during the sensitive period at 8-15 weeks of gestation may lead to a reduction of the Intelligence Quotient by 30 points per Sv. Except for mental retardation, the most frequent malformations observed are growth delays, central nervous system and eye problems. Other malformations are rare and the threshold of teratogenicity seems to be situated between 0.1 and 0.5 Sv. The risk of cancer being induced during the foetal period is relatively constant during pregnancy, and is clearly more important than at adult age. Moore has stated that an exposure in utero of 0.01 Sv would lead to a risk of developing a cancer before the age of 15 of $4-5 \times 10^{-4}$ [4]. An acute exposure just before or at the moment of the formation of the embryo could lead to genetic effects for the foetus, such as Down's syndrome, but with a very low probability. Since the works of Gardner [5], some studies have been performed to assess whether childhood leukaemia and non Hodgkin's lymphoma may result from the father's or the mother's exposure to ionising radiation before conception. Relative risks vary widely in these studies and it is therefore difficult to conclude the magnitude of the risk.

While the risk to medical personnel associated with the acute radiation is nowadays not of sufficient magnitude to be a major concern, the cumulative risk associated with a lifetime exposure could become significant, concerning stochastic effects, especially if appropriate precautions are not taken.

Dose limits

The limit for effective dose recommended by the ICRP Publication No. 60 for occupational exposure is 20 mSv a year, with the possibility to go to 50 mSv in a single year provided that the total effective dose in five consecutive years does not exceed 100 mSv, which gives an average annual dose of 20 mSv. Additional limits apply to the lens of the eye (150 mSv in a year), the hands and feet (500 mSv in a year) because these tissues may not be adequately protected by the limit on effective dose [6]. Furthermore, the annual dose limit for the skin of radiation workers is 500mSv at a depth of 20-100 μm averaged over any 1 cm^2 regardless of the area exposed.

Concerning pregnant women, the early part of pregnancy is considered by the ICRP to be covered by the normal protection of workers. The Commission recommends that the working conditions of a pregnant worker, after the declaration of pregnancy, should be such as to make it unlikely that the additional equivalent dose to the foetus will exceed about 1 mSv during the remaining time of pregnancy. The US National Council on Radiation Protection and Measurements (NCRP) recommends a maximum permitted dose for the foetus of a pregnant worker of 0.5 mSv per month, or a total gestational equivalent dose of 5 mSv [7].

Nevertheless, special restrictions concerning the exposure of individuals may not need to be applied automatically merely because their doses have slightly exceeded a dose limit, because such exposure will not lead to onset of deterministic effects, and the risk for stochastic effects from subsequent exposures will not be affected by previous doses. Such events, however, should call for a thorough examination, usually by the regulatory authority or the occupational health physician, of the design and operational aspects of protection in the installation concerned, rather than for restrictions or penalties applied to an exposed individual. Furthermore, to remove a worker without determining causes of the increased exposure is punitive, encourages poor compliance with monitoring requirements and ultimately endangers the other workers and possibly the patients. However, if the investigation reveals that the overexposed worker is consequently setting aside established radiation protection measures, replacement might be the solution of choice.

Main exposures

Many studies have demonstrated that conventional radiodiagnostics nowadays does not lead to major, nor even sometimes detectable, exposures to ionising radiation, provided that the basic principles of radiation protection are followed. Furthermore, new technologies in conventional radiodiagnostics may lead to a further decrease in the worker's and patient's exposure, while improving the quality of the diagnostic outcome. However some of these new technologies can occasionally lead to an increased worker's exposure. For example it was reported that helical computed tomography can produce a more than three times higher radiation dose to patients (and probably also to personnel) as compared to thin-section computed tomography, although this is not a general feature of this technique [8].

On the other hand, exposures during invasive and interventional radiology are of increasing concern, especially in the practice of cardiology [1]. For example, in one recent study, the majority of personal dose badges in hospital revealing exposure above established dose limits was worn by staff in the cardiology division. Furthermore, it seems that cardiologists are sometimes negligent in their use of badges and appropriate shielding [9]. Radiation exposures levels during various diagnostic or interventional procedures have been summarised by Limacher and Coll. [1]. The measurements vary widely, depending on the examination technique, the duration of fluoroscopy, the collimation of the X-ray beam, the distance from the source and the wearing of leaded aprons and thyroid collars. For example, the calculated effective dose for a physician who manipulates catheters from the femoral area during an ablation procedure is 0.018 mSv per case with an exposure of 55 minutes of fluoroscopy [1]. The mean collar-level exposure per case for physicians who perform coronary angiography and percutaneous transluminal angioplastic has been reported to be 0.04-0.16 mSv.

Concerning radiotherapy, the main sources of exposure are external radiation therapy equipment and the use of radionuclides for intracavitary and interstitial therapy, the latter being responsible for more than 70% of radiation exposure to the staff [10]. The use of radionuclide such as ^{32}P handled in thin-walled laboratory or clinical containers such as polypropylene vials or syringes is a common source of exposure of skin to beta radiation. Taking ^{32}P for example, activities of the order of 200 MBq are frequently administered in concentrations of 40 MBq g^{-1}. In such cases, skin exposure of the clinician who administers the radionuclide can reach 3 Gy h^{-1} over an area exceeding 1 cm^2, leading to an excess of the annual dose limit for skin in less than 10 minutes [11]. Contact with patients who had been administered ^{137}Cs or ^{192}Ir may lead to considerable radiation exposure. For example, the dose rate at 1 m from a patient who is being treated with 10 GBq of ^{137}Cs is 0.5 mSv h^{-1}.

In addition, the use of radioactive material can sometimes lead to internal contamination via inhalation or contact with a non-intact skin. The level of exposure will then depend on the activity of the source, the amount and the radiological half-life period, but also on bioavailability and biological half-life period of the compound.

Radiological protection - basis

The basic components of radiological protection, according to ICRP recommendations are justification, optimisation and application of individual dose limits.

The justification of practice means that what is done should do more good than harm. This can be a generic justification, e.g. promoting one or another technique or promoting routine radiological screening for some types of cancer, but also a justification on an individual patient level. The latter is to protect patients, but reducing the doses for patients is also an effective way to reduce exposure to staff.

The optimisation of protection, i.e. within a practice, to maximise the net benefits, economic and social factors being taken into account. This is usually applied at two levels: the design and construction of equipment and installations and the day-to-day methods of working (working procedures). The change for one protection option to another should, at least, provide a reduction in exposures that compensates for the extra use of resources. Thus, the optimisation of protection involves weighing up the relative importance of the exposures, the use of resources and the quality of the final outcome. Nevertheless, in practice, it is often difficult to make a quantitative balance between loss of diagnostic information and reduction of dose to the patient or the staff. This is the basis of the ALARA (As Low As Reasonably Achievable) principle, which means that the risks should be minimised by utilising techniques and procedures that keep exposure to a level as low as reasonably achievable.

The application of individual dose limits implies monitoring of worker's exposures, for external exposure but also for intake of radioactive materials. Individual monitoring for external exposure is simple and does not require major commitment of resources. Personal dosimetry monitors include those using X-ray film (film badges) or thermoluminescent dosimeters (TLDs) which use lithium fluoride crystal. Both allow the dosimetry laboratory to make an estimate about the type and energy of the radiation. They are typically worn in holders, under the apron at waist or chest level and outside the apron at collar level, for one month before being submitted for processing. A ring dosimeter can be used during some procedures since the hands are often the closest part of the body to the beam. In medicine, individual monitoring for external exposure should be used for all those who work in controlled areas. Moreover, it should be considered for those who work regularly in supervised areas unless it is clear that their doses will be consistently low. Nevertheless, this monthly monitoring provides only information on the cumulated exposure of the past month, but does not provide reliable data on exposures during single events. This can be achieved using pocket ionisation chambers or some electronic devices that permit case-by-case exposure readings.

Monitoring of exposure is of particular importance in some circumstances such as nursing of brachytherapy patients once the sources have been implanted, palpation of patients during fluoroscopy or interventional radiology. Furthermore, the development of measurement of the doses delivered to the patients for every single act is increasing and will be mandatory in an increasing number of countries. This should provide useful information on the doses delivered to the staff during these procedures.

In some special risk areas, e.g. radiotherapy, continuous stationary measurement is warranted.

Monitoring for internal exposure is much more complex since it uses bioassay, i.e. measurement in biological samples containing radionuclides. It should be used routinely only for workers who work regularly in areas that are designated as controlled areas specifically in relation to the control of contamination and in which there are grounds for expecting significant intakes [2]. Bioassays should also be done if any pregnant staff members are internally or externally contaminated.

The results of the monitoring of exposure should be analysed by a person responsible for radiation in the institution and possibly by an occupational health physician. Furthermore, the results should be filed for each individual so that it is possible to calculate yearly and lifetime dose. These results should also be recorded on a personnel document stating the type, amount and duration of exposure (e.g. a register card), which is to be given to the employee when he/she leaves the institution.

National laws and regulations usually exist for the regulation of radiation protection.

Radiological protection - in practice

In practice, reducing the risks can be achieved through applying some fundamental principles such as designation of workplaces into controlled and supervised areas, increasing distance, decreasing time, limiting scattered X-rays and using of shielding in diverse settings and procedures.

A system of designated areas is suggested to avoid unreasonable complexity in the control of occupational exposure. In "controlled areas", normal working conditions, including the possible occurrence of minor mishaps require workers to follow well-established procedures and practices aimed specifically at controlling radiation exposures. "Supervised areas" are those in which the working conditions are kept under review, but special procedures are normally not needed. In areas where there is no problem of contamination by unsealed radioactive material, designated areas may be defined in terms of the dose rate at the boundary. For example, "controlled areas" may be those in which normal working conditions may lead to personal exposure exceeding one third of dose limits, and "supervised areas" those in which working conditions may lead to exposure of less than one third of dose limits. Signs should be used to indicate to employees, especially to maintenance staff, limits of controlled areas. Furthermore, entrance to such areas should be restricted to employees with special accreditation. In addition to its primary function of providing information for the control of exposures, a programme of individual monitoring may be helpful in confirming the classification of workplaces and in detecting fluctuations in working conditions.

The intensity of X-rays is inversely proportional to the square of the distance. This law also applies to radioisotope sources. Thus, direct contact with radiation sources should be minimised. Radioactive materials should be transported in a shielded container, preferably on a cart to avoid hand carrying. A separate waiting area should be considered for patients injected with radioactive material, and imaging rooms should be large enough to permit the technician to operate the console at a reasonable distance from the patient.

Scattered X-rays should be taken into account. For example, the scatter at a 90-degree angle and at one meter from the patient is 0.1% of the beam entering the patient [1]. In addition, the larger the beam size entering the patient, the greater the amount of scatter. Collimation and keeping the image-intensifier as close to the patient as possible are two operational methods that can be used to reduce scatter levels. Use of appropriate shielding is of major importance in reducing doses to the staff. Nevertheless, personal shielding is designated to attenuate scatter X-ray levels, but not primary beam exposure. The effectiveness of attenuation decreases with increasing kV or energy of radiation. For example, a 0.5 mm lead apron reduces the intensity of the radiation to 50% for a 100-kV beam. Wraparound two-piece aprons, thyroid shields and eye protection are the most important personal shields. Additional shielding available includes ceiling-mounted lead acrylic face shields, table-side drapes and mobile "door-type" shields that can be used to reduce exposure to staff during long procedures.

In addition to the technical considerations concerning radiation safety, it is of major importance to promote a safety culture among health care workers. This implies education and training in radiological protection for existing and future professional and technical staff in medical practice. This training programme should include initial training for all incoming staff and regular updating and retraining.

Other sources of electromagnetic radiation

Lasers, ultraviolet radiation and magnetic fields are non-ionising radiation sources. They are usually far less hazardous than ionising radiation but can be encountered in medical settings and require special care to prevent injury [12].

Lasers are used more and more intensively in medical settings, for various purpose (e.g. to position patients in radiology or in surgery). World-wide standards are based on a hazard classification system, which groups laser products into four broad hazard classes according to the laser's output power or energy and its ability to cause harm. Class 1 lasers cannot emit potentially hazardous laser radiation and pose no health hazard. Classes 2 through 4 pose an increasing hazard to the skin and eye, with possible partial to total loss of vision. Virtually all surgical lasers are Class 4. The higher the laser's output power or energy, the more dangerous are the effects. Furthermore, for class 3B and class 4 lasers, the blink reflex which occurs within 250 ms is not effective in protecting the retina. The accidental reflection of the laser beam during surgical procedures can also result in injury to the staff. Other than the obvious rule - not to point a laser at a person's eyes - there are no control measures required for a Class 2 laser product. For lasers of higher classes, safety measures are clearly required and laser users should wear protective goggles specifically designed for each type of laser and should take care not to focus the beam on reflecting surfaces.

Another hazard of lasers in medical settings is that during surgical procedures using a laser unit, the thermal destruction of tissue creates smoke as a by-product, and this may contain toxic gases and vapours (benzene, hydrogen cyanide and formaldehyde) and bioaerosols (dead and live cellular material, for example human papillomavirus). Such exposure can be effectively controlled by proper ventilation of the treatment room.

Last, because of the high voltage supply required, all lasers present the risk of electrical shock [13].

Ultraviolet radiation is used in germicidal lamps, in certain dermatological and dental treatments and in air filters in some hospitals. Exposure of the skin to ultraviolet light causes sunburn, ages the skin and increases the risk of skin cancer. Eye exposure can result in temporary but extremely painful conjunctivitis. Long-term exposure can lead to partial loss of vision. The best approach to prevention is education and wearing shaded protective eye-glasses [14].

Since medical settings use many 50/60 Hz electric material, exposure to magnetic fields (mainly extremely low frequencies) is frequent. Therapeutic equipment has been reported to lead to magnetic flux exposures of 1 - 16 microTesla at 1 meter distance. In NMR-units, exposure of the staff is usually lower than 1 milliTesla, but may reach 100-150 milliTesla during short periods. In recent years interest has increased in the biological effects and possible health outcomes of weak electric and magnetic fields [15]. Epidemiological studies seem to indicate a slight leukaemia and brain tumour risks increase in "electrical" occupations, for average workday field strengths of 0.2 - 0.4 microTesla, but with a lack of clarity as to exposure characteristics. Adverse pregnancy outcomes and childhood cancer after maternal or paternal exposure to magnetic fields remains controversial, as well as neurobehavioural reactions. For people having a pacemaker, exposure to magnetic field should be limited and the International Radiation Protection Agency has proposed a threshold of 0.5 milliTesla.

Assessment of magnetic fields exposure is difficult to achieve, and many people are exposed to substantial levels out of their work environment, though for shorter periods, in their homes (mean magnetic fields in homes is 0.16 microTesla) or during rest time, e.g. while travelling or staying under or near power lines. The effects of magnetic fields still warrant further investigation, concerning health personnel as well as other workers.

References

1   Limacher MC, Douglas PS, Germano G, Laskey WK, Lindsay BD, McKetty MH, Moore ME, Park JK, Prigent FM, Walsh MN. Radiation safety in the practice of cardiology. JACC 1998;31(4):892-913
2   ICRP. Radiological protection and safety in medicine. ICRP Publication 73. Annals of the ICRP 1996;26(2):1-47
3   Committee on the Biological Effects of Ionizing Radiation (BEIR V). Health effects of exposure to low levels of ionizing radiation. National Academy of Science. Washington (DC): NRC, 1990
4   Moore RH. Childhood cancer after prenatal exposure to diagnostic X-ray examination in Britain. British Journal of Cancer 1990;62:152-168
5   Gardner MJ, Snee MP, Hall AJ, Powell CA, Downer S, Terell JD. Results of case-control study of leukemia and lymphoma among young people near Sellafield nuclear plant in west Cumbria. British Medical Journal 1990;300:423-429
6   ICRP. 1990 Recommendations of the ICRP. New York: Pergamon Press, 1991; ICRP Pub. No 60.
7   National Council on Radiation Protection and Measurements. Limitation of exposure to ionizing radiation. Bethesda (MD): NCRP, 1993; NCRP Report No. 116
8   Lucidarme O, Grenier P, Coche E, Lenoir S, Aubert B, Beigelman C. Bronchiectasis: comparative assessment with thin-section CT and Helacal CT. Radiology 1996;200:673-679
9   McKetty MH. Study of radiation doses to personnel in a cardiac catheterization laboratory. Health Phys 1996;70:563-567
10   Leung PMK. Personnel radiation exposure analysis in a radiotherapy center: fourteen year retrospective study. International Journal of Radiation, Oncology, Biology, Physics 1983;9:1705-1713

11 Beddoe AH, Kelly MT. Absorbed dose in the skin from beta emitters in medical and laboratory containers. British Journal of Radiology 1994;67:54-58

12 Lewy RM. Exposure to physical agents. In: ILO Encyclopaedia of Occupational Health and Safety. 4th edition 1998(3):97.1-97.73

13 Sliney DH. Lasers. In: ILO Encyclopaedia of Occupational Health and Safety. 4th edition 1998(2):49.16-49.18

14 Sliney DH. Light and infrared radiation. In: ILO Encyclopaedia of Occupational Health and Safety. 4th edition 1998(2):49.13-49.16

15 Knave B. Electric and magnetic fields and health outcomes. In: ILO Encyclopaedia of Occupational Health and Safety. 4th edition 1998(2):49.2-49.4

Occupational Health for Health Care Workers - A Practical Guide
H.-M. Hasselhorn, A. Toomingas and M. Lagerström (Editors)

Noise problems in health care facilities

Norman Tran, Daria McLean, Annalee Yassi

Health effects and noise exposure limits

Noise exposure is the cause of noise-induced hearing loss (NIHL) and is possibly linked to other undesirable effects on mental and physical health such as headaches, stress, increased blood pressure, and increased irritability [1-4]. Noise can affect a worker's ability to perform work efficiently and safely [5]. Current control measures will not eliminate occupational NIHL. The permissible noise exposure level is a political compromise balancing feasibility with cost. The Occupational Safety and Health Administration (OSHA) in the United States requires implementation of feasible administrative or engineering controls at 90 dBA for an eight-hour time-weighted average (TWA) sound level and at levels above 85 dBA TWA sound level, a hearing conservation program is required [6].

Occupational risk for health care workers

Occupational NIHL is an irreversible but entirely preventable disease that continues to be one of the ten leading causes of disability caused by occupational exposures [7-8]. Health care facilities are not noise free workplaces [9-10]. Exposures to hazardous noise levels that can cause NIHL and nuisance noise levels (sound levels that affect worker's ability to concentrate) occur in many hospital departments. For example, in a dietetics department, levels of 89 dBA have been measured in the pot washing area (Table 1).

Hearing conservation program

A hearing conservation program (HCP) can be implemented in health care facilities to eliminate or reduce NIHL and to address noise concerns in areas where nuisance noise levels are detected. The HCP measures required increase with the level of worker exposure and include noise exposure monitoring, engineering and administrative controls, audiometric testing, personal hearing protection devices, education, and record keeping.

Identification of risk

Potentially noisy areas within health care facilities can be identified from the existing knowledge and experience of the investigators, and from concerns expressed by the workers or managers. Workers and managers must be made aware of their responsibility to share their knowledge about the work environment and hazardous areas with investigators. Hazardous noise levels can be assessed initially using a calibrated sound level meter, which is the basic instrument for measuring noise levels. Areas or tasks that produce instantaneous noise levels in excess of 80 dBA can be further evaluated using a calibrated personal noise dosimeter, which is also an integrating sound level meter. This measures and stores sound energy over time giving a TWA. A dosimeter is worn in the pocket or attached to the belt. The microphone is positioned on the shoulder in the hearing zone of the worker, who goes about a normal work shift while wearing the dosimeter.

Prevention of exposure

Engineering and administrative controls

Some examples of engineering and administrative controls of noise in hospital departments are shown in Table 2. Recommendations to control noise at the source include replacing nozzles on air hoses, panel damping, vibration isolation, equipment maintenance, and fitting larger tyres on transport vehicles. Recommendations to contain noise in an environment or along the path include isolating noisy equipment and/or installing noise barriers and enclosures. Administrative noise controls to limit workers exposure by reducing time spent in noisy areas can also be implemented.

Audiometric screening

Audiometric testing and evaluation is crucial to monitor the success and effectiveness of a HCP, and it is the only way to determine whether NIHL is being prevented. If workers are exposed to noise levels in excess of 80 dBA, audiometric evaluation should be conducted as soon as possible, preferably before the first exposure to noise. In this way, a baseline audiogram will be obtained for all workers before they are exposed or potentially exposed to hazardous noise levels in excess of 80 dBA. The baseline audiogram documents the hearing status of the worker and is the standard by which future hearing tests are compared. If a significant hearing loss (15 dBA or more) is discovered, the worker must be informed and have their hearing test repeated. If a significant threshold shift is confirmed when compared to the baseline audiogram, a referral for further audiological and/or medical examination is necessary to rule out pathology in the auditory system. Discussion regarding proper hearing protective devices (HPD) is necessary.

Hearing protective devices

Workers who are exposed to noise levels of 80 dBA or higher after implementation of engineering and/or administrative controls must wear HPD, for example, earplugs or earmuffs. Earplugs are HPD, which are worn within the external ear canal or at the entrance to the external ear canal. Earmuffs are HPD consisting of a headband and earcups with a soft outer ring or cushion. Several types of HPD should be made available for the workers to choose from. Compliance with HPD is improved by ensuring comfort and suitability for the job. The HPD should be fitted by someone experienced in hearing protection and the worker should be instructed in its use and educated about its limitations.

Education

All workers potentially exposed to hazardous noise levels should be regularly educated in scheduled training sessions. The workers must be informed of the noise exposure levels and the associated hazards. Workers failing to wear the required HPD should be re-educated. All elements of the HCP should be documented and records kept for follow-up. The records can also be used by management to ensure proper resource allocation.

Program enforcement and costs

Hazardous and nuisance noise levels remain problematic for health care facilities. A HCP is essential to eliminate or reduce the potential for occupational NIHL. Active enforcement is required as recommendations alone are generally not followed. Engineering controls should be implemented as a long term solution to eliminate or reduce the noise levels to below 80 dBA such that workers can be totally excluded from the HCP. This will result in ultimate saving due to reduction of the costs associated with the HCP.

Table 1. Noise survey results in a large hospital (TWA=8-hours continuous sound exposure level)

Area / Work Task	TWA (dBA)
Cast Room	77 - 82
Central Energy	82 - 110
Computer Room	74 - 76
Dietetics • Bakery • Cooking • Pot Washing • Stripping/Dishwashing • Cafe Dishroom	<80 - 86 80 - 84 89 82 <80 - 86

to be continued on page 155

continued
Table 1. Noise survey results in a large hospital (TWA=8-hours continuous sound exposure level)

Area/Work Task	TWA (dBA)
Housekeeping	
• Autoscrubbers	72 - 80
• Burnishers	90 - 100
Laundry	
• Dryer/Washer Operator	86 - 99
• Flat Irons	83 - 89
• Cart Drivers	79 - 86
Magnetic Resonance Imaging	
• Patient Bed/MRI Machine Area	102
Mailroom	
• Tube Feed	83
• Postage Meter	82
Maintenance	
• Carpentry	82
• Equipment/Furnishing	73 - 80
• Mechanical	81 - 83
• Grounds	84
Material Handling Cart Drivers	76 - 91
Operating Rooms	
• Compressor Air Drying	88
Print Shop	
• Copier	75 - 82
• Press Operator	81 - 90
Rehab Engineering	
• Orthotics	80 - 94
• Prosthetics	79 - 87
• Machine Shop	80
Self Care Dialysis- Reverse Osmosis Water Treatment Unit	77
Ultrasound-Air Conditioners	68 - 72

Table 2. Noise control options for various equipment / processes for the work areas with hazardous noise levels, as proposed for one hospital.

Work Areas	Equipment / Process	Control Options
Cast Room	Saws	Purchasing criteria
Central Energy	Generators, fans, pumps, compressors, boilers, air hoses	Enclose the source, personnel acoustic booth
Dietetics	Washing and unloading dishes, pot washing, garborator, blenders	Automate process, use sound barriers and deflectors, enclosure
Housekeeping	Autoscrubbers, burnishers	Purchasing criteria
Laundry	Washers and dryers, compressed air/flat irons	Isolate certain processes, modify air jets, use sound barriers, reposition machines
Mailroom	Tube feeder, postage meter	Enclosure
Maintenance	Grinders, saws, surface planer, shaper router, driller, motor miter box, radial arm and band saws, compressed air, pneumatic tube system	Purchasing criteria, preventive maintenance, relocation, damping materials
Material Handling/ Transport/Linen Services	Loose wheels, metal transport cages, grid-like sewer traps, rough floors in tunnels	Preventive maintenance, smoother floors, reduce vibration, damping materials, larger wheels
Print Shop	Photocopiers, off-set printer, puncher	Preventive maintenance
Rehabilitation Engineering	Buffers, grinders, air hoses, welding torches, saws, fans	Purchasing criteria, sound absorbing materials, sound barriers and deflectors.

References

1   Topf M. Noise-induced occupational stress and health in critical care nurses. Hospital Topics 1988;66:30-34
2   Verbeek JHAM, van Dijk FJH, de Vries FF. Non-auditory effects of noise in industry. IV. Afield study on industrial noise and blood pressure. Int Arch Occ Envir Hlth 1987;59:51-54
3   Stasiow AP. Some non-auditory effects of industrial noise exposure. Annals Am Confer Gov Ind Hyg 1986;14:225-230

4   Melamed S, Luz J, Green MS. Noise exposure, noise annoyance and their relation to psychological distress, accident and sickness absence among blue collar workers - the cordis study. Israel J Med Sci 1992;28:629-635

5   Smith A. Noise, performance efficiency and safety. Int Arch Occ Envir Hlth 1990;62:1-5

6   Occupational Safety and Health Administration (OSHA). Oh XVII 1910-176. Code of Federal Regulations. Washington, DC: US Government Printing Office, 1988.

7   Alleyne BC, Dufresne RM, Kanji N, Reasal MR. Costs of workers' compensation claims for hearing loss. J Occ Med. 1989;31:134

8   Leading work related diseases and injuries - United States. MMWR. 1986;35:12

9   Yassi A, Gaborieau D, Gillespie I, Elias J. Noise hazards in a large health care facility. J Occ Med 1991;33:1067-1070

10   Falk SA, Woods NF. Hospital noise levels and potential health hazards. New Eng J Med 1973;289:774-781

Further reading

- www.cdc.gov/niosh/hearing.html
- www.cdc.gov/niosh/noisepg.html
- www.hearingconservation.org/links.htm
- www.osha-slc.gov/Osh-Std_data/1910_0095.html

Occupational Health for Health Care Workers - A Practical Guide
H.-M. Hasselhorn, A. Toomingas and M. Lagerström (Editors)

Psychosocial aspects of health care work

Bengt B. Arnetz

Current status of the health care sector

The health care sector is currently undergoing profound changes all over the world. There is a multitude of factors driving these changes. Increased competition and the privatisation of health care are some important determinants of change. However, structural and demographic changes, changes in the financing and organisation as well as rapidly changing attitudes among health care consumers also play an important role.

Health care personnel expect a more flexible and less hierarchical work structure. Younger people expect responsive patient-orientated health care organisation. They also expect a work organisation that fosters appropriate skills development and deployment. They expect flexibility, challenging job content and a less hierarchical management structure.

Medical professionals are socially disadvantaged by their dedication to constant caring. Thus, divorce rates are increased in some medical professions, such as physicians. Recently long-term sickness has been reported to be on the increase for both hospital-based and primary care physicians in Sweden. However, compared to the population at large it appears that health care personnel are healthy, at least with regard to physical health.

Although there are numerous and difficult stresses in health care practice it is important to remember that overall, health care personnel are very satisfied with their work. However, they are in a transition period. As in any period of change, this implies opportunities as well as threats.

Awareness and action

It is important to be aware of threats to the health and wellbeing of health care workers that arise from continuous change. There is a need for a system that monitors the health and well being of health care workers as well as practical programs to counteract the negative effects of changes. The inherent risks in health care work will continue to require attention.

Hazardous psychosocial exposures

Uncertainties and suffering

Health care personnel are exposed to numerous and well-recognised potential psychosocial stressors. Dealing with people in need, death, hopelessness and uncertainty, are a few. Others include the threat of 'brownout', which is a feeling of loss of mental energy but not at a level that can be classified as 'burnout'. These conditions are the consequence of constantly using oneself as the most important instrument to help patients.

Malpractice claims

Another psychosocial stress in health care is the constant threat of causing harm or even death by erroneous decisions or failure to detect potentially dangerous conditions. Physicians and nurses have to make numerous and many times critical decisions, commonly in the face of limited facts. Various reports have highlighted occupational stresses arising from the risk of malpractice claims. There is heightened readiness among patients to report physicians and other health care workers. Even though organisation stressors may have contributed to an erroneous decision it is rarely accepted as an excuse by the legal institutions. The individual physician's perception of the threat of malpractice appears to change his/her practice patterns. Nurses and other health care professionals are also at risk of malpractice claims. Patients are increasingly willing to report health care personnel, not only for, what they perceive as poor medical competence, but also for poor behaviour and attitudes. There are numerous examples of the anguish physicians, as well as nurses and other health care professionals, have to go through between the time they have been reported for a possible error and the final judgement. Regardless of outcome many physicians report long-term effects from a patient-physician mishap.

Increasingly more demanding patients

Patients are increasingly demanding more thorough information and an active part in the decision making process. They are more knowledgeable and search for information and answers, using the World Wide Web and other sources which are now readily available to them.

Striving for quality enhancement

The focus on enhancing the quality in health care has a direct impact on work routines, reporting structure and skills development. Staff are expected to contribute to enhancing the overall quality of the health care systems. Individual performance records are no longer anonymous and the team is expected to ensure that the care they provide is up to par. "Total quality management" (the entire organisation strives to improve quality and all actions taken should consider the impact on quality) is increasingly applied in health care. There has been little debate on how the quality focus impacts on other aspects of the organisation, such as skills development. Occupational health personnel need to ensure that their advice and knowledge is considered in quality enhancement initiatives.

Night time and shift work

Night work is an inherent part of health care. Suffering and diseases do not respect regular day-time work hours. Extended working hours and on-call duties among physicians lead to measurable sleep deprivation, subjective feelings of mental fatigue and an inability to perform efficiently. A study of physicians on night duty reported an increase in mental fatigue and increased electroencephalographic signs of sleepiness during the latter part of the first night on duty. Residual effects from night work could be detected two days following night work. There are few scientific studies of the performance of health care personnel. Experimental studies of sleep-deprived physicians working night duty have demonstrated errors reading electrocardiographic print-outs. These studies suggest that physicians that have been actively working for a period of 16-20 hours are more likely to make judgement errors. Approximately 5% of physicians report that their clinical performance is severely disturbed during night duty. As many as 20% rate themselves to be clinically impaired the day following night duty. It is therefore imperative, both from the physician and the patient point of view, that total working hours for physicians are regulated. Typically, physicians carry out regular daytime work prior to night duty while nurses and other health care professionals work in shifts, working either daytime or night time hours and rotating between day and night. It can be assumed that physicians having worked 36 hours at a stretch are more affected than professional groups only working a regular night shift. However, that remains to be determined.

Job strain and skills utilisation

Studies of health care workers reveal that their work has high mental and physical demand levels, with relatively limited influence over the decision making processes. Commonly there is sub-optimal skills utilisation and development in their job. During the latter part of the 1990's there has been financial cut-backs in health care that have added further to an already high stress level.

    Various independent assessments, in numerous countries around the world, of the impact of current changes on health care personnel's working conditions seem to suggest that there has been an overall increase in workload coupled with unchanged or even decreased influence over workplace decisions. Thus, the strain of the job has increased. It is also noted that health care personnel, facing increased workload and more complex disease panoramas, commonly report that they lack sufficient skills to manage the situation satisfactory. Personnel, that have high demands and at the same time limited skills to meet those demands, report higher mental stress levels as well as more musculoskeletal symptoms.

    The rapid expansion as well as the fast ageing of medical knowledge requires health care personnel to constantly upgrade their knowledge and work practices. There is a need to ensure task-relevant skills development for the individual as well as the entire workplace. A department needs to think strategically and ensure that present and future demands from patients are met with relevant skills.

New technologies – threats and opportunities

Information technologies have enriched many jobs in health care but also increased the demand for employees to change the way they organise and do their job as well as upgrading their skills. Initially, information technologies were used to improve the administrative aspects of health care. More recently it is being used to improve patient care and the overall quality of care. Medical information is now available on the World Wide Web and patients increasingly turn to 'the Net' to get a second opinion or seek out the most recent information on how to diagnose and treat various diseases. Information technologies are becoming an integrated part of modern health care organisations. In order to reap the maximum benefit from information-technologies health care personnel should take an active part in the development and deployment of information technology systems. When new technologies are used in a proper way, they should make work more effective and thus provide free time for health care personnel to do things that they do not have enough time for, such as reading medical literature. There is also a rich arsenal of new instruments, machines and methods that increase the risk of malfunction and erroneous decisions on part of health care personnel. Advanced machines are used to supervise patients. In many cases, health care personnel lack sufficient knowledge about these new machines. Commonly, health care personnel have to oversee more than one machine at a time. This may result in cognitive overload. Some of the claims about the abilities of new machines are overstated and may put operating personnel in difficult positions.

Negative health effects

Health care employees represent a great number of professions, socio-economic backgrounds and exposure profiles. Therefore, it is unlikely that there would be specific diseases that are characteristic for health care employees in general.

Work related exhaustion

More commonly discussed risks of the medical professions are mental exhaustion, commonly referred to as 'burnout'. Even though this is not a specific and easily diagnosed mental disorder, numerous studies suggest an increased risk of mental exhaustion among health care workers. Factors linked to mental exhaustion are health care personnel who constantly nurture other peoples need for emotional support and the need for constant presence, and who deal emotionally with sick people and their relatives. However, organisational factors, such as stress, poor definition of goals and low perceived organisational efficacy also contribute to the development of emotional exhaustion. Employees suffering from mental exhaustion report less skills development in their jobs. Thus, most likely there is an interaction between individual, organisational and patient-related factors in the development of mental exhaustion.

Increased work pressure, as a result of ongoing cut-backs within health care and more demanding and complex patients, are accompanied by decreased mental energy and increased level of mental exhaustion.

Suicide and mental disorders

There is a preponderance of medical profession suicide studies and there is an established increased risk for female physicians. In some, but far from all studies, increased rates have also been reported for male physicians, especially surgeons. Psychiatric nurse assistants have also been highlighted as at increased risk in some studies as well as male registered nurses. However, internationally, the most consistent findings is the increased suicide risk among female physicians.

Suicide is the final result of a long and complicated pathway. Some studies have pointed out that physicians are at an increased risk of suicidal feelings. Mental disorders, notably depression, are a major risk factor for subsequent suicide. Admission rates for mental disorders have been reported to be elevated for health technologists, practice nurses, nurses' aides and dental assistants.

There are indications that work-related stress and mental exhaustion ('burnout') is related to feelings of hopelessness and moodiness in physicians and nurses as well as low self-esteem. Higher work-load seems to be related to decreased mental well being as does poor professional management and perceived low organisational efficacy.

Cardiovascular health

Some studies have pointed out a similar or even higher risk for cardiovascular disease among physicians as compared to socio-economically equivalent professions. In a study of Swedish surgeons it was found that surgeons run an increased risk of fatal cardiovascular events compared to other physician groups. It has been suggested that intensive work schedules, the stress of surgery combined with long work hours contribute to the risk of cardiovascular disease for surgeons.

Working climate

Numerous psychosocial and other environmental hazardous exposures will lead to a poor working climate with poorly functioning work teams and bad team spirit. The final outcome might well be reduced well-being among staff with increased turnover, absenteeism and sickness. This is a vicious cycle resulting in a negative spiral.

How to detect risky exposure

Psychosocial exposure at levels that pose a risk to the well-being and health of staff should not be allowed. However, in contrast to traditional exposure guidelines that apply to physical and chemical exposures, there are no firm guidelines for psychosocial stressors. Unspecific and rather vague guidelines are provided. Based on today's knowledge it should be possible to provide more specific guidelines.

The first step to detect potentially unhealthy exposures is to institute continuous and regular monitoring of the psychosocial work conditions. Not only is this of importance to secure the long-term wellbeing of the staff, it is also a necessity to ensure patients are provided with best quality care. It will also ensure a productive and high-quality workforce.

Questionnaire

By means of a questionnaire it is possible to measure some key areas that define a healthy and productive work place. Survey methods used should focus on enhancing the psychosocial work environment as well as the processes of health care organisations. The view of patients also needs to be obtained on the quality of care as well as their view of the work environment [1, 2].

To get a valid perception of the psychosocial work environments key areas for assessment are:
- Mental energy and well-being (measures the total mental energy available among staff to perform their job)
- Work climate (congenial atmosphere and relationship)
- Work load/stress (time available to plan, execute, enhance and reflect over work)
- Management performance feed-back (clearness of work directives and feed-back in term of how well one performs the tasks)
- Participatory management (degree to which employees are engaged in the change process and enhancing the way work is being done)
- Skills development (use of existing skills as well as development of new skills)
- Mission clarity (whether the mission of the department and goals are clear, realistic, and measurable)
- Organisational efficacy (employee rating of how efficient they consider the work process is in their own unit)
- Leadership (ratings of various aspects of immediate supervisor)
- Employee ownership (to what degree employees seek information, push for change, commit to enhance work and provide feed-back to one another).

In addition the following are important: Regular monitoring of the psycho-social situation, clear setting of goals concerning various aspects of the psycho-social work environment and feed-back of results and acting upon the results.

Work place discussions based on facts to enhance work and total quality

It is important to encourage discussions among the leadership and personnel based on facts. Regular surveys provide such facts. Detailed analysis of surveys will also add to a better understanding of the cause-and-effect relationships. Based on such results, improvement initiatives become more efficient. It is important to focus on clear and well-defined issues and provide definite suggestions on how to improve the situation. Improvement initiatives can be further developed in small working groups that have been given clear directives on the limitations of authority.

Regular defusing

Debriefing following severe and emotionally taxing events are commonplace in health care today. However, regular defusing, that is at-the-end-of-the-day talks in the work team to touch on the daily experience, concerns and emotions, is an easy way of monitoring the psychosocial work environment and its consequence for health and wellbeing. Defusing does not demand an outside process leader but encourages the personnel themselves to briefly discuss today's happenings. It is important to have systems in place that allow for the identification of needs as they appear, not months later.

Management awareness

Simply asking co-workers how they are doing is a simple means by which managers keep up-to-date with the status of their staff.

Prevention and the creation of psychosocial health

In order to create psychosocially healthy work places, it is important to integrate psychosocial issues with the overall business. Merely trying to understand psychosocial stressors by looking at physical and mental workload does not suffice.

Increase organisational efficacy

Departments and work places that are able to increase participatory management, efficacy and clarity of goals actually manage to handle organisational and process changes much better. The psychosocial environment in which the work is being done is a major determinant of how employees are going to react. Thus, increased production does not necessary result in increased stress.

Since work load is a major concern to health care organisation, given the ongoing cut-backs and restructuring, it is important to engage all employees in discussions focusing on the goal of the workplace, realistic production volumes as well as means to enhance efficacy.

Studies using the QWC-Quality-Work-Competence method to assess and enhance work organisations (see below) have reported that in departments where employee-perceived organisational efficacy increased, self-rated emotional well-being improved as well. In departments where employees develop and utilise more of their own professional skills, mental energy and wellbeing increased at the same time. In contrast, in departments where efficacy decreased and skills were not used or not further developed, mental fatigue increased. There is also a positive relationship between staff-rated organisational wellbeing and patient rating of global quality of care [1].

Clarify goals

Another important determinant to improve mental energy, and thus counteract 'burnout', is to clarify the overall goals of the work units. Employees that are not aware of the overall goals of the workplace are not able to prioritise various competing obligations.

Leadership – a strategic resource for enhancing the psycho-social work environment

Leadership skills also play an important role for mental wellbeing. In units where leadership skills are further developed employees also improve in mental wellbeing. An important determinant to enhance organisational efficacy is enhanced performance feedback from the immediate manager.

Skills development

There is a rapid development of new skills in the health care area. Employees therefore need to constantly develop their skills. The organisation of work must also ensure that employees also get to use their entire competence for the job. It is all too common that health care professionals report that they do not get to use their full range of skills and neither do they develop necessary new skills.

Health care workers need skills to be more professional in their interaction with patients to ensure that they do not over-commit themselves emotionally with the result that they are at risk from emotional and intellectual 'burnout'.

Participatory management

Participatory management is an important aspect of healthy work organisations. Employee ideas need to be incorporated into everyday work processes in order to ensure healthy and efficient work practices. Management that does not facilitate such engagement will create a sub-optimal work environment and frustrated workers, who will be more likely to leave the organisation.

Cross-functional work teams

Health care organisations also need to encourage cross-functional work teams and more efficient team efforts. Still today, health care organisations are characterised by sub-optimisation through fragmentation based on departments and professional groups.

Professional counselling

Employees in need should be offered professional counselling, both individually as well as in groups. Group counselling may be very beneficial following stressful circumstances, such as a major event or unexpected complication in the medical care process. However, groups focusing merely on dealing with emotional reactions to an unhealthy workplace and emotionally demanding and draining patients should not be the sole or core strategy to deal with occupational stressors.

Description of an intervention program

QWC-Quality-Work-Competence is a method tried in a number of different health care settings which is based on assessing the psychosocial work environments in terms of stress, skills development, efficacy, clarity of goals, leadership, employeeship and related factors. The base for the assessment is a questionnaire. The questionnaire has been, as far as possible, calibrated against biological stress markers.

There are 6 distinct steps in the QWC assessment and improvement method:
1. Assessment: Following organisational wide information, a questionnaire is distributed to all personnel. The questionnaire is most often mailed to the employee's home address and furnished with a self-addressed, pre-paid envelope that is returned directly to the independent evaluator.
2. Feed-back: Following the analysis of the questionnaire, results are fed-back to each organisational level, that is workplace level and higher. Each level is compared to the immediate higher level. The entire organisation is compared to external organisations, representing both private and public organisations. Factors contributing to high stress-levels, are identified statistically and presented to the work group. Following the presentations of the results to individual units, results are discussed. At first in general, then more in detail. Internal and external challenges facing the workplace and its effect on psychosocial measurements are discussed.
3. Engagement: Three key areas for improvement are identified and agreed upon as the target for the enhancement process. These should be the areas most in need of improvement, that is the lowest scoring. Specific factors that will improve the situation are discussed.
4. Resolution: A smaller project group is appointed to be responsible for developing further ideas and implementation strategies. The group's responsibilities and rights are clearly defined by management and a time schedule is agreed.
5. Implementation and commitment: Following the implementation of ideas the impact on the psycho-social environments is reassessed. Results are fed back to the group.
6. Reassessment: The last step is to once again assess the effect of the enhancement program that has been implemented throughout the organisation. Then the process starts all over again, beginning at step 1.

Conclusion

The solutions to many of today's challenges to health care might not be found solely within the health care organisation. The financing of health care as well as societal changes impact greatly on the conditions under which health care operates. However, there are a number of initiatives that can be taken to enhance the organisational structure, counteract unhealthy workplaces and engage all healthcare workers in forming a healthy, efficient and flexible workplace that is shaped for the future. Merely dealing with these challenges on an individual level will not suffice.

The organisation of health care must ensure that the work environments offered are stimulating and challenging to all professionals, not solely to certain groups. Health care of today is a knowledge industry. Up-to-date skills and knowledge are two key ingredients for high quality patient care. This demands the creation of environments that are appealing to employees with the right credentials and characteristics to work as knowledge workers. Key ingredients in such environments are participatory management style, less bureaucratic decision making, flexibility, skills development and utilisation of existing knowledge as well as use of modern technologies to create rich and rewarding work organisations.

References

1   Arnetz JE, Arnetz BB. The development and application of a patient satisfaction measurement system for hospital-wide quality improvement. International Journal for Quality in Health Care 1996;8:555-566
2   Arnetz BB. Physician's view of their work environment and organization. Psychotherapy and Psychosomatics 1997;66:155-162

Further reading

- Cooper CL, Cartwrigt S. Healthy mind, healthy organization – a proactive approach to occupational stress. Human Relations 1994;47:455-471
- Health care quality. Management for the 21st century. James B. Couch (Ed). The American College of Physician Executives. American College of Medical Quality. Tampa, Florida, 1991
- Stress and coping in mental health nursing. J. Carson, L. Fagin, Ritter SA (Eds). Chapman & Hall, New York, 1994
- Schaufeli WB, Maslach C, Marek T. Professional burnout: Recent developments in theory and research. Taylor & Francis, London. 1993

Occupational Health for Health Care Workers - A Practical Guide
H.-M. Hasselhorn, A. Toomingas and M. Lagerström (Editors)

The risk of making mistakes - a neglected occupational health problem

Carin Sundström-Frisk

Health care work is centred on humans, who may be weakened by disease and in physical and emotional distress. Unpredictable complications occur frequently, creating demands on complex decision making. The use of risky methods and complicated technology can tax to the maximum the motor, cognitive, emotional and social skills of the health care worker (HCW). When demands on human behaviour exceed human capacity the probability of making errors increases. Stressful situations due to time pressure, inadequately trained staff, badly designed equipment or tiredness due to shift work etc. increases the error rate.

Human errors occur in all professions. However, the consequences of such errors in health care may be disastrous for the patient and are becoming less and less acceptable. Demands for cures are steadily increasing as a result of better informed and less passive patients. This has created a hitherto neglected occupational stressor - the worry the HCW might make a mistake and harm a patient.

Causing harm

Among nurses and assistant nurses in intensive care units, it has been shown that the risk of making mistakes gives rise to greater concern than other established work stressors, like physical exertion, infections, psychological strain, and violence [1]. All those interviewed reported making mistakes that had or might have harmed a patient. More than half of the HCW were more or less emotionally affected by these events regardless of the outcome in terms of manifest patient injury, discovery, or legal aftermath. Thus, the emotional burden of guilt was more disturbing than other outcomes. Being involved in an incident also resulted in feelings of inferiority and uneasiness, even when the mistake has passed unnoticed by the patient or was corrected in time. According to the same study, 88% of the subjects blamed themselves, even when the mistakes were attributable to circumstances beyond their control. Half of them reported lasting negative effects such as sleep disturbances, nightmares and general anxiety. Of these 53% found it hard to keep their minds off what had occurred and thought about it over and over again. 48% were quite concerned that they might meet the same situation again, (a stressor that increases the probability of repeating the mistake).

There are no figures available to assess the general impact that the worry of making mistakes may have on the HCW. The problem attracting most attention is the worry of doctors to be reported to the authorities. Studies showed that 33% of the doctors at a university hospital expressed fear and anxiety about being reported [2]. In the sample studied, 31% had in fact been reported, 17% more than once.

The effect on those involved depends on the underlying legal and cultural situation. Consequences for staff involved could be summarised as follows:

Consequences related to legal issues:
* Economic and professional consequences of a juridical verdict.
* The mere fact of being reported to the authorities induces, regardless of the outcome, feelings of stigmatisation, and low self-esteem. Publicity in the media, which usually implies guilt before investigation generates feelings of unfair treatment. (Usually, only a small percentage of reported cases leads to legally based sanctions).

Other consequences:
* Feelings of guilt,
* Stressful fantasies about mistakes where the possible outcome is unknown or likely to have a delayed appearance,
* Feelings of professional inadequacy and the related worry of making new mistakes,
* Patient distrust.

The size of the problem

There is a massive underreporting to the authorities of mistakes due to feelings of shame, fear of informal punishment and legal sanctions. This makes it difficult to estimate the size of the problem by relying on official reports [3]. In an extensive American study, however, the frequency rate was assessed by reviewing 30100 randomly selected records. Adverse events were identified in 3.7% of the hospitalised patients, whereof 28% were due to negligence that was equally common in the different clinical specialities. By negligence was meant that personnel did not meet expected standards of behaviour. The proportion of cases due to negligence increased with age of patient and severity of the iatrogenic injury [4].

Using the same data Leape analysed the 1331 cases of adverse events involving medical actions [5]. Technical errors during treatment accounted for 44% of all cases and error in diagnosis for 17%. The commonest errors due to negligence were "delayed treatment" (70%), and "failure to use indicated tests" (91%). Most errors were slips, lapses, and mistakes, which anyone might commit, related to attentional and memory failures that are more influenced by physical and mental stressors than by professional skill. A minor proportion was due to professional inadequacy.

Underreporting means that certain diagnoses and types of problems perceived by HCW never become visible in official statistics about work environment problems. Sensitivity among occupational health personnel to these more or less disguised problems is essential to prevent or take care of work-related problems and illness among HCW. Ongoing research shows that 14% of randomly selected HCW, consulting for psychosomatic or psychological symptoms, bring up during therapy the worry of committing errors as a significant stressor to them, without having reflected on its impact on their health status.

Human errors

Traditionally individual characteristics have been used to explain human errors. The insight that all human beings make mistakes, and that behaviour varies with mental and physical demands have made it obvious that individual traits alone cannot account for the errors. The perspective has been widened and today we look for causes in the pattern of interaction between human, technical, and organisational factors.

Human behaviour is regulated on different levels of consciousness, and varies from non-intentional reflexive or automated routine behaviour to highly conscious complex, cognitive processes like problem-solving. Errors are committed at all levels. Strategies to reduce the probability of making errors must be based on an analysis of what type of error is involved since different types demand different means of prevention [6].

Prevention

The fundamental counter-measure in the workplace is to build up expertise, routines and organisational arrangements to reduce the risk of making a mistake, i.e. to identify and remedy conditions that provoke error.

Since there are no zero risk activities, near-accidents and accidents will continue to occur. This is why supportive and rehabilitative efforts have to be made, including providing psychological care to the persons involved.

Identification and prevention of errors

Management commitment
The hospital management should give priority to safety issues. This involves a well-developed strategy by management and the allocation of resources in the form of personnel time, and finance.

Information systems and risk analysis
Procedures for reporting and investigating incidents and accidents need to be developed [7]. To reduce underreporting, systems should be introduced independent of the official ones where mistakes could be admitted and investigated without fear of judicial sanctions. It is important to promote an atmosphere of understanding and support for the HCW who has made a mistake. Risk analysis techniques need to be used, especially when introducing new technological and organisational systems.

Systems for feed-back and auditing
Auditing (follow-up and quality evaluation), and publicising investigation data should be developed to improve employees' knowledge of errors.

A broad arsenal of safety measures
Preventive strategies are directed towards the individual, the work environment, the job and the organisation. This implies furnishing staff with adequate knowledge, skills and

resources – as well as designing procedures and equipment with due regard to new techniques and human capacity. An ever growing speed of change due to new technology and new knowledge demands a continuous assessment and updating of individual professional skill.

Training in communication skills

HCW should be trained to deal with the injured patient following a failure or error. This not only reduces the risk of being reported but also reduces the anger among those involved and may prove to be helpful for debriefing.

Individual stress coping strategies

Individual stress-coping strategies may reduce mental stress, which is a frequent underlying cause of errors.

Emotional debriefing (crisis intervention)

Psychological care after serious accidents decreases the risk for post-traumatic symptoms. Teams and sessions for emotional debriefing are becoming ever more frequent in hospitals and techniques for crisis therapy are developing rapidly. Supporting networks for doctors with personal or work-related psychological problems exist in several countries already [8].

References

1   Sundström-Frisk C. Near accidents in the use of advanced medical equipment. In: Smith MJ, Salvendy G (Eds). Advances in Human Factors/Ergonomics, 19A. Human Computer Interaction: Applications and Case Studies, Amsterdam: Elsevier 1994:821-826
2   Arnetz BB. Physician's view on the work environment and organisation. Psychotherapy and Psychosomatics 1997;66:155-162
3   Hellström M, Sundström-Frisk C. Critical incidents in the use of medical equipment-documentation and feedback of users' experiences. In: Westlander G, Hagberg M (Eds) Pro Health Care, Book of Abstracts. Stockholm: National Institute for Occupational Health, 1994: 116
4   Brennan TA, Leape LL, Laird NM, Herbert L, Localio AR, Lawthers AG, Newhouse JP, Weiler PC, Hiatt HH. Incidence of adverse events and negligence in hospitalized patients. Results of the Harvard Medical Practice Study I. New England Journal of Medicine 1991;324:370-376
5   Leape LL.The Preventability of Medical Injury. In: Bogner MS (Ed). Human Error in Medicine. New Jersey UK: Lawrence Erlbaum Associates Publishers Hillsdale, 1994:13-25
6   Reason J. Human Error. University of Cambridge, Lawrence Erlbaum Associates Publishers, Hillsdale, 1994:13-25
7   Van der Schaf T, Lucas D, Hale A. A near miss reporting system as a safety tool. Oxford: Butterworth-Heinemann, 1991
8   Hardt F, Dalsgaard U. Collegial network for Doctors in Denmark 1.5.1992-30.4.1997. Copenhagen: Danish Medical Association, 1997

Occupational Health for Health Care Workers - A Practical Guide
H.-M. Hasselhorn, A. Toomingas and M. Lagerström (Editors)

Violence at the health care workplace

Judith E. Arnetz

Violence in health care: definition and background

Violence in the health care sector was traditionally recognised as a problem only in psychiatric settings, where violent behaviour from mentally ill patients was viewed, simply, as "part of the job." In recent years, however, violence has gained recognition as an occupational hazard for health care workers generally [1]. The traditional definition of violence as the intentional use of physical force to inflict harm has been broadened to include verbal aggression, threats and sexual harassment. This broader perspective developed after an increasing number of studies revealed negative health effects of threats and verbal aggression on health care workers.

Exposure

Measuring the prevalence and incidence of violence towards health care workers is hampered by wide variation in the use of definitions and methods of measurement, and by the sensitive nature of the issue [2]. Violent incidents are often not reported in many psychiatric care environments, where violence occurs frequently and is considered by staff to be routine. In studies of homicide as well as non-fatal assault, health care workers have been shown to be at increased risk in comparison to other professional groups. The health care environments at greatest risk for violence from patients are psychiatric, emergency and geriatric settings. Research has shown that nursing personnel are at greatest risk for violence from patients, followed by physicians, while paramedical personnel are not at increased risk [3]. Recent changes in health care organisation have implied an increase in outpatient and home-health care. There is a need to assess possible risks for violence to health care personnel working alone, and in patients' homes.

Negative health effects

Mezey and Shepherd describe possible psychological, physical and behavioural effects of physical assault in health care professionals [4]. The majority of violent incidents directed towards health care workers do not result in serious physical injury [2]. However, several studies have pointed to both short- and long-term psychological effects, including symptoms of burnout and post-traumatic stress [4]. Swedish health care workers have reported feelings of anger, fear, helplessness, irritation, and humiliation as the result of violence from patients [2]. In a survey of a representative national sample of Swedish nurses, experience with violence was significantly correlated with occupational as well as certain lifestyle factors, such as smoking, coffee drinking, and use of alcohol to unwind after work. The study was cross-sectional, and cause and effect can not be determined. However, nurses expressing dissatisfaction with work were at increased risk for violence [5]. Health care workers have a tendency to blame themselves when patients become aggressive, feeling that they have failed as care-givers [4].

Detection of risk situations and negative health effects

The aetiology of violence must be understood in order for effective management and prevention methods to be established. The earliest strategies dealt with attempting to predict violent behaviour in psychiatric patients. To focus solely on patient or staff behaviour is insufficient. Studying only the serious violent events, i.e., those that are reported as official work injuries, also gives the organisation incomplete information. Inclusion of all types of violent incidents, including those of a low-level nature that do not necessarily result in physical injury, is a first step in the risk assessment process [2]. The Violent Incident Form (VIF) is a 20-item checklist for registration of all types of violent incidents in the health care workplace, including those where little or no physical injury is incurred [2]. It was designed to complement official work injury reports, as a practical tool for the individual workplace. Results of a controlled, longitudinal intervention study at 47 health care work sites showed that use of the VIF instrument, in combination with a structured program of regular discussion of registered incidents, was an effective method for improving staff awareness of risk situations for violence. Regular review of threatening or violent events is the key to better understanding of risk and safety factors at one's own workplace. Routine monitoring of events may also improve the possibility to detect negative health effects on staff, both physical, psychological, and emotional, that can have a negative impact on work satisfaction and, ultimately, on the quality of care provided.

Strategies for dealing with violence in the health care workplace

The individual health care workplace should have an established safety policy regarding violent or threatening behaviour. Debriefing, i.e., discussion with support and understanding on the part of colleagues and supervisors can be a significant source of help to the victim of a violent incident. More serious incidents may require professional counselling outside the workplace. Staff should receive training on a regular basis to recognise risk situations for violence, and to familiarise themselves with safety practices. Alarm systems, either personal or installed at the workplace, may be necessary at certain work sites, or for health care staff who work in isolated areas. The physical work environment should be safeguarded to minimise risks for violence, for example with adequate lighting and easy access to and from all rooms. Staff training in non-violent self-defence techniques may be useful, although such training often requires regular practice and refresher courses.

All types of violent events must be reviewed in order for an accurate assessment of workplace violence to be made. Violence towards health care workers must be openly discussed at the workplace if strategies for management are to be developed. A non-punitive environment, with willingness on the part of both management and staff to review and discuss actual incidents, is a necessary prerequisite to prevention of violence at the workplace.

References

1   Lipscomb JA, Love CC. Violence towards health care workers. An emerging occupational hazard. AAOHN Journal 1992;40,219-228
2   Arnetz JE. The Violent Incident Form (VIF): a practical instrument for the registration of violent incidents in the health care workplace. Work & Stress 1998;12,17-28
3   Arnetz JE, Arnetz BB, Söderman E. Violence towards health care workers. Prevalence and incidence at a large regional hospital in Sweden. AAOHN J 1998;46,107-114.
4   Mezey G, Sheperd J. Effects of assault on health-care professionals. In Shepherd J. (Ed). Violence in Health Care. Oxford: Oxford University Press, 1994, 1-11
5   Arnetz JE, Arnetz BB, Petterson IL. Violence in the nursing profession: occupational and lifestyle risk factors in Swedish nurses. Work & Stress 1996;10,119-127

Further reading

•   Shepherd J (Ed). Violence in Health Care. A practical guide to coping with violence and caring for victims. Oxford: Oxford University Press, 1994
•   Wykes T (Ed). Violence and Health Care Professionals. London: Chapman & Hall, 1994

Occupational Health for Health Care Workers - A Practical Guide
H.-M. Hasselhorn, A. Toomingas and M. Lagerström (Editors)
© 1999 Elsevier Science B.V. All rights reserved.

Alcohol and substance abuse among health care workers

Walter Lenz, Monica Lagerström

Size of the problem

Alcohol and substance abuse, also called chemical dependency, has been recognised as the third leading health problem in US and other developed countries [1]. In the USA and Sweden the national prevalence of alcoholism is estimated at 10% of the male adult population. 1-2% of the adults are known to be drug dependent. There is a higher proportion of males with alcohol dependency than females in most countries. Women use more than 2/3 of the total consumption of tranquillisers to calm down in stressful situations. Mixed abuse of alcohol and tranquillisers is more common among women than among men. Alcohol is regarded as a remedy for coping with life. Among female blue-collar workers their low job decision latitudes stand for the most important relationship to alcohol problems. Irregular working hours and part time work belong to the factors which make it more difficult to see and identify persons who belong to the category that might need help in solving their drinking problems [2].

The health care sector has traditionally been looked upon as a workplace with several risk factors as far as abuse of alcohol and drugs is concerned. One risk factor for health care workers is that alcohol and drugs are part of the work environment. The prevalence of narcotic dependency among doctors is usually higher than in the general population which is seen as a consequence of availability. Also psychoactive drug use among medical doctors is higher than in the general population [3]. In the USA, UK and other countries there is particular concern about misuse of benzodiazepines among junior hospital doctors [4]. Among Finnish doctors, alcohol consumption was higher than that of the general population and heavy drinking was associated with stress and burn-out problems [5]. In the "Johns Hopkins precursors study" where 1014 male medical students/doctors have been studied for several decades it was found that 131 doctors (12.9%) had alcohol problems [6].

A US survey stated that at least 40 000 nurses out of 2 millions (2%) are known to be alcohol dependent. Nurses' prevalence of drug or alcohol problems is estimated to be 6 to 8% [7]. However, generally nurses in USA do not experience more problems with alcohol or use of illicit drugs than other women [2, 7].

A main problem has been for health professionals to define their roles and identify alcohol and substance abuse as a special problem. Other health care workers often have more traditional relationships with alcohol and drug use.

Main hazardous exposure factors and negative health effects

Nursing is frequently acknowledged to be a stressful occupation and nurses often state increased stress as a result of many responsibilities, limited time for contact with the patients and low social support at work.

Auxiliary nurses and state enrolled nurses are submitted to physically strenuous work as well as low job decision latitude. Nurses and doctors, on the other side, have to take qualified decisions and often under time pressure which contributes to stress. Plant et al. pointed out that working conditions gave the highest stress among female nurses, in particular female medical nurses while psychiatric nurses had the lowest stress levels. Alcohol and substance abuse was connected to specific conditions like a high level of sickness absence among nurses, back pain and sleep disorders, gastric disorders, depression, uncertainty concerning treatment, burn-out signs etc. [8].

Other risk factors which might lead to the use of alcohol and substance abuse as a coping strategy are long working hours, shift work, sleep deficit, fear of making errors, threats and violence, harassment, competition, ethical and emotional conflicts, close contact with suffering and death, and last but not least access to alcohol and drugs within the work environment.

Among health professionals alcohol is the drug that is the most used followed by psychoactive drugs (specifically benzodiazepines), and narcotics like cannabis, amphetamine, cocaine, morphine, and derivates. Female health professionals more often than male abuse alcohol together with psychoactive drugs while male health professionals mainly misuse alcohol. (Definitions see table 1).

Early individual problems are for example sleeping disorders, irritability, gastric symptoms, and psychosocial problems. Some early signs of misuse can be seen by co-workers and supervisors. These signs include a red-face, perspiration, trembling, nervousness, and a smell of alcohol or an attempt to disguise this. In the case of misuse of drugs, dilated pupils and uncoordinated movements, and loss of balance can be seen. These early signs may be followed by a change in work performance such as unexpected frequent short term absences from work, impaired productivity, mood change, aggressiveness, frequent accidents, avoidance of co-workers. These will have an impact on relationships within the working team.

The well-known cortege of alcohol linked disorders and diseases includes alcoholic psychosis, e.g. delirium tremens , alcoholic dementia, Korsakov's psychosis, peripheral neuropathy, gastric disease, pancreatic disease, alcoholic hepatitis and liver cirrhosis, heart disease, skin troubles, infectious diseases, impairment on to the haemopoetic and endocrine system, and finally effects on the foetus. To these physical diseases we must add psychological and social increased risks: violence, accidents, suicide, sex abuse, child abuse, family disturbances etc. [9].

How to detect and handle new suspected cases of alcohol and substance abuse

The workplace is the most important and powerful place to detect alcohol and substance abuse. This statement is important for all people working in the health care sector. There is a close relationship between alcohol and substance abuse and poor job performance. Co-workers and supervisors need to be aware of how the early signs lead to changed behaviour at work.

In the early stage co-workers and supervisors often are apt to deny the problem which might lead to some form of co-dependency. In a more advanced stage of the problem the complaints increase and tolerance of impaired behaviour decreases among co-workers and others.

There is a special problem with health professionals, such as doctors, nurses, psychologists, physiotherapists, dentists, pharmacists, hospital engineers, and students in health professions. They are trying to hide on hiding their alcohol or drug abuse problems because of their real fear of losing their fitness to practice after disciplinary procedures. They also risk being sued for incorrect practice and management. Sometimes it may be difficult to intervene with a colleague at work because of issues of confidentiality. On the other hand it would be unethical not to act. This ethical dilemma has been pointed out by different professional associations in all countries whose members are offered training in how to intervene effectively when necessary. Rather than waiting for legal action from the authorities it is important to take early steps to forestall serious problems.

Table 1. Definitions of terms concerning alcohol and substance abuse

Term	Source	Definitions
Alcohol intoxication	(DSM-IV) [10]	Recent ingestion of alcohol with maladaptive behavioural changes (e.g. inappropriate sexual or aggressive behaviour, mood lability, impaired judgement, impaired social or occupational functioning).
Psychoactive Substance Abuse (alcohol, drugs, chemical substance or psychoactive substance)	(DSM-IV) [10]	A maladaptive pattern of substance use leading to clinically significant impairment and distress by at least one of the following: 1. Recurrent use despite knowledge of having a persistent or recurrent social, occupational, psychological or physical problem that is caused or exacerbated by use of the psychoactive substance. 2. Recurrent use in situations in which it is physically hazardous (e.g. driving when impaired by substance use).

to be continued on page 178

continued
Table 1. Definitions of terms concerning alcohol and substance abuse

Term	Source	Definitions
High/risky consumption	(ICD-10) [11]	Risk of developing alcohol related damages and /or dependency: Females: > 210 g alcohol/week (WHO = 175 g/week). Males: > 280 g alcohol/week (WHO = 245 g/week).
Harmful use	(ICD-10) [11]	A pattern of psychoactive substance use that is causing damage to health. The damage may be physical or mental.
Dependency syndrome	(ICD-10) [11]	A cluster of behavioural, cognitive, and physiological phenomena that develop after repeated substance use and that typically include a strong desire to take the drug, difficulties in controlling its use, persisting in its use despite harmful consequences, a higher priority given to drug use than to other activities and obligations, increased tolerance, and sometimes a physical withdrawal state.

Tools for detection of chemical dependency

One of the most useful ways to detect chemical dependency is to use questionnaires that measure habits, behaviour, and dependency factors. There are several questionnaires which can be used for both alcohol and substance abuse like Minnesota Assessment of Chemical Health (MACH) while some only focus on alcohol abuse; Alcohol Use Disorders Test (AUDIT), Michigan Alcohol Screening Test (MAST), and Cut down Annoyed Guilty Eye opener (CAGE) [12].

There are different tests to detect alcohol and substance abuse in blood and urine. For example alcohol testing of promille contents in blood and/or breath and drug tests can be used when accidents have occurred at work etc.. Similar tests exist for narcotics (for example cannabis, amphetamine, cocaine, and heroin) and their presence and levels can be analysed in blood and urine.

There are biological markers sensitive to alcohol induced damage to the organs of the body. They may give quick or delayed response but there is no single certain pathognomonic test that detects high consumption (Table 2). Most tests like GammaGT, and ALAT show the effect on the liver of high consumption and requires 1-2 months or more of misuse. CDT, on the other hand shows the effect on transferrin which reflects high consumption of alcohol of 60-120 g daily during as little as two weeks or more.

Biological markers can be used both for identification and follow up of high consumption levels.

Table 2. Tests for detecting and follow-up of alcohol and drug induced damage #

Body region	Biological marker
Influence on liver	• ASAT-Aspartate Amino Transferase • ALAT-Alanine Amino Transferase • GT-Gamma Glutamyl Transferase
Influence on erythrocytes:	MCV-Mean Corpuscule Volume
Influence on serum transferrin	CDT-Carbohydrate Deficient Transferrin
Influence on pancreas	Amylase
Other tests (less specific that the above)	• Thrombocytes • Uric acid, Creatinin etc.
Blood and urine (test of narcotics)	Occurrence and level of substance (drug)

\#   Higher than normal values may arise due to factors other than alcohol and substance abuse

Medical treatment and rehabilitation

In most industrialised countries employers have access to some form of Occupational Health Service system (OHS) which normally contains medical and technical service. Large OHS often have specialised nurses and doctors who know how to handle alcohol and substance abuse correctly. Employers might also have access to an Employee Assistant Programme (EAP) with psychological expertise.

In early interventions there is an urgent need for the supervisor to hold a discussion with the affected health care worker about well being. Absence from work and other signs should be carefully documented. The staff member should be sent to the OHS and EAP for medical opinion and/or help with psychosocial problems.

There are three main approaches to providing help to affected health care workers and to assist staff in this area.

Individual approach

- Medical examination and interview, whenever the employee/patient calls for treatment because of sickness that may arise due to alcohol or substance abuse.
- Health check-ups including enquiry into work-related and other problems, lifestyle e.g. diet, physical exercise and drinking habits.
- Focused health check-ups for those with increased sick-leave and/or who might be exposed to night or shift work, chemical hazards, accidents, etc. which could be related to alcohol and substance abuse.

Organisational approach

With an epidemiological perspective on alcohol and substance abuse, the focus is within the organisation and should include investigation of special risk groups. Experts investigate occupational groups e.g. nurses, doctors and others in order to raise awareness of alcohol and substance abuse in relation to other health risks and working environments. The organisational approach entails the hospital/health organisation providing and implementing an alcohol and substance policy and to informing all officials and staff, as well as working for changed attitudes about affected workers. Training of key-persons in how to detect and how to handle these cases should also be provided.

Examples of how to put into practice such a policy might include:
- to distribute leaflets about the policy and information on how to handle the problem
- to educate supervisors and all employees of the organisation
- to inform personnel at regular meetings
- to have certain regulations banning alcohol and promoting alcohol-free drinks

Rehabilitation groups

The hospital/ organisation has a responsibility to set up some type of rehabilitation group consisting of the patient, his/her union support, work supervisor and the staff at the OHS/EAP. They should all meet regularly and check on how matters are going according to a mutually agreed contract. If anything occurs outside the terms or in breach of the rehabilitation plan, the group should arrange a new meeting. Help from Alcoholics Anonymous (AA) may be recommended. A study has shown that following intervention, affected full time hospital staff showed the same level of sick-leave, late arrivals and other problem behaviours as the unaffected control groups [1].

Strategies for prevention

Alcohol- and substance policy strategies

The most important issue is to create and implement a policy. The policy must include strategies how to change attitudes towards making use of alcohol less permissive, increase awareness of seriousness of the problem, and of how to detect the problem. Everybody in the organisation has to know who to talk to and they should know that the OHS has to handle the problem with full confidentiality. The policy should stress openness about the problem and point out that dependency is a disease and not a personal failure. Affected health care workers need help to become aware of the problem, and they need treatment. The aim of the program is to enable the employed health care worker to continue at work.

Alcohol and substance abuse is not only a medical problem but also a problem related to organisation and leadership. Thus there is also a need for different strategies to reach out to staff in different stages of alcohol consumption or dependence:
- Social drinkers who do not have high/risky consumption (Table 1) and whose job performance is not yet affected need information about alcohol and drugs. They also need education to help them decrease their intake in times of personal crisis.
- Abusers of alcohol (high/risky consumption, Table 1) need to lower their consumption.
- Alcohol dependent persons (Table 1) need medical treatment as they are unable to stop drinking without long term support. Those who are abusers or dependent on drugs/substances should be treated in the same way.

Education and co-workers support

It is necessary to train staff in how to support and to confront abusers, their denial of their problems, their manipulative behaviour and psychological mechanisms of defence. To succeed in the treatment of abusers among health care workers there is a need for good information and education about the process of recovery. In the workplace, co-workers and voluntary peer assistants have important missions to give concrete support and help as well as encouragement and hope. Nurses and doctors post recovery experience many problems when re-entering their jobs due mainly to co-workers' suspicion and disbelief.

These problems are, however, widespread and alcohol dependency is an increasing problem also in the third world. In the developed countries, on the contrary, alcohol consumption may be decreasing but substance abuse is ever more widely spread and must be seen as a new threat to health care workers.

References

1   Calley Y. Chemical abuse rehabilitation for hospital employees. AAOHN J 1994;32(2):67-75
2   Blazer LK, Mansfield PK. A comparison of substance use among female nurses, clerical workers and blue-collar workers. J Adv Nurs 1995;21:305-313

3   Domenighetti G, Tomamichel M, Gutzwiller F, Berthoud S, Casabianca A. Psychoactive drug use among medical doctors is higher than in the general population. Soc Sci Med 1991;33:269-274

4   Aach RD, Girard DE, Humphrey H, McCue JD, Reuben DB, Smith JW, Wallenstein L, Ginsburg J. Alcohol and other substance abuse impairment among physicians in residency training. Annals Intern Med 1992;116:245-254

5   Juntunen J, Asp S, Olikinuora M, Äärimaa M, Strid L, Kauttu K. Doctors'drinking habits and consumption of alcohol. BMJ 1988;297:951-954

6   Thomas CB, Santora P, Shaffer JW. Health of physicians in midlife in relation to use of alcohol: a prospective study of a cohort of former medical students. Johns Hopkins Med J 1980;146:1-10

7   Trinkoff A, Eaton W, Anthony J. The prevalence of substance abuse among registered nurses. Nursing Research 1991;40:172-175

8   Plant M, Plant M, Foster J. Stress, alcohol, tobacco and illicit drug use amongst nurses: a Scottish study. J Adv Nurs 1992;17:1057-1067

9   Allebeck P, Rydberg U. Risks and proctective effects of alcohol on the individual. Alcoholism Clin Exp Res 1998;22:269S

10   American Psychiatric Association. Diagnostic and Statistical Manual of Mental Disorders. (Fourth Edition ed.) Washington DC: 1994

11   WHO. International Statistical Classification of Diseases and Related Health Problems. (Tenth Revision ed.) Geneva: 1992

12   Ewing J. Dectecting alcoholism: The CAGE questionnaire. JAMA 1984;252:1905-1907

Health care workers with mental disorders

Manfred Glatzel

According to official estimates about 10-12% of the German population need psychiatric treatment in any year, mainly due to depression. Consequently psychiatric disorders are common in employment including health care work. These include psychoses, affective disorders, anxiety states, and personality disorders. Drug and alcohol abuse/dependency are dealt with in a separate chapter in this book.

Occupational consequences of mental disorders

The mental disorders listed above may lead to impairment of performance at work or interpersonal relationships. This may appear as impaired concentration, difficulty working under pressure, a reduced capacity to deal with novel situations and deterioration in interpersonal skills.

This may have serious consequences in a hospital:
* A nurse with a decompensated bipolar disorder may put patients and colleagues at risk if he/she is unable to follow medical instructions or misinterprets examination results.
* Deterioration in interpersonal relationships can affect teamwork.

The impaired performance of a worker with a mental disorder may be misinterpreted by colleagues and seen as incomprehensible, hurtful or damaging to the work of the team.

The role of the occupational health service

When consulting the occupational health physician (OHP), the superior of the (suspected) mentally ill health care worker (HCW) should describe the changes in performance and behaviour. Vague references to "strange behaviour" are insufficient.

Dealing with mentally ill personnel is a demanding task for the occupational health service. Confidentiality must be assured, but the OHP should notify those who need to know e.g. a "support group" (see below), of any additional support or restrictions required in employment. Clinical details must not be disclosed without the consent of the worker.

The OHP should serve as an advocate for the mentally ill HCW where possible. The views of the HCW with a mental disorder should be included as much as possible when considering the employment consequences of the illness.

The management of a HCW with suspected mental illness may require the OHP to consider referral to a psychiatrist.

It is possible that a HCW who is unpopular or seen as a threat by management or colleagues can be incorrectly labeled as mentally ill (e.g. a refractory pro-union nurse) and referred to the Occupational Health Service. The OHP should be aware of this possibility.

Rehabilitation of the mentally ill HCW

The occupational health team has a central and demanding role in the rehabilitation to work of the mentally ill HCW. A number of measures described below may be supportive in this task.

Stepwise integration

After a long phase of disease related sick leave the mentally ill HCW should start working with a reduced amount of work hours. As an example, the HCW could begin working 2 hours/day for 4 weeks thereafter gradually increasing working hours.

Work restrictions

Work restrictions should be specifically defined by the occupational health physician and reported to the employer. These may include:
- Avoidance of work known to be stressful e.g. in intensive care units
- Night work may result in lack of sleep and provoke an acute exacerbation of the mental disorder e.g. in affective psychoses. In addition, a HCW may be alone when working at night with little support. Dayshift work can benefit the mentally ill HCW where there is close support within a team.
- Work tasks may require to be limited. For example, an orthoptist recovering from a psychosis could be limited to visual field examinations.

Redeployment

It may become necessary to redeploy a mentally ill HCW, e.g. a physician from patient care to administrative work, or a nurse to non-clinical duties.

The use of a "support group"

When dealing with a mentally ill HCW, occupational health personnel often need the support of others within and outside the hospital setting. By creating a "support group" with the consent of the HCW, it becomes possible to promote understanding and acceptance among those involved. Members of this group may include the HCW's superior (when informed about the HCW's disease), a staff representative, and a member of the personnel department.

Co-operation with the HCW's psychiatrist

Close co-operation with the HCW's psychiatrist is of importance in the course of rehabilitation, for example in questions concerning pharmacotherapy. This requires the consent of the HCW.

The long term employability of mentally ill health care workers

Rehabilitation to the original job can be a stabilising factor for the mental, social and economic well-being of the mentally ill HCW. On the other hand, the reintegration of mentally ill personnel has become increasingly difficult due to harder working conditions in health care. The long-term prognosis of rehabilitation measures is, therefore, difficult to make.

Occupational Health for Health Care Workers - A Practical Guide
H.-M. Hasselhorn, A. Toomingas and M. Lagerström (Editors)

Night and shift work

Yuichiro Ono

Many researchers regard it as difficult for the human biological clock to adjust completely to night and shift working schedules. Realignment of biological phase will seldom occur in night and shift workers in contrast to travellers crossing time zones by jet: the latter's circadian rhythms are gradually adjusted to new local clocks. The body clock is adjusted to 24-hour cycles by a mechanism which is achieved by external factors called "zeitgebers". The daylight/darkness cycle is regarded as the major zeitgeber in most animals including human beings. Behaviour such as social interaction and meal timing also plays the role of a zeitgeber. The daylight/darkness cycle competes and slows the adjustment process of biological clocks in night and shift workers, which explains why complete adjustment to night shift is considered quite unfeasible for them.

Shift systems

There are many types of shift system in workplaces. The shift systems worked by nurses and midwives have been classified according to the degree of flexibility for shift rostering (regular, irregular, or flexible) and the speed of rotation between night and day work (permanent night, fast or slow rotation, see below)[1]. In a study of larger general hospitals in England and Wales, the majority of systems were flexible and included permanent night shift systems. Flexible systems, there, meant an unfixed roster in which nurses were consulted before the roster was drawn up. The distribution of the types of shift systems for nurses, however, are quite diverse from country to country. For example, permanent night shift is quite uncommon among hospital nurses in Japan.

Shift systems according to the degree of flexibility:
- Regular shift: A fixed roster is repeated when the cycle of shifts finishes.
- Irregular shift: The duty roster does not repeat in any regular manner. Individuals' preferences are not taken into account.
- Flexible shift: The duty roster does not repeat in any regular manner. Individuals' are consulted before the roster is drawn up.

The organisation of night shift cover (speed of rotation):
- Permanent night shift: Nurses work on the night shift only and do not engage in day work at all.
- System of fast (internal) rotation: Nurses generally work on the day shift, yet also work a few nights each month.

- System of slow (internal) rotation: Nurses generally work on the day shift, yet also work a few small blocks of night duty each year.

Occupational risk

As there are needs of whole day care of patients and clients, hospitals and social welfare facilities, in general, have night and shift work systems. Thus, many kinds of health care workers have to face shift work as part of their jobs. Inter-individual differences in susceptibility to shift schedules are described below.

Individual differences

Inter-individual differences in health effects of shift work have often been reported. Factors suspected to make individual differences include morning / evening types, extroverts / introverts, ageing, gender, social and family responsibilities, physical fitness, and sleep habits [2, 3]. It was reported that morningness (morning larks) have more difficulties with shift work than eveningness (night owls). In other words, morning types who are more alert in the morning than evening types, decrease the circadian adjustment to shift work. Neurotic extroverts were also reported to have greater circadian ability to adjust to night and shift works than neurotic introverts. There has been evidence on the effects of ageing on circadian adjustment to shift work. Chronobiologically, middle-aged or elderly workers are less tolerant to shift work than younger ones. The critical age reported in studies is around 40-50 years. Gender differences regarding tolerance to shift work are not clear. However, sleep will be sacrificed more easily in women than in men by shift work or a compressed work week because women often have to deal with more household duties than men in many countries. Rigidity in sleep habits and ability to overcome drowsiness were also reported to have relations with shift work tolerance in some studies. There is a study reporting an effect of exercise on reducing the complaint of general fatigue in the night shift. Physical fitness is supposed to be an important factor because it may improve sleep at home and alertness during work. As the above mentioned factors will or may influence the shift work tolerance of workers, they should be taken into account in planning preventive measures.

Effects on sleep

Studies on the sleep of night and shift workers often report reduction in the number of hours slept. One study indicates a reduction in the average sleeping time of nurses; a reduction of 2 hours sleeping time in those working on permanent night shift and 30 min in those on a rotating night shift [4]. Sleep quality also often deteriorates in night and shift workers; they experience difficulties in sleeping, intermittent sleep, and early waking. One study reported that the number of shifts per week (more than 4.1 shifts) and duration of shift work (more than 13.6 years) was correlated with the presence of sleep disorders [5]. In some studies, EEG findings indicated the alteration of normal sleep/wake rhythm and of REM/non-REM sleep patterns among shift workers. These changes in sleep length and quality will be brought about by unfavourable bedtime with regard to circadian rhythms and environmental noise in the daytime.

Reduced alertness and job performance decrements

In night shift, workers often experience markedly reduced alertness around 4-6 am and have to fight against sleep. Some studies observed an increase of alpha and theta bands or even found workers falling asleep with EEG monitoring in night shift.

There are some studies on variations in job performance over 24-hour period, which can be classified into three categories; speed, accuracy, and attention/vigilance [6]. One such study concerned a frequency of minor accidents in hospital [7]. The findings showed that performance was worse during night hours and also showed a post-lunch dip. Gradual decline in performance was also observed in a succession of night shifts in another study.

Accidents

As mentioned above, the frequency of accidents will increase during night and shift work. In 1994, a consensus regarding accidents and sleepiness, endorsed by many researchers, was reported by an international group of scientists studying human performance safety, and prevention of accidents associated with work schedules, night activity, and inadequate sleep [8]. The consensus indicated that the risk of errors and accidents is increased by the deleterious effects of insufficient and disturbed sleep, chronic sleep deprivation, and prolonged wakefulness. For medical workers, the risk will also endanger the safety of patients. An increase of the risk of accidents related to frequent dozes and involuntary falling asleep while driving home, was also noticed in the consensus.

Gastrointestinal problems

Shift workers often complain of gastrointestinal symptoms such as increased/decreased appetite, constipation, or diarrhoea. As the circadian system controls appetite and gastrointestinal functions, working and taking meals at odd hours do not follow the normal circadian variation and may disrupt normal function. Several studies reported higher incidence or prevalence of peptic ulcer and/or gastrointestinal disorders in shift workers than in day workers [3]. These disorders may have some relation with excessive alcohol and caffeine consumption or smoking habits in shift workers. However, the results of these studies remain inconsistent and further studies are needed.

Cardiovascular problems

In some studies, smoking and higher blood pressure were found more common in shift workers than in day workers. An increase in serum cholesterol and urinary catecholamin levels was also reported in workers who were abruptly transferred from day work to night work. Thus, it is reasonable to suppose that the risk of coronary heart disease would increase in shift workers. In a review paper, Kristensen [9] concluded that epidemiological studies of good quality consistently found a modestly higher incidence of cardiovascular diseases among shift workers. A study evaluated as "best" in the review, found the relative risk of 1.4 for ischaemic heart disease in shift workers. Recently, a prospective study on coronary heart disease also reported that multivariate adjusted relative risks were 1.2 among female nurses with less than 6 years of shift work and 1.5 among those with 6 or more such years, compared with those who had never worked shifts [10]. The association of shift work with occurrence of cardiovascular diseases may also explain the large proportion of shift workers in all sudden death cases reported as "Karoshi" (death from overwork) in Japan.

Mental health

In a longitudinal study on shift workers, an increase in neuroticism and somatic/neurotic complaints was found. Gordon et al. [11] also reported higher prevalence of job stress and severe emotional problems in variable shift workers than in non-variable shift workers. However, it is not clear whether shift work plays a role as a risk factor in the occurrence of depression, although some dysfunction of circadian rhythm is found in depressed patients.

Pregnancy

McDonald et al. [12] found a statistically significant increased risk (1.25) of spontaneous abortion in rotating shift workers. They also reported an association of low birth weight with rotating shift work, which suggested foetal growth retardation and increased risk of pre-term birth. Some researchers reported similar results that the increased risks of miscarriage and premature birth were associated with work at irregular hours or shift work. Although the number of studies is too limited to have conclusive views, it seems reasonable to advise female shift workers especially during pregnancy to avoid simultaneous exposure to potential risk factors of obstetric problems such as weight lifting, physical effort, and standing for long hours.

Social and family life

Many adverse effects of shift works on social and family life have been reported. Family members often have problems in scheduling events because of variable shift work schedules. Communication among family members and companionship between wife and husband also tend to be disturbed. Parenting roles in child care and spouse roles as a social companion and a sexual partner are often adversely affected by shift work. In some studies, nurses on fixed shift spent more time with their family than those on rotating shifts. Sometimes there are few child-care facilities or other support found around night and shift workers. Additionally, it is often very difficult for them to participate in recreational and learning events that are usually scheduled for day workers. When shift work is connected with weekend work, family and social activities of workers are furthermore disturbed. It is indicated that rotating shift workers get free day-time for going to banks and public offices or enjoying recreation. Physical and mental conditions of shift workers, however, may often be deteriorated during day-time by sleep insufficiency related to shift work.

Prevention

Individual coping strategies

In order to prevent and/or alleviate adverse effects of night and shift works, individual coping strategies and preventive measures in the workplaces have been recommended. Shift workers often experiment with different strategies to alleviate the harmful effects of night and shift work (Table 1).

Table 1. Individual coping strategies for night and shift workers [13-15].

Individual habits	Coping strategies
Improvement of sleep environment	• Noise and light reduction • Ask co-operation of family members • Use good beds
Sleep behaviour modification	• Attempt to sleep on arrival at home and in the evening after night shift, • Relaxation training
Eating and drinking	• Avoid drinking caffeinated drink within 5 hours of bedtime, • Eat lightly before bedtime, • Avoid alcohol before bedtime
Activity and exercise	• Avoid strenuous physical and mental activity just before bedtime, • Exercise at least three times a week
Social activities	• Plan to co-ordinate family's social life
Medication	• Use sleep medication only temporarily as a final measure
Coping with night shift	• Consumption of little caffeine prior to 3 am for a night shift worker, • Avoid dangerous or critical tasks around 4-6 am slump • Provide bright lighting and a stimulating environment in night shift, • Use public transport instead of cars for commuting

Preventive measures in workplaces

There are preventive measures to be recommended to the employer and occupational health staff, which are related to shift work schedule, legal aspects, medical check and support, education, and provision of resources.

Shift work schedules
Many shift systems in workplaces exist. Even though all systems have advantages and drawbacks, some systems are considered more favourable than others from physiological, psychological, and social viewpoints. Knauth [16] discussed key characteristics of shift systems in proposing recommendations, which were: 1. permanent night work versus slowly and quickly rotating shift systems, 2. duration of shifts, 3. timing of shifts, 4. distribution of leisure time within the shift system, 5. direction of shift rotation, and 6. other characteristics of shift systems. As research evidence of shift system preferences over others with regard to these characteristics are limited and often controversial, recommendations should be tentative. For example, views on permanent night shift are sharply conflicting. Some researchers reported a better adjustment to night work and day sleep in permanent night shifts than in two or three rotation shifts. Their studies, however, were criticised by opponent researchers, as they did not take masking effects into consideration and may have overestimated the degree of adaptation of human endogenous clocks. An accumulation of sleep deficits and social isolation were also the reasons why permanent night shift does not seem to be advisable. In the same way, evidence is very limited regarding the key characteristics of shift systems. We can, however, still find some guidelines or recommendations, like those listed below, which appear to be widely approved by many researchers and shift workers.

In some countries, an extended (compressed) working day of up to 12-hour shifts is reported as a recent trend. The duration of shifts is sometimes extremely prolonged even up to16 hours or more by combining two consecutive shifts in some hospitals in Japan. Plausible justification of this extreme length is that it is adopted for the purpose of restricting the frequency of night shift and commuting as well as improving the quality of patient care during the night. Extended work-days are, however, viewed as definitely unacceptable according to the recommendations by Knauth [16], without strict preventive measures to minimise the accumulation of fatigue. In this context, it seems reasonable that many nurses regarded 12-hour shift as suitable only for some specialities with a slow pace of work, low levels of patient contact, and high patient turnover [17].

Some recommendations for better shift systems are [16]:
- Night work should be reduced as much as possible.
- Quick rotating shift systems are preferable to slowly rotating ones.
- Permanent night work is not recommended for the majority of shift workers.
- Extended workdays (9-12 hours) should only be contemplated, if the nature of work and the workload are suitable; the shift system is designed to minimise the accumulation of fatigue; overtime will not be added; there are adequate arrangements for cover of absentees.
- An early start for the morning shift should be avoided.

- Quick changeovers must be avoided.
- The number of consecutive working days should be limited to 5-7 days.
- Every shift system should include some free weekends with at least two successive full days off.
- The forward rotation of shifts (morning to evening to night shifts) would seem to be recommended at least in continuous shift systems.

Legal aspects (The ILO Convention and Recommendation)

The International Labour Organization (ILO) adopted the Night Work Convention (No.171) and Recommendation (No. 178) in 1990. Those standards apply to night workers, irrespective of gender. Definition of night is a period of at least seven consecutive hours which involve the interval from midnight to 5 am. The Convention documented specific measures required for night workers, which included safety and health, transfer to day work, maternity protection, compensation, social services, and consultation of workers' representatives [18]. The Recommendation listed additional measures as follows; limitation of normal working hours (do not exceed eight hours in any 24-hours period), avoiding overtime, taking at least 11 hours of rest between shifts, a break or breaks for resting and eating, maternity assignment to day work, measures for social services, consideration for workers with family responsibilities and older workers, benefit from training opportunities, and so on. It is expected that these comprehensive international standards contribute to helping night and shift workers to a great degree in many countries. Unfortunately, the number of countries having ratified the Convention is still limited.

Medical surveillance and support

Scott and LaDou [3] propose definite and relative contraindications for shift work. Relative contraindications include conditions shown below, which should be used at pre-employment screening for counselling prospective employees and for establishing adequate medical surveillance. As the disorders or conditions listed below might be influenced by shift work, applicants should be counselled with respect to the potential for aggravation before employment or placement. Definite contraindications listed below, are comprised of disorders or conditions for which physicians should consider recommending a medical restriction from shift work. Then, medical surveillance should be periodically carried out to monitor the effects of shift work. Occupational health staff should give advice and support shift workers who are suffering certain disorders or are at increased risk of health problems. Referral to specialists including sleep clinicians may sometimes be necessary.

Relative contraindications for shift work are [3]:
- Extreme "morningness"
- Sleep rigidity
- Insomnia
- Mild asthma
- Non-insulin-dependent diabetes mellitus (NIDDM)
- Age over forty

- Cardiac risk factors such as cigarette smoking, family history of coronary artery disease, elevated cholesterol, or hypertension
- History of depression
- Use of a medication known to have circadian variation in effectiveness
- History of seizures, but not currently requiring medication and no episodes for at least a year
- Frequent indigestion
- Mild irritable bowel syndrome
- Crohn's disease
- Family instability
- Excessive family responsibilities
- Long commute to work

Definite contraindications for shift work are [3]:
- Epilepsy requiring medication within the last year
- Coronary artery disease, especially if there is unstable angina or history of myocardial infarction
- Asthma requiring regular medication, especially if the patient is steroid dependent
- Insulin-dependent diabetes mellitus (IDDM). (IDDM workers may be able to tolerate a permanent night shift if regularity in meals, activity, and medication can be maintained during work days and days off.)
- Hypertension requiring multiple drugs
- Polypharmacy in general if there are circadian variations in the effectiveness of any medication - especially if a rotating schedule is being considered
- Recurrent peptic ulcer disease
- Irritable bowel syndrome if symptoms are severe
- Chronic depression or other psychiatric disorder requiring medication
- A history of shift maladaptation syndrome

Education and provision of resources
Special emphasis should be put on education of shift workers with regard to health effects of shift schedules, coping measures, and other preventive strategies. Employers should also provide canteen and recreational resources for supporting shift workers.

References

1   Barton J, Spelten ER, Smith LR, Totterdell PA, Folkard S. A classification of nursing and midwifery shift systems. Int J Nurs Stud 1993;30:65-80
2   Härmä M. Individual differences in tolerance to shiftwork: a review. Ergonomics 1993;36:101-109
3   Scott AJ, LaDou J. Shiftwork: effects on sleep and health with recommendations for medical surveillance and screening. Occup Med 1990;5:273-299
4   Escribà V, Pérez-Hoyos S, Bolumar F. Shiftwork: its impact on the length and quality of sleep among nurses of the Valencian region in Spain. Int Arch Occup Environ Health 1992;64:125-129

5   Barak Y, Achiron A, Lampl Y, Gilad R, Ring A, Elizur A, Sarova-Pinhas I. Sleep disturbances among female nurses: comparing shift to day work. Chronobiology International 1995;12:345-350
6   Folkard S, Monk TH. Shiftwork and performance. Human Factors 1979:21;483-492
7   Folkard S, Monk TH, Lobban MC. Short and long-term adjustment of circadian rhythms in 'permanent' night nurses. Ergonomics 1978;21:785-799
8   Åkerstedt T, Czeisler CA, Dinges DF, Horne JA. Accidents and sleepiness: a consensus statement from the International Conference on Work Hours, Sleepiness and Accidents, Stockholm, 8-10 September 1994 J Sleep Research 1994;3:195
9   Kristensen TS. Cardiovascular diseases and the work environment. Scand J Work Environ Health 1989;15:165-179
10 Kawachi I, Colditz GA, Stampfer MJ, Willett WC, Manson JE, Speizer FE, Hennekens CH. Prospective study of shift work and risk of coronary heart disease in women. Circulation 1995;92:3178-3182
11 Gordon NP, Cleary PD, Parker CE, Czeisler CA. The prevalence and health impact of shiftwork. Am J Public Health 1986;76:1225-1228
12 McDonald AD, McDonald JC, Armstrong B, Cherry NM, Côté R, Lavoie J, Nolin AD, Robert D. Fetal death and work in pregnancy. Br J Ind Med 1988;45:148-157
13 Monk TH, Folkard S. Making shiftwork tolerable. London: Taylor & Francis, 1992
14 Wedderburn A. Guidelines for shiftworkers. Dublin: European Foundation for the Improvement of Living and Working Conditions, 1991
15 Åkerstedt T. Wide awake at odd hours. Stockholm: Swedish Council for Work Life Research, 1996
16 Knauth P. The design of shift systems. Ergonomics 1993;36:15-28
17 Reid N, Robinson G, Todd C. The 12-hour shift: the views of nurse educators and students. Journal of Advanced Nursing 1994;19:938-946
18 Kogi K, Thurman JE. Trends in approaches to night and shiftwork and new international standards. Ergonomics 1993;36:3-13

Occupational Health for Health Care Workers - A Practical Guide
H.-M. Hasselhorn, A. Toomingas and M. Lagerström (Editors)
© 1999 Elsevier Science B.V. All rights reserved.

Reproductive health hazards among health care workers

Peter A. Czeschinski

Occupational hazards can have adverse effects on human reproduction in the form of marked changes in sexual behaviour, hormone balance, as well as oogenesis and spermatogenesis, pregnancy outcome and foetal malformations. Reproductive disturbances can potentially be induced by physical, chemical, biological as well as psychological factors.

Due to the lack of empirical data it is very difficult to determine specific hazards for health care employees. For this reason, some *noxae* are mentioned that could have an effect on reproductive capacity, although there is to date no data to support these claims.

Reproductive disturbances induced by chemical influences

Cytotoxic agents

It has already been established that some cytotoxic agents affect the reproductive capacity of both male and female patients who undergo cytotoxic therapy. However, data regarding health hazards for health care personnel who work with cytotoxic agents are not available. Nonetheless, some recent investigations have described a significantly increased infertility rate in nurses who were regularly exposed to cytotoxic agents. The infertility rate of male health care workers has also been found higher than among members of corresponding age groups in other occupations. Definite evidence of an increase in abortion rates due to teratogenic effects is not available [1, 2].

Health care workers exposed to cytotoxic agents
Medical staff (nurses, physicians, pharmacists, laboratory technicians, cleaning staff and other auxiliary medical personnel) involved in the preparation, application and disposal of cytotoxic agents and material contaminated with cytotoxic agents (e.g. patient's faeces and urine).

Prevention
* Technical measures: Closed systems for preparation, application and waste disposal (e.g. urine collection).
* Organisational measures: Instruct and inform personnel, labelling of therapeutic substances, removal of the pregnant woman from hazardous work.
* Personal protective equipment: Gloves, coats, masks and eye protection suitable for handling cytotoxic agents.

Waste anaesthetic gases

It has been suggested in various studies that exposure to waste anaesthetic gases is a factor in triggering early abortion. In addition, increased infertility rates of unknown origin have been observed in women with occupational exposure to waste anaesthetic gases. Fertility disorders have also been described for males exposed to waste anaesthetic gases.

Germicides

Ethylene oxide merits particular mention as an established cause of spontaneous abortion [2]. In addition, it is probable that ethylene dibromide, which is used for room disinfection, contributes to reproductive problems in the health care sector as well. Indeed, spermatocyte abnormalities and infertility have been described for men exposed to this substance [1, 3, 4].

Health care workers exposed to germicides
Mainly sterilisation specialists, disinfectors, dental assistants and other staff performing related tasks.

Prevention
- Technical measures: Use of less hazardous substitutes or sterilisation methods if possible, regular inspection and maintenance of medical equipment, use of other sterilisation substances, e.g. formaldehyde where possible.
- Organisational measures: see above.
- Personal protective equipment: Suitable respiratory protection and protective clothing during room disinfection and also when opening sterilisers.

Other chemical substances

In medical laboratories, in particular, exposure to reproductive and teratogenic health hazards cannot be excluded. These substances include solvents, e.g. N,N-dimethylformamide or carbon disulphide, and solubility mediators e.g. dimethyl sulphoxide or ethylene glycol ethers as well as ethidium bromide, which is known to be mutagenic. Adverse effects on human fertility may be expected from heavy metals, too (e.g. dentists' exposure to mercury vapour) [1,2,4,5].

Health care workers exposed to chemical substances
Medical personnel (physicians, nurses, laboratory technicians, cleaning staff and other auxiliary personnel) in medical or research laboratories, dentists and auxiliary dental personnel, dental technicians.

Prevention
- Technical measures: Use less hazardous substitutes if possible, biological monitoring, regular maintenance and inspection of medical equipment.

- Organisational measures (see above).
- Personal protective equipment: Suitable gloves, clothes, masks, and eye protection.

Disturbances of reproductive capacity induced by physical factors

Ionising radiation

Exposure to ionising radiation especially x-rays can give rise to infertility in both men and women. For women, even low doses of radiation can have serious consequences prior to nidation of the fertilised ovum, which can in turn cause a significant increase in spontaneous abortions. Radiation at later stages of pregnancy is known to induce congenital malformations. In men, a marked reduction in sperm count has been demonstrated even with exposure to very low doses of radiation (20centiGy). Azoospermia can occur at doses greater than 75centiGy; and for doses greater than 300centiGy this condition is frequently irreversible. These doses, however, occur only in the course of radiation accidents [2].

Health care workers exposed to potential health hazards
Medical personnel (physicians, nurses, laboratory technicians, cleaning staff and other auxiliary personnel) in X-ray-units, radiation therapy and/or nuclear medicine units.

Prevention
- Technical measures: Shielding of radiation sources and accurate dosimetry.
- Organisational measures: Establishment and enforcement of limited access zones, use of examination techniques that minimise radiation.
- Personal protective equipment: suitable protective clothes such as lead aprons.

Non-ionising radiation

To date, the impact of non-ionising radiation (high frequency electromagnetic fields, microwaves) on female fertility has been inadequately investigated. It has been established, however, that thermally induced malformations and miscarriages can occur following therapeutic treatment of the abdominal cavity of pregnant women. However, these treatments involved doses that were significantly above 10mW/cm², and such doses are unlikely to occur in the workplace. In addition, disorders in spermatogenesis after testicular hyperthermia from high-energy doses have been observed [2, 6].

Health care workers exposed to potential health hazards
Potentially, medical personnel employed in physical therapy or in nuclear magnetic resonance therapy (NMR).

Prevention
- Technical measures: Shielding of radiation sources.
- Organisational measures: Establishment and enforcement of limited access zones.
- Personal protective equipment: None known.

Heavy physical strain

In several studies an increased risk of pre-term delivery has been found in women whose jobs include a combination of stressful factors such as standing upright for long periods and repetitive heavy lifting, especially in later stages of pregnancy [1, 10].

Health care workers exposed to potential health hazards
Medical staff (nurses, physicians, cleaning staff) involved in lifting or transfer of patients and in activities with long periods of standing.

Prevention
- Technical measures: Use of mechanical lifting equipment and ergonomic systems of work.
- Organisational measures: Removal of pregnant women from hazardous work.

Disturbances in reproductive capacity induced by biological agents

Infections, especially mumps, and in some rare instances cocksackie viruses or other pathogens such as pneumococci and brucella can give rise to orchitis, which frequently results in permanent azoospermia. In women, occupational infections that give rise to irreversible sterility are rarely encountered. If infertility occurs, it is caused by extremely severe infections, rather than by specific pathogens. Spontaneous abortions may be induced by several infections e.g. human *Parvovirus B19*, and *Listeria monocytogenes*. Teratogenic effects may be observed at different stages of pregnancy after infectious diseases such as rubella, cytomegalovirus infection, toxoplasmosis, chickenpox (*Varicella zoster*), herpes (HSV2), measles etc.

Health care workers exposed to infections
Medical personnel, especially male (physicians, nurses, laboratory technicians, cleaning staff and other auxiliary personnel) exposed to infectious agents.

Some infectious diseases affecting reproduction, e.g. HIV may place at risk the partners of medical personnel and their children without effective prophylaxis being available. Moreover, infertility can also occur as an effect of the treatment of specific infections, e.g. ornidazol therapy for protozoal infection.

Prevention
- If possible, immunisation of the personnel involved.
- Technical measures: Systems of work minimising exposure to pathogens, e.g. closed systems for taking blood samples.
- Organisational measures: Labelling of infectious materials, removal of the pregnant woman

from hazardous work.
- Personal protective equipment: Appropriate protective gloves, coats, masks, and eye protection.

Disturbances in reproductive capacity induced by psychosocial factors

To date, the impact of psychosocial factors on human reproductive capacity has not been sufficiently studied. Medical practitioners, however, do not dispute the considerable impact of intensive care work combined with the stressful effect of nightshift and/or stand-by for emergency duties at night, on sexual behaviour and libido. Among other symptoms, an increased occurrence of menstrual disorders has been described. Prolonged significant stress in males leads to markedly lowered testosterone levels with implications for sexual behaviour and reproduction [2, 8, 9].

Health care workers exposed to adverse psychosocial conditions
Medical personnel (especially physicians and nurses) exposed to high levels of psychological stress, e.g. in intensive care and oncology units, and when dealing with natural or man-made disasters etc.

Prevention
Reduction of stress on personnel, reduced work hours, assistance with coping with problems, e.g. teaching stress reduction and coping techniques, discussion- or Balint-groups, and psychological counselling.

References

1   Paul M. Occupational reproductive hazards. Lancet 1997;349:1385-1388
2   Baranski B. Effects of the Workplace on Fertility and Related Reproductive Outcomes. Environmental Health Perspectives 1993;101:81-90
3   Ahlborg Jr G, Hemminki K. Reproductive effects of chemical exposures in health professions. J Occup Environ Med. 1995;37:957-961
4   Rowland AD, Baird DD, Weinberg CR, Shore DL, Shy CM, Wilcox AJ. Reduced fertility among women employed as dental assistants exposed to high levels of nitrous oxide. N Engl J Med 1992;327:993-997
5   Rowland AD, Baird DD, Weinberg CR, Shore DL, Shy CM, Wilcox AJ. The effect of occupational exposure to mercury vapour on the fertility of female dental assistants. Occup Environ Med 1994;51:29-34
6   Lundsberg LS, Bracken MB, Belanger K. Occupationally related magnetic field exposure and male subfertility. Fertil Steril 1995;63:384-391
7   Bernton E, Hoover D, Galloway R, Popp K. Adaption to chronic stress in military trainees. Ann NY Acad Sci 1995;774:217-231
8   Nilsson P, Moller L, Solstad K. Adverse effects of psychosocial stress on gonadal function and insulin levels in middle-age males. J Internal Med 1995;237:479-486
9   Christiansen K, Hars O. Effects of stress anticipation and stress coping strategies on salivary testosterone levels. J Psychophysiol 1995;3:264
10 Luke B, Mamelle N, Keith L, et al. The association between occupational factors and preterm birth: a United States nurses study. Am J Obstet Gynecol 1995;173:849-862

Occupational Health for Health Care Workers - A Practical Guide
H.-M. Hasselhorn, A. Toomingas and M. Lagerström (Editors)

Occupational health aspects in dentistry

Tobias Walker, Tore Dérand, Eva Bejerot

Biological hazards

Needles and other sharps, contaminated instruments, splatter and aerosols can be sources of viral and bacterial infectious agents.

Health care workers (HCW) in dentistry are at risk of acquiring hepatitis B. There is also a theoretical risk for hepatitis C and HIV transmission but such cases have not yet been reported. There is no statistically increased risk for hepatitis A (HAV) even though single cases of HAV transmissions from patients to dentists have occurred. No hepatitis B transmissions from infectious dentists to patients have been reported since 1987, which may indicate that using gloves and applying universal hygiene precautions is protective in these cases. HIV has been transmitted by one dentist suffering from AIDS to 6 of his patients. There have been no subsequent reports and the mode of transmission remains unclear. No case of dentist-to-patient transmission of hepatitis C is known (see chapter Hepatitis C). Except for common cold viruses, herpes simplex is the most commonly transmitted virus in the dental practice. Occupational herpes simplex transmission from patients to HCW does not only lead to oral lesions (labial herpes) but also to infection of the fingers (resulting in herpetic whitlow) and the eyes. Surgical gloves, safety glasses and appropriate sterilisation procedures can provide adequate protection (see chapter Herpes simplex). There is also data showing an increased risk for Epstein Barr virus and cytomegalovirus infection but occupational transmission to HCW is rare. Respiratory infections are more common among dental personnel than other medical workers or the general population.

Although there are many potential bacterial infections in the dental office, the major areas of concern are syphilis, tuberculosis and legionellosis. Syphilis in the primary and secondary stages is highly infectious and a problem for dentists because of the patient's oral lesions. It is common among AIDS patients. Patient-to-staff transmission of tuberculosis is rare in dentistry. There are some reports of transfer from an infected dentist to patients. Legionella is widely distributed in soil and water. *Legionella pneumophila* can cause legionnaires' disease or - more common - non-pneumonia influenza like illness known as Pontiac fever. Most infections are subclinical and antibodies to Legionella are relatively common in the population (5-25%). In dental clinical personnel this is 20% of the employees, in dental practices 50% of dentists and among dental technicians 20%. The most likely source of potential infection is aerosol spread of contaminated water from the dental units. Legionella can proliferate in units that stand idle for many days. Dental units should be flushed with fresh water before and after use. Periodical rinsing with a disinfectant, such as hypochlorite, is also recommended. So far, however, there have been no case reports of occupationally acquired legionellosis among dental personnel.

Prevention

All dental HCW should be protected from / vaccinated against hepatitis B, influenza, measles, mumps, rubella, varicella, tetanus, diphtheria and possibly other diseases (depending on local epidemiological conditions). The measures following a suspected/verified percutaneous or mucocutaneous exposure to HIV contaminated blood should be well defined and known to all personnel at risk. Careful sterilisation and disinfection, use of masks, plastic face-shields, gloves and careful handling of needles and other sharps should be commonplace.

Chemical hazards

Skin problems

Skin problems are a common hazard in dentistry. Several studies had shown that dental technicians and dentists including dental assistants have an elevated prevalence of skin problems on the hands and fingers compared to the general population. A variety of materials used in the dental office can cause direct skin irritation or a delayed allergic reaction. The lists of irritations include soaps and detergents, adhesives, germicides, filling materials, metals (especially nickel), organic solvents and X-ray processing chemicals. Disposable gloves should prevent skin reactions. But the use of latex gloves itself causes allergies and skin problems in a large number of HCW (see chapter dermatoses). Latex gloves used should be powderless. In addition, working in wet conditions increases the risk of skin irritation. Therefore proper hand care is important and should include use of non-irritating hand-wash and disposable paper towels. Cloth towels should be used only once before being laundered.

Acrylates/ Cyanoacrylates

Acrylates have been used in dentistry for removable dental protheses, impression trays, orthodontic devices, occluses splints, and various fixed crowns and bridges since 1940. Methacrylates, which are chemically distinct from cyanoacrylates, serve as a basis for acrylic resins, which have various applications, including use as adhesives and fillers in dental procedures. Polymethyl methacrylate, the most used acrylate in dentistry, is usually prepared by mixing liquid monomethyl methacrylate with polymethyl methacrylate powder. The plastic could be auto cured (self-curing) or heat cured. Diffusion through the skin after direct contact of the monomer is the most critical uptake mechanism and cause of symptoms. In addition the inhalation of acrylate containing vapours and dust (cutting, polishing) may lead to symptoms. Acrylic monomers are irritating to the eyes and mucous membranes and have been reported to produce allergic and irritating contact dermatitis and sometimes to local neurotoxic effects of the hand.

Dental laboratory technicians are handling acrylates much more than dentists and are therefore a more obvious risk group. Some investigations estimate that nowadays 10% of all dental HCW suffer from symptoms due to acrylates. The greatest health risk derives from acrylate monomers which is why thorough hardening (polymerisation) is of special importance as totally polymerised acrylates never cause any allergic contact reactions. When handling monomers gloves should be worn. Polyethylene copolymer gloves provide the best protection. Latex gloves are useless as a barrier to monomers.

Cyanoacrylate based glues give a high bond strength between a variety of materials and are used in dental laboratories. They should be handled with care because they can stick together fingers or eyelids. Furthermore, cyanoacrylate causes irritations of the upper respiratory system.

It is of utmost importance that all dental personnel know about the risks deriving from acrylates and the necessary precautions to be taken. Persons with history of allergic diseases who intend starting training in dental professions should be tested for acrylate sensitivity and be counselled.

Another group of resins which should be handled with care is the bonding agents which are used to attach prosthetic constructions to teeth. Most of them contain hydroxyethyl methacrylate (HEMA) which is a hydrofil substance that quite easily penetrate dentin (under the enamel layer) and also skin. Precautions should be taken not to come in contact with the monomer with unprotected fingers. The resin is often sold in small plastic bottles and it is easy to let the liquid wet the outside of the container.

Used sticks and small cups should be put in plastic parcels which can then be disposed of in normal waste. Again, polymerised HEMA, which often is done with blue light, is a harmless material and never causes allergic reactions.

Amalgam

Concern about amalgam handling has existed since the 1930' s. Exposure to mercury vapour occurs during direct clinical work with amalgam restorations - that is during cutting, filling and polishing operations. In several recent studies the mercury vapour levels in the breathing zone of dentists and dental assistants was far below the national occupational exposure limits. However, even in modern dental offices significant mercury vapour levels can be detected. High occupational exposure to mercury vapour can cause biological damage. Numerous studies with controversial results exist about the occupational risk by exposure to amalgam in dental settings. In one study, elevated mercury levels in dentists were detected in body fluids, i.e. blood, urine and saliva but this was not found in other investigations. Several studies indicate that female dental personnel do not need longer time to become pregnant and that there is no increased risk of spontaneous abortions, foetal malformations, and low birth-weight. Also for wives of amalgam exposed men no increased risk of spontaneous abortions was found. Yet, the exposure to mercury should be kept as low as possible. Prevention of exposure includes replacement of amalgam by other fillings. If this is not possible using sealed amalgam capsules, working in well-ventilated areas, using water spray when grinding amalgam, storing amalgam in closed containers will reduce exposure. In modern dental offices the mercury vapour content today is so low that almost all risks are eliminated, however, all personnel should be informed about the need for good mercury hygiene.

Eugenol

Temporary cements are sometimes used between two treatments. One type contain zinc oxide powder and eugenol which is an aromatic ether. Eugenol is derived from oil of cloves and is a mixture of several chemicals and is used primarily in the hardening process but has also an anti-inflammatory effect. However, it has been shown that it is possible to cause contact irritations or allergic reactions among some patients. The diagnosis is easy to make but also dental personnel should be aware of the possible risk and handle contaminated instruments and cotton rolls with care.

Hydrofluoric acid

In dental treatment planning ceramics have become an alternative to metals in crowns and bridges. Their use is increasing and the aesthetic properties and the non-metal content have let to their high acceptance among patients. The method of fixing the prosthesis to the tooth substance often requires the use of adhesive bonding. Porcelain etchants are used to create micro-mechanical retention on the inside of bonded ceramic restorations. Here hydrofluoric acid (HF) is the active ingredient in practically all porcelain etchants. The current types are gels in concentrations around 10% and they are used both extra- and intraorally. They have a certain caustic effect on tissues and should therefore only be applied where reliable tissue protection could be employed for both patient and dental personnel.

Physical hazards

Musculoskeletal disorders

Among the main occupational problems in dentistry are musculoskeletal disorders (MSD). Main risk factors for MSD include long periods of work in static and awkward postures, demands on extreme precision and pre-existing conditions (disease, trauma, malformations). Studies among dentists showed a lifetime prevalence for musculoskeletal disease of 30-70 percent. Recent studies noted a higher incidence of pain and discomfort in the neck, shoulders and lower back among dentists than for other groups. Intensive or repetitive hand motions can lead to cumulative trauma disorders like carpal tunnel syndrome, tenosynovitis, and ulnar neuropathy. Scaling procedures are a primary cause of these disorders among dentists.

Reports of musculoskeletal pain continue despite equipment design improvements and the increase in sit-down and four-handed dentistry. Although sitting provides less opportunity for twisting and contorting the body, it does exert pressure on the intervertebral disks.

The risk for occupationally related MSD can be reduced by frequent changes of position while working. Alteration of sitting and standing postures reduces fatigue by shifting muscular support to opposing muscular groups.

Ionising radiation - X-ray

In recent years, radiographic equipment and techniques have advanced so that direct radiation injury to fingers or skin of HCW in dentistry is uncommon. There is, however, still concern about the cumulative total-body radiation. Good radiation practice in the dental office, high film speed and proper processing protects both the patient and the dental HCW. Today, scattered radiation when taking X-rays is the most significant concern. Ideally, the operator should stand behind a protective barrier such as a leaded shield or a wall. If that is not possible, a safe position during exposure is behind the patient's head at a distance of at least 1.5 m. Dentists or dental assistants should never hold the film in the patient's mouth or the X-ray head in position. Staff should wear radiation monitoring badges and radiological equipment should be checked regularly.

Non-ionising radiation - ultraviolet light, blue light

New occupational hazards have arisen with the use of composite resin restorative materials, bonding agents and sealants. These materials were originally polymerised with ultraviolet light (UVA). UVA, especially in the wavelengths between 320 and 400 nm can cause cataracts and retinal damage. In recent years UVA lights have increasingly been replaced by blue light polymerising units which function in the 400-500 nm range. Although much safer than UV units, blue light is not without hazard. Intensive light can cause thermal or photochemical injury to the retina. Manufacturers of blue light units recommend safety shields and glasses. Such protective lenses can absorb virtually all of the radiation in the 200-800 nm range.

Non-ionising radiation - lasers

Lasers are also a potential hazard in the dental office. Because lasers generate energy that can burn or alter the target tissue, they should never be directed toward the eyes, non-target tissues or onto reflective surfaces. The operator and staff should all be shielded to minimise the risk of reflected energy. Use of black or anodised instruments when working with lasers can minimise reflection.

Illumination

Visual stress is increased by inadequate illumination. Further the amount and the quality of work output is reduced and the viewer is more fatigued at the end of his work-day. Adequate illumination increases the worker's alertness with the result that more work is done without necessarily increasing the amount of energy expended. Therefore, the minimum amount of light required should be determined by finding what quantity of light on the task area allows the task to be completed without creating visual stress. National guidelines may regulate illumination requirements at the dental workplace.

Vibration

High-frequency vibration from handpieces may produce finger receptor dysfunctions or vibration white finger in dentists and dental technicians. The neurological reactions consisted of symptoms such as numbness, often combined with a prickling and tingling sensation in the fingers. In some cases the fingers were cold and white or subject to spasms or reduced holding power. The majority of the neurological finger reactions were attributed to unspecified work-related causes.

Dusts - metals, acrylates, minerals

Dental personnel are exposed to several potentially hazardous dusts. Metal dusts can contain chromium, cobalt, molybdenum, beryllium and nickel. These metals are used in the production of crowns, bridges and dentures. Acrylates are also used in the preparation of dentures. Silica is used as a sandblasting abrasive and is also present in porcelain. Polishing materials contain iron, aluminium, silica, and chromium. Pneumoconiosis has been described in dental technicians caused by various presumed agents: beryllium, silica, and metals (cobalt, chromium, tungsten, molybdenum) with or without silica. Analysis of lung biopsy specimens has shown the presence of various metals and silica.

Pregnancy

Pregnant women in dentistry are exposed to special hazards: there may be an increased risk of infectious diseases that are potentially hazardous to the unborn, such as cytomegalovirus, rubella, varicella. These risks are discussed in the respective chapters in this book. In addition, certain chemicals may pose a risk for the mother and foetus. Finally, musculoskeletal symptoms among pregnant women in dentistry increase due to the special postures required. Usually, laws and regulations limit the activity of a pregnant dental HCW, but in reality – especially in private practices – it is often difficult to abide by these regulations.

It is recommended that pregnant dental HCW:
- must not be exposed to ionising radiation,
- must not be exposed to anaesthetic gases,
- must not be exposed to carcinogenic or harmful agents,
- should not use formaldehyde containing disinfectants,
- should minimise risk of infection by strictly abiding by universal hygiene measures (masks, gloves),
- should minimise contact with mercury containing substances/vapours,
- should not work at night and
- should not work with sharps or needles (injections).

Psychosocial problems in dentistry

Except for musculoskeletal disorders, stress related illnesses have been found to be the most important group of diseases causing premature retirement among dentists. Several studies based on questionnaires indicate that dentists also perceive their profession as being stressful in many ways. Burnout and elevated suicide levels among dentists are reported from several countries.

In dentistry six major sources of stress have been identified: 1. patient pain and anxiety, 2. interpersonal relations with patients and staff, 3. physical strain of work, 4. economic pressures, 5. third-party constraints and 6. the strain of perfectionism and seeking ideal results. Another classification of specific occupation-related stressors in dentistry is based on two dimensions: task or organisation (i.e. high concentration level, isolation, financial pressure), and interpersonal relations (i.e. anxious patients, treating intricate cases, interaction with staff). These two dimensions are mirrored in one way or another in almost every study of dentistry as an occupation. In most studies chemical and biological hazards are not listed as sources of stress. A clear picture of current stressors in dental work would help the dental team to develop effective coping strategies.

A survey of European studies published during the 1990's show that job satisfaction for dentists is connected to such factors as relations with patients, delivery of quality care, autonomy at work, and relations with colleagues – while job dissatisfaction is connected to factors such as lack of stimulation and promotion prospects, time pressures, conflict between profit requirements and professional ethics, the running of a practice, and lack of rewards and respect. Another stressor is related to the excess of dental manpower in some countries, and the detrimental effects of the increase in competition among dentists.

The problems described as applying to dentists is similar to the stressors of the hygienists and dental surgery assistants. The reports also show that in both these groups there is often a feeling of being undervalued by dentists. In regard to dental surgery assistants, the work conditions are very dependent on the management skills of the dentist. Unplanned overtime, low salaries and lack of respect are the chief sources of stress, as well as the role as a buffer between dentists and patients. For hygienists, relations with the auxiliary staff often make them feel like outsiders in the clinic.

Several studies indicate that dentists are rather pessimistic about the future in the occupation. Especially, there seems to be a somewhat unhappy situation for the staff in the public dental health service. One problematic area is the perception of high organisational demands and management control of work patterns, which are high predictors of low job satisfaction.

To sum up, a large part of the psycho-social problem in dentistry is of a character that could be changed. It is important, however, to understand that the problem cannot be solved primarily on the individual level, but requires measures on the structural and organisational level, and also developments in the training of all the personnel in the dental team.

Further reading

- CDC. Recommended Infection-Control Practices for Dentistry, 1993. MMWR May 28, 1993;42(RR-8):1-10
- Chopp GF. Kaufmann EG. Mercury vapor related to manipulation of amalgam and to floor surface. Operative Dentistry 1983;8:23-27
- Jacobsen N, Pettersen AH. Self-reported occupation-related complaints among dental laboratory technicians. Quintessenz International, 1993;24:409-415
- Lervik A. Hazards in the dental environment – curing lights and high-speed handpieces in the Health Care Professions. In: Brune D, Edling C (Eds). Occupational Risks in the Health Care Professions. Boca Raton, Florida: CRC Press, 1989:291 – 297
- Miller CH, Cottone JA. The Basic Principles of Infectious Diseases as Related to Dental Practice, Dental Clinics of North America, 1993;37:1-20
- Persson B, Brune D. Dental laboratories in the Health Care Professions. In: Brune D, Edling C (Eds). Occupational Risks in the Health Care Professions. Boca Raton, Florida: CRC Press, 1989:333-346
- Persson BRR. Radiation hazards. In: Brune D, Edling C (Eds). Occupational Risks in the Health Care Professions. Boca Raton, Florida: CRC Press, 1989:163-263
- Katsuno K, Manabe A, Kurihara A, Itoh K, Hisamitsu H, Wakamuto S, Yoshida T. The adverse effect of commercial dentin-bonding systems on the skin of guinea pigs. J Oral Rehab 1998;25:180-184
- Pick RM, Powell GL. Lasers in dentistry. Dent.Clinics of N. Am., 1993;(2), 281 – 296
- Widström J. Methyl methacrylate. In: Brune D, Edling C (Eds). Occupational Risks in the Health Care Professions. Boca Raton, Florida: CRC Press, 1989:141-145
- Hagberg M, Hagberg C. Risks and Prevention of Musculoskeletal Disorders among Dentists. In: Brune D, Edling C (Eds). Occupational Risks in the Health Care Professions. Boca Raton, Florida: CRC Press, 1989: 323-332
- Bejerot E. Dentistry in Sweden - Healthy work or ruthless efficiency? Solna: Arbete och Hälsa 1998:14

Occupational Health for Health Care Workers - A Practical Guide
H.-M. Hasselhorn, A. Toomingas and M. Lagerström (Editors)

Occupational hazards in the laboratory environment

Xavier Guardino

Hospital laboratories present characteristic risk situations for staff: the occupational hazards may be great, variable and several risks may exist simultaneously. Biological risks occur when handling infectious samples. Hepatitis B, Hepatitis C and HIV are the infectious diseases most commonly associated with transmission in the laboratory environment. Among physical risks, ionising radiation can be a hazard in the laboratory work environment, mainly due to the widespread use of isotopic radioactive compounds in radioimmunoassay and other analytical techniques. Specific and strict regulations have been established for the purchase, handling and waste disposal of radioactive isotopes. Since biological and ionising risks are described elsewhere in this book, this chapter will deal with laboratory specific risks, mainly those related to the use of chemicals.

Occupational risks

The chemical hazards for laboratory personnel are associated with the hazardous properties of chemicals (Table 1) and the methods of handling them. The risks may derive from short and/or long-term exposure to substances due to inadequate working procedures, malfunctioning apparatus/devices or accidents. *All* personnel working in the laboratory, including cleaning staff, may be exposed to risk from chemicals.

Table 1. Hazardous characteristics of chemicals

Physicochemical	Explosive
	Comburent (oxidising)
	Flammable (highly, extremely)
	Radioactive
Toxicological	Toxic ("*very toxic*", "*toxic*")
	Harmful
	Irritant (eyes, skin, respiratory tract)
	Sensitising (skin, inhalation)
	Carcinogenic
	Mutagenic
	Teratogenic
	Other reproductive hazards
Environmental hazards	Harmful for biosphere, ecological systems, ozone layer, etc.

Long term exposure

Long term exposure to certain substances may cause severe health problems in laboratory personnel. For many substances the effects of long term exposure are not known. Therefore, all long-term occupational exposure to chemicals must be minimised.

Accidents

Accidents in the laboratory environment are frequent. They include:
- chemical spills,
- skin contact or eye contact with caustic or corrosive substances,
- irradiation or contamination with radioactive compounds,
- electric shock,
- fires,
- explosions,
- thermal (high and low temperature) and electric burns,
- explosion or implosion systems working at high pressure or vacuum, respectively,
- stumbling, falling, hitting against object.

Risk awareness

Staff in hospital laboratories do not always work safely in accordance with the actual existing risks in the working environment. This may be due to a number of circumstances including:
- Employees lack information about the specific hazards and protective behaviour to avoid risk situations.
- Negative health effects due to the laboratory hazards are often those with rare occurrence.
- Some risks are difficult to estimate and assess.
- Safe procedures may be uncomfortable and/or time consuming.
- Protective devices may be uncomfortable to work with and/or expensive.

Prevention of chemical risks

General aspects

Hazards in the laboratory environment must not be underestimated. When working with substances with specific hazards, proper precautions should be taken. Strict safety instructions must be developed and included in all standard written protocols prepared and established in the laboratory. It should be assumed that any mixture will be more toxic than its most toxic component and that all substances of unknown toxicity are to be considered as toxic. Even for substances of no known significant hazard, exposure should be minimised. Skin contact with chemicals should always be avoided as a fundamental rule.

Legislation and responsibilities

All current laws and regulations concerning chemical substances, personal protective equipment and control measures must be known by the responsible persons. All levels of hospital management are involved in the responsibilities for minimising occupational risks. The supervisor of the section or unit is responsible for the general working conditions in the unit. Staff must know and follow the rules and undertake regular housekeeping inspections including routine examination of emergency equipment.

Safety and health programmes

A hygiene programme designed to minimise exposure is essential. Specific assessment programmes must be developed to evaluate possible exposure and measures put in place to reduce exposure. General precautions for handling all laboratory chemicals should be adopted, rather than specific guidelines for particular chemicals.

Design and organisation

Installations must be appropriate to the work conducted regarding size, distribution of rooms, exits, etc. They must be equipped with appropriate ventilation systems, well-ventilated stockrooms/storerooms, safety equipment, and arrangements for waste disposal. The design of the laboratory must recognise that the risks associated with a procedure affect not only the workers involved in it. Dangerous operations must be conducted under special safety (preventative and protective) conditions. Working alone in the laboratory should be strictly avoided.

Ventilation

The general laboratory ventilation system should provide a source of fresh air for breathing and for supply to local exhaust ventilation devices, but it should not be relied on for protection from toxic substances released into the laboratory. The ventilation system must ensure that laboratory air is continually replaced to prevent the increase of atmospheric concentrations of toxic substances during the working day. Supply air should come from uncontaminated areas and exhaust air should be released outside the hospital. General airflow should not be turbulent and should be relatively uniform throughout the laboratory, with no areas of high velocity or static air. Ventilation rates of 4-12 room air changes/hour provide adequate general ventilation if local exhaust systems such as hoods are used as the primary method of control.

　　The best way to prevent exposure to airborne substances is to use hoods and other ventilation devices combined with general ventilation to minimise residual airborne contamination. A laboratory hood with at least 75 cm of hood space per person should be provided for every two workers if they spend most of their time working with chemicals. It is suggested that every hood should have a continuous monitoring device to allow instantaneous confirmation of adequate hood performance before and during use. If this is not the case, work with substances of unknown toxicity should be avoided or other types of local ventilation devices should be provided. Airflow into and within the hood should not be turbulent and with a suitable face velocity (typically 0.3-0.8 m/s).

Ventilated storage cabinets, canopy hoods, snorkels, etc. should be provided as needed. Each canopy hood and snorkel should have a separate exhaust duct.

The characteristics (quality and quantity) of the ventilation system should be evaluated on installation, regularly monitored (at least every three months) and re-evaluated whenever a change is made. Any alteration to the ventilation system should be put into operation only after thorough testing indicates that worker protection from airborne toxic substances is not reduced.

Chemical procurement, distribution and storage

Before a substance is received, staff who will be using the chemical should have information on proper handling, storage and disposal. No container should be accepted without an identifying label. In this way the establishment of a strict control of chemicals entering the laboratory, by a means of a register of all chemicals purchased, could be an excellent preventative measure. This register can provide very useful information about chemicals present in the laboratory (bought, stored and used) but also about their disposal, substitution programmes and the reduction in the use of very toxic agents (such as carcinogenic, mutagenic or teratogenic agents). This register should extend to all chemicals used in the hospital. The manufacturer must also provide the specific Safety Data Sheet with the first delivery of each product. These Safety Data Sheets should be easily accessible to all personnel handling chemicals since they will describe the methods of controlling chemical risks in the laboratory. Specific procedures should be used to label products and solutions prepared in the laboratory. Highly toxic substances should be segregated in a well-identified area with local exhaust ventilation. Stored chemicals should be examined periodically (at least annually) for replacement, deterioration and container integrity. Stockrooms/storerooms should not be used as preparation or repackaging areas; they should be open during normal working hours and controlled by only one responsible person. When chemicals are hand-carried, the container should be placed in an outside container or bucket. Freight-only elevators should be used if possible. Amounts permitted into the laboratory should be as small as practicable. Storage on bench tops and in hoods is inadvisable. Exposure to heat and direct sunlight should be avoided. Periodic inventories should be conducted, with non-essential items being discarded or returned to the storeroom/stockroom.

Environmental and biological monitoring

Regular instrumental monitoring of airborne concentrations is usually not justified or practical in laboratories but may be appropriate when testing or redesigning hoods or other ventilation devices or when a highly toxic substance is stored or used regularly. It can be also used for the periodic testing for the absence of residual formaldehyde in pathology laboratories. An adequate biological monitoring programme can also substitute for environmental monitoring, i.e., for organic solvents, such as xylenes or methanol, and mercury

Housekeeping, maintenance and inspections

Floors should be cleaned regularly and formal housekeeping and chemical hygiene inspections should be held at least quarterly for units that have frequent personnel changes, and semi-annually for others. Informal inspections should be made more often.

Eye wash fountains should be inspected at intervals of no less than three months. Other safety equipment such as safety showers and fire extinguishers should be inspected regularly according to respective guidelines. Procedures to prevent restarting of out-of-service equipment should be established.

Stairways and passageways should not be used as storage areas. Access to exits, emergency equipment and utility controls should never be blocked or locked (for security reasons).

Protective clothing and equipment

Protective equipment has to be available and in working order. Appropriate training has to be provided for all personnel.

The following should be available in each laboratory:
• Protective clothing appropriate for the required degree of protection for substances being handled, mainly protective gloves with specific resistance to the chemical being used - these must be worn. In addition eye or face protection could be required or total or partial body protection by means of an apron or pinafore,
• an easily accessible drench-type safety shower,
• an eyewash fountain,
• fireproof blankets,
• fire extinguishers,
• fire alarms and telephone for emergency use should be available nearby,
• first aid equipment,
• other items designated by the laboratory supervisor.

Signs and labels

Prominent signs and labels of the following types should be posted:
• Identity labels showing contents of containers (including waste receptacles) and associated hazards.
• Location signs for safety showers, eyewash stations, other safety and first aid equipment, exits and areas where food and beverage consumption and storage are permitted.
• Warnings at areas or equipment where special or unusual hazards exist.

Spills and accidents

A written emergency plan should be established and communicated to all staff. This should include procedures for spills, splashing, accidents, ventilation failure and evacuation. First aid measures must be co-ordinated with emergency room personnel.

There should be an alarm system to alert people in all parts of the facility including isolation areas such as cold rooms.

A spill control policy should be developed and this should include consideration of prevention, containment, cleanup and reporting.

All accidents or near accidents (incidents) should be thoroughly analysed and the results distributed to all who might benefit.

Information and training programme

The training and education programme must be a regular, continuing activity - not simply an annual presentation. All new staff must be trained before starting work in the laboratory. Every laboratory worker should know the location and proper use of available protective clothing and equipment. Some full-time staff in the laboratory should be trained in the proper use of the emergency equipment and procedures.

Receiving and stockroom/storeroom staff should know about hazards, handling equipment, protective clothing and relevant regulations.
Literature and advice concerning chemical risks should be readily available to laboratory staff, who should be encouraged to use these information resources.

Waste disposal programme

To minimise risk for laboratory workers, the general population and the environment from waste laboratory chemicals a waste disposal programme must be established. The programme should specify (according to the General Hospital Waste Disposal Programme) how waste is to be collected, segregated, stored and transported and should include consideration of what materials can be incinerated. Transport from the institution must be in accordance with local regulations and the General Hospital Waste Disposal Programme.

Waste should be removed from laboratories to a central waste storage area at least once a week and from the central waste storage area at regular intervals.

Incineration outside the hospital, in an environmentally acceptable manner by a specialised company, can be a practical disposal method for combustible laboratory waste. Indiscriminate disposal by pouring waste chemicals down the drain or adding them to mixed waste containers for landfill burial is unacceptable. Hoods should not be used as a means of disposal for volatile chemicals. Disposal by recycling or chemical decontamination should be used whenever possible.

Further reading

- CEC-IPCS (UNEP, ILO, WHO). International Chemical Safety Cards. CEC-IPCS, Luxembourg, 1991
- Stellman JM (Ed). Encyclopaedia of Occupational Health and Safety. 4th ed. Vol III. Chapter 97: Health Care Facilities and Services. Geneva: International Labour Office, 1998
- Lunn G, Sansone EB. Destruction of Hazardous Chemicals in the Laboratory. New York: John Wiley and Sons, 1990

Managing hospital waste

Kazuya Fujishiro, Toshiaki Higashi, Hans-Martin Hasselhorn

In the course of daily activities, a hospital produces waste. A waste is any solid, liquid, or contained gaseous material no longer used. Medical waste includes all types of waste generated by health care organisations, including hospitals, clinics, doctor's offices and veterinary facilities. The federal Environmental Protection Agency (EPA) estimates that the generation rate of hospital waste is at a rate of 5.9 kg/bed/day, but some independent estimates put the generation range between 7.3 and 10.4 kg/bed/day [1].

Hospital waste management includes aspects of occupational and community health together with environmental protection. This paper will place most emphasis on the issues relating to occupational health, but the others remain of the utmost importance. In addition, most countries will have legislation which regulates or influences hospital waste management policies.

The basis of effective waste management is an adequate classification and sorting system. Whereas in earlier years most hospital waste was classified as hazardous, a more differentiating view is applied today [2]. Differentiated classification allows separate collection and handling of waste thus reducing exposure and costs.

Hospital waste can be classified according to its nature and source (modified from [2]):
- Group I: Recyclable hospital waste
- Group II: Non recyclable hospital waste that does not pose a risk to health or to the environment when handled as ordinary urban refuse (e.g. blood-stained-material and used medical equipment)
- Group III: Specific hospital waste or hazardous waste
    - Sharp instruments (e.g. needles, scalpels)
    - Infectious waste: Waste contaminated with biological agents of infectious diseases, e.g. brucellosis, diphtheria, cholera, Creutzfeld-Jakob encephalitis, tularaemia, anthrax, plague, rabies, Q-fever, tuberculosis. This includes infectious laboratory waste and also filters from biological cabins of class II and class III where hazardous biological agents have been handled.
    - Chemical waste: Waste containing substances which are classified as toxic and/or hazardous, e.g. pharmaceuticals, reagents used in the laboratory, filters of chemical safety cabinets, heavy metals such as mercury or cadmium from batteries etc.

        Cytotoxic waste: All surplus anti-neoplastic drugs that are not fit for therapeutic use, as well as all single-use material that has been in contact with the same (needles, syringes, catheters, gloves and so on). Also included are the filters from safety cabinets for preparing cytotoxic drugs.

- Radioactive waste: All material contaminated with radioactive isotopes which exceeds the threshold levels of radiation (according to national laws)
- Group IV: Human biological material where disposal may have ethical implications (placentas, parts of human body, e.g. following surgery or pathology examinations). Usually, national laws regulate the procedures for eliminating aborted foetuses as well as anatomical pieces of larger size.

Hospital waste may be recycled, dumped or incinerated. Certain waste may be discharged into the sanitary sewage system and some gaseous waste may be released through laboratory hood vent ducts, sometimes after filtering. Community health and environmental protection aspects must always be considered, however. For most types of waste, laws and regulations exist which regulate their handling: these include radioactive, chemical and potentially infectious waste.

Occupational risk and prevention

A large number of health care workers (HCW) are involved in the collection, cleaning and disposal of hospital waste, which, should be considered to be potentially biologically and chemically hazardous. Exposure to hospital waste depends largely on the appliance of safety measures by all people involved. If rules for safe systems of work exist (e.g. by means of a hospital waste management plan) and are followed, the health risk can be effectively reduced. Hospital personnel at risk are not only medical and laboratory personnel, but include cleaning staff, portering staff, maintenance staff, laundry workers, kitchen staff and others. This should be taken into account when assessing risks and implementing preventive measures (e.g. vaccinations, equipment for personal protection, working procedures etc.).

Basic principles of prevention

- The basis of all waste hazard reduction is prevention at source. Waste producing procedures should be reviewed and hazardous substances should be replaced by less hazardous, where possible.
- Waste should be separated and classified at the point of production. This should occur as conveniently as possible for all involved. All persons involved in waste production should know the procedures for safe handling and disposal, whilst all employees should be fully aware of the existence and contents of a hospital waste management plan.
- It should be possible to estimate the risk of the contents of waste disposal containers from the outside, e.g. by using bags with defined colours or by thorough and highly visible labelling.
- All persons or organisations handling waste should be informed about its nature, risks and proper handling.

Group I and II waste

For environmental reasons group I waste should be recycled whenever possible. Group II waste contains materials that are not recyclable. It may also be stained with blood or other biological fluids, making recycling not suitable. Group II waste usually does not pose a risk for the environment or community and may be disposed of in a manner similar to urban waste. In some countries guidelines or regulations may exist for special treatment of group II waste (e.g. incineration).

Group III waste

Group III waste may pose a risk if not handled properly. To facilitate the removal and reduce risks to a minimum, single use rigid containers should be used for collection. They should never be compacted and must not be filled to total capacity so that they easily can be hermetically closed. The containers should be disposed of by authorised personnel following the methods of treatment established for disposal of such waste by national laws.

Sharps

The risk of contracting hepatitis B, hepatitis C or HIV by accidental needle-stick injury or injury by other "sharps" is well known. Sharp instruments, once used, must be placed in specifically designed, rigid "sharps" containers that have been strategically placed throughout the hospital. Such materials will be disposed of as hazardous waste even if used on uninfected patients.

Infectious waste

Infectious waste of the group III type will be placed in single-use, rigid, colour-coded polyethylene containers and hermetically sealed. The containers should be clearly labelled as "Hazardous hospital waste" and kept in specified areas until collected. Waste classed as a biohazard should not be disposed of by dumping directly into the drainage system. All personnel possibly exposed to infectious waste (including housekeeping and service workers) should be informed about the risks of infection, the measures to be taken in case of percutaneous or mucocutaneous contact, and should be vaccinated against hepatitis B.

Chemical waste

Medical work often produces chemical waste that may cause serious health problems if not handled and disposed of properly. Chemicals in health care settings can be broadly categorised as disinfectants, sterilising agents, pharmaceutical agents, laboratory reagents, and agents used in housekeeping/maintenance etc. Health care institutions are heavy users of chemicals and employ large numbers of people. The health care environment is complex and incorporates a wide range of professions and services, many of which involve potential exposure to chemical hazards.

Medical technology uses appliances which if handled or altered during disposal may release toxic compounds. For example, many dental and surgical procedures involve the implantation of prostheses that may be glued in place with a form of acrylic resin. The cutting of such material has been shown to release fumes containing allergens.

The range of chemicals used in hospitals is very broad and such waste often receives less attention than infectious waste. For example, mercury compounds (e.g. mercuric chloride) used in hospitals have, in some cases, been simply poured down the drain for disposal.

All hospital personnel must take particular care when handling chemicals, whilst storage of chemical waste before disposal should be for as short a time as possible. Waste liquids need to be collected separately according to type and labelled. Most chemical waste can be controlled by observing manufacturer's recommendations and Material Safety Data Sheets. A hospital wide computerised register for chemicals as proposed in the chapter "Occupational hazards in the laboratory environment" could provide quick access to necessary information about disposal. In some countries (e.g. Sweden) specialised companies exist for collection, disposal or recycling of chemical waste.

Cytotoxic waste

Exposure to cytotoxic drugs may lead to irritation of the skin, allergic reactions, but may also include teratogenic risks (see chapter "Cytotoxic drugs"). Cytotoxic waste may be found in materials used for preparation and administration (e.g. used drug bottles, syringes) but also in the urine, faeces and other body fluids from treated patients. Thus hospital linen and similar materials may be contaminated, potentially leading to exposure of cleaning, laundry, and maintenance staff servicing drains, etc.

Given the danger it poses to persons and the environment, cytotoxic hospital waste must be collected in rigid, watertight, sealable single-use, colour-coded containers which should be clearly labelled "chemically contaminated material: Cytotoxic agents". These containers must be disposed of according to appropriate guidelines. In some countries, material contaminated with cytotoxic agents may be treated like solid urban waste, but incineration is preferred. Usually, faeces and urine of patients treated with cytotoxic drugs are flushed into the drainage system, resulting in more than 90% of all cytotoxic substances being disposed of via this route. Thus, comprehensive measures for management of cytotoxic waste other than faeces and urine would only catch up to 10% of the total cytotoxic waste. Nevertheless, bottles containing remnants of cytotoxic drugs should be incinerated at high temperatures. Central preparation of cytotoxic drugs does not only lead to better protection of HCW but also contributes to less cytotoxic waste.

Radioactive waste

Radioactive waste may be radioactive material or radioactively contaminated material, such as used equipment, cleaning material and reagents or chemicals. It may be solid, liquid or gaseous. The risks of handling radioactive substances and thereby also radioactive waste are well recognised and usually strictly regulated.

Disposal of radioactive waste depends on the half-life of the radionuclide. Solid or liquid radioactive waste with long half-life radionuclides must be disposed of by specialised organisations. Those with short half-life radionuclides may be stored until radioactivity has decayed. Faeces and urine may be flushed down the toilet, which should then be flushed several times. If the patient has received large doses of radioactive iodine, the urine may be stored for e.g. two days and flushed after verifying low levels of residual radioactivity. Radioactive waste gases in hospitals may usually be released into the outside air, ensuring that re-entry into buildings cannot occur.

All personnel having possible contact with radioactive waste should be constantly monitored for exposure to ionising radiation (see chapter "Radiation problems in the health care professions").

Group IV: Substances with ethical impact

Biological material classified in group IV (e.g. placentas, parts of human body) should from the point of physical health risk be treated like infectious waste. Their handling, however, may have a strong impact on the psychological wellbeing of individuals and even the community. Guidelines should exist in all health care institutions concerning handling of these materials. Even respective national regulations may exist.

Transportation of waste

Waste disposal also involves transport inside and outside hospitals. The comparatively large volumes of waste involved nowadays must be considered when designing new hospitals. Corridor and lift spaces need to be large enough to cope with the vehicles that are used for the internal transport of waste. The disadvantages of chutes for the internal transport of waste outweigh their advantages. Other devices, such as compactors, may be useful for those types of waste that can be safely disposed of by landfill or incineration. Usually, national guidelines exist for transportation of hazardous waste.

Waste management strategies

All hospitals should develop waste-disposal strategies and training programmes that are designed to cope with local problems. These should be based on the national guidelines. Indeed, in many countries, passage of "right to know" laws, which seek to assure that workers be informed of the name and nature of the chemicals to which they may be exposed to on the job, has introduced a major administrative challenge to occupational health and safety specialists in health care institutions.

Waste management plan

For each hospital, the site waste manager should develop and implement a waste management plan following these stages:
- informing the site management
- designating those responsible at the executive level
- creating a committee on hospital waste made up of personnel from the general services, nursing and medical departments that is chaired by the waste manager.

For different types of waste, specific "waste management plans" may be formulated. As an example an infectious waste management plan could be set up in the following way:

1. Determination/definition of "infectious waste".
2. Segregation of infectious and non-infectious waste at source.
3. Packaging and storing. It should be determined which type of infectious waste should be packed and stored in storage areas marked with the universal biological hazard symbol. Storage of infectious waste should be for the shortest possible time.
4. Disposal. For each type of infectious waste the method of disposal must be determined considering community health and environmental protection aspects. The methods will often be dictated by local or national guidelines.
5. Emergency plan. An emergency plan should exist for all types of emergency which might occur when handling infectious waste (e.g. rupture of waste bags, waste spills)
6. Education and training. All personnel handling infectious waste should be educated about the characteristics and risks of infectious waste and how to handle it. They should know what to do in emergency situations.
7. Information. All hospital personnel should know the content of the "infectious waste management plan" as well as which person is responsible for its implementation.

ISO Standards for managing waste

A formal Environmental Management System, using the International Organisation for Standardisation (ISO) standard 14001 as the performance specification, has been developed and is being implemented in many hospitals [3]. The ISO 14000 standards system is a continuous improvement model based on a controlled management system.

References

1   Cheremisinoff PN, Shah MK. Hospital waste management. Pollution Engineering 1990;22:60-66
2   Arias MP. Hospital Waste Management. In: Stellman JM (Ed). Encyclopaedia of Occupational Health and Safety. 4th ed. Vol III. Geneva: International Labour Office 1998:97.61-97.64
3   Spiegel J, Reimer J. Management of Hazardous Waste Disposal under ISO 14000. In: Stellman JM (Ed). Encyclopaedia of Occupational Health and Safety. 4th ed. Vol III. Geneva: International Labour Office 1998:97.64-97.67

Further Reading

- WHO. Management of waste from hospitals. EURO reports and studies 97:1-49
- EPA. Standards for the tracking and management of medical waste. Federal register 54: 12371-12395
- European Union. Council Directive on Hazardous Waste, 91/689/EEC, 1991

Authors

Dominique Abiteboul, MD
GERES, Occup. Health Service
Hôpital Bichat-Cl. Bernard
46, rue Henri Huchard
F-75 877 Paris Cedex 18, France

Jacob Amir, Prof.
Head of Dept. of Paediatrics C.
Schneider Children´s Medical Center of Israel
Sackler School of Medicine
Tel Aviv University, Petach Tikvah, Israel
phone: +972-3-925-3700
fax: +972-3-925-3801

Judith E. Arnetz, PhD
Division of Psychosocial Factors and Health
Karolinska Institute, Box 220
S-171 77 Stockholm, Sweden
phone: +46-8-728 67 83
fax: +46-8-33 43 96
judy.arnetz@phs.ki.se

Peter A. Czeschinski, MD
Institute of Occup. Medicine
Westphalian Wilhelm University Münster
Domagkstr. 11, D-49149 Münster, Germany
phone: +49-251-835-6081
fax: +49-251-835-5051
czeschi@uni-muenster.de

Tore Dérand, Prof.
Dept. of Oral Technology
School of Dentistry
S-214 21 Malmö, Sweden
phone: +46-40-32 21 34
fax: +46-40-32 21 36
Tore.Derand@od.mah.se

Raymond Agius, MD, FRCP, FFOM,
Sen. Lecturer in Occup. and Environ. Health
The University of Edinburgh Medical School
Edinburgh EH8 9AG, UK
phone: +44-131-650-3231
fax: +44-131-650-6909
Raymond@agius.com

Bengt B. Arnetz, MD, PhD, Prof. of Social
Medicine, Dept. of Public Health
Uppsala University
S-751 85 Uppsala, Sweden
phone: +46-18-66 30 00
fax: +46-18-51 16 57
Bengt.Arnetz@medhs.ki.se

Eva Bejerot, PhD
National Institute for Working Life
S-171 84 Solna, Sweden
Phone: +46-8-730 91 02
Eva.Bejerot@niwl.se

Feroza Daroowalla, MD, MPH, Medical Officer
National Institute for Occup. Safety and Health
1095 Willowdale Rd., B-163
Morgantown, WV
USA 26505
fax: +1-304-285-5861

Markus Dettenkofer, MD
Inst. of Environ. Med. and Hospital Epidemiology
Hugstetter Str. 55
D-79106 Freiburg, Germany
phone: +49-761-270-5483
fax: +49-761-270-5485
mdet@iuk3.ukl.uni-freiburg.de

Madeleine Estryn-Behar, MD, PhD
Hôpital Saint-Louis
Service de médecine du travail
1, ave Claude Vellefaux
F-75010 Paris, France
Estryn.Belfer@chu-stlouis.fr

Jean-François Gehanno, MD
Occupational Medicine Service
Assistance Publique
Hôpitaux de Paris
1, place du parvis Notre Dame
F-75004 Paris, France
fax: +33-142-348-520
Jean-Francois.Caillard@htd.ap-hop-paris.fr

Xavier Guardino, PhD
CNCT Instituto Nacional de Condiciones de
Trabajo
Dulcet, 2-10, E-08034 Barcelona, Spain
phone: +34-93-280-0102
fax: +34-93-280-3642

Heléne Harder, RN, Labour inspector
National Board of Occupational Safety and
Health
Ekelundsvägen 16
S-171 84 Solna, Sweden
phone: +46-8-730-9550
helene.harder@arbsky.se

Hans-Martin Hasselhorn, MD
Dept. of applied physiology, occupational
medicine & infectiology
University of Wuppertal, FB 14
Gaußstr. 20, D-42097 Wuppertal
phone: +49-202-439-2112
fax: +49-202-439-2068
Hans-Martin.Hasselhorn@arbmed.uni-wuppertal.de

Kazuya Fujishiro, MD, PhD, Associate Prof.
Occup. Health Training Center,
University of Occup. and Environ. Health
Iseigaoka 1-1, Yahatanishi-ku, Kitakyushu,
807-8555, Japan
phone : +81-93-691-7171
fax : +81-93-692-4590
fujisiro@med.uoeh-u.ac.jp

Manfred Glatzel, MD, Arzt für Arbeitsmedizin,
Leitender Betriebsarzt
Ärztlicher Dienst der Stadt Karlsruhe
Moltkestrasse 132
D-76187 Karlsruhe, Germany
phone: +49-721-133-1111
fax: +49-721-133-1119

Mats Hagberg, MD, PhD
Dept. of Occup. and Environ. Medicine
Sahlgrenska University Hospital
Göteborg University
St Sigfridsgatan 85
S-412 66 Göteborg, Sweden
mats.hagberg@ymk.gu.se

John Harrison, MD, Senior Lecturer in Occup.
Medicine, University of New Castle
Dept. of Environ. and Occup. Medicine
The Medical School, NE2 4HH
Framlington Place, Newcastle upon Tyne, UK
phone: +44-191-222-8718
fax: +44-191-222-6442
john.harrison@ncl.ac.uk

Toshiaki Higashi, MD, Dr. Med.Sci, Prof.
Dept. of Work Systems and Health
Institute of Industrial Ecological Sciences
University of Occup. and Environ. Health
1-1 Iseigaoka Yahatanishi-ku Kitakyushu city 807-
8555, Japan
phone: +81-93-691-7470
fax: +81-93-601-2667
thigashi@med.uoeh-u.ac.jp
yoshimura@wshiivx.med.uoeh-u.ac.jp

Friedrich Hofmann, MD, PhD, Prof.
Dept. of applied physiology, occupational
medicine & infectiology
University of Wuppertal, FB 14
Gaußstr. 20, D-42097 Wuppertal, Germany
phone: +49-202-439-2088
fax: +49-202-439-2068
Hofmann@arbmed.uni-wuppertal.de

Philippe Kiss, Occup. Health Physician
Progecov, Occupational Health Service
Vogelmarkt 11, B-9000 Gent, Belgium
phone: +32-9-265-8150
fax: +32-9-265-8155
DrKiss.Progecov@pophost.cevi.be

Nenad Kralj, MD, Facharzt für Arbeitsmedizin
Dept. of applied physiology, occupational
medicine & infectiology
University of Wuppertal
Dept. of Safety Engineering, FB 14
Gaußstr. 20, D-42097 Wuppertal, Germany
phone: +49-202 439 2902
fax: +49-202 439 2068
kralj@arbmed.uni-wuppertal.de

Patrick Ledosseur, MD
Pediatric-Radiology-Rouen Hospital
1, rue de Germont
F-76031 Rouen, France
Patrick.Ledosseur@chu-rouen.fr

Roberto Lucchini, MD
Institute of Occup. Health, University of Brescia
P. le Spedali Civili 1, I-25125 Brescia, Italy
phone: +39-30-3995-735
fax: +39-30-3996-080
lucchini@cci.unibs.it

Christer Hogstedt, MD, Prof. of occup health
National Institute for Working Life
S-171 84 Solna, Sweden
phone: +46-619 67 16
fax: +46-619 67 28

Thomas Kistemann, MD, MA
Institute of Hygiene, University of Bonn
Sigmund-Freud-Str. 25
D-53105 Bonn, Germany
boxman@mailer.meb.uni-bonn.de

Monica Lagerström, RN, Associate Prof.
National Institute for Working Life
S-171 84 Solna, Sweden
phone: +46-8-730-96 30
fax: +46-8-730-19 67
monica.lagerstrom@niwl.se

Walter Lenz, MD
Lenz-Taguchi Education
Burevägen 16A
S-182 63 Djursholm, Sweden
fax: +46-8-753-2272

Lars Magnius, MD, PhD, Associate Prof.
Dept. of Virology
Swedish Inst. for Infectious Disease Control
S-171 82 Solna, Sweden
phone: +46-8-457 26 37
fax: +46-8-32 83 30
lars.magnius@smi.ki.se

Daria McLean, RN, COHN(C), CIAT,
Occup. Health Nurse, Dept. of Occup. and
Environ. Medicine, Health Sciences Centre
618-700 McDermot Avenue, Winnipeg
Manitoba R3E 0T2, Canada
phone: +1-204-787-4817
fax: +1-204-787-1172
dmclean@exchange.hsc.mb.ca

Olle Nygren, Associate Prof.
Dept. of Chemistry
National Institute for Working Life,
Box 7654, S-907 13 Umeå, Sweden
phone: +46-90-786-6393
fax: +46-90-786-5027
Olle.Nygren@niwl.se

Christophe Paris, MD, PhD
Institute of Occup. Health
University Hospital Charles Nicolle
F-76031 Rouen Cedex, France
phone: +33-2-32-888-285
fax: +33-2-32-888-184
christophe.paris@chu-rouen.fr

Antoon De Schryver, MD
Dept. of Public Health, UZ Blok A
De Pintelaan 185, B-9000 Gent, Belgium
phone: +32-9-240 36 21
fax: +32-9-240 49 94
antoon.deschryver@rug.ac.be

Carin Sundström-Frisk, Sen. Researcher, MSc. psyc.
National Institute for Working Life
S-171 84 Solna, Sweden
fax: +46-8-730 19 67
frisk@niwl.se

Birgitta Meding, MD, PhD, Associate Prof.
Dermatology Division
National Institute for Working Life,
S-171 84 Solna, Sweden
phone: +46-8-730 98 62
fax: +46-8-730 98 92
birgitta.meding@niwl.se

Yuichiro Ono, MD, DMS, Associate Prof.
Dept. of Public Health
Fujita
Health University School of Medicine
1-98 Dengakugakubo, Kutsukake-cho
Toyoake 470-11 Aichi-ken, Japan
phone: +81-562-93-2452 or -2453
fax: +81-562-93-3079
yono@fujita-hu.ac.jp

Monika A. Rieger, MD
Dept. of applied physiology, occup. medicine &
infectiology
University of Wuppertal, FB 14
Gaußstr. 20, D-42097 Wuppertal, Germany
phone: +49-202-439-3838
fax: +49-202-439-2068
rieger@arbmed.uni-wuppertal.de

David Snashall, MD, Senior Lecturer in Occup.
Medicine, Clinical Director Occup. Health Services
Guy`s & St Thomas` NHS Trust
Lambeth Palace Road, London SE1 7EH, UK
fax: +44-171-922-8378
david.snashall@gstt.sthames.nhs.uk

Ian S. Symington, MD
Glasgow Occupational Health
20 Cochrane Street, Glasgow G1 1JA
Scotland/UK
phone: +44-141-287-4422
fax +44-141-287-4133
Glas_occup@cqm.co.uk

Allan Toomingas, MD, PhD, Auth. psychologist
National Institute for Working Life
S-171 84 Solna, Sweden
phone: +46-8-730 97 37
fax: +46-8-730 19 67
allan.toomingas@niwl.se

Tobias Walker, MD
Dept. of applied physiology, occup. medicine &
infectiology
University of Wuppertal, FB 14
Gaußstr. 20, D-42097 Wuppertal, Germany

Karin Wrangsjö, MD, PhD
Dept. of Occup. and Environ. Dermatology
Karolinska Hospital
S-171 76 Stockholm, Sweden
karin.wrangsjo@smd.sll.se

Annalee Yassi, MD, MSc, FRCPC, Prof.
Director Dept. of Occup. and Environ. Medicine
Health Sciences Centre, University of Manitoba
112-750-Bannatyne Avenue, Winnipeg,
Manitoba
Canada
phone: +1-204-789-3289
fax: +1-204-789-3905
Yassi@cc.umanitoba.ca

Norman Tran, B.Sc., Occupational Hygienist
Dept. of Occup. and Environ. Medicine
Health Sciences Centre
618-700 McDermot Avenue, Winnipeg
Manitoba R3E 0T2, Canada
phone: +1-204-787-1898
fax: +1-204-787-1172
ntran@exchange.hsc.mb.ca

Myriam van Winckel, MD
Dept. of Pediatrics, UZ 5 K6
De Pintelaan 185, B-9000 Gent, Belgium
phone: +32-9-240-3966
fax: +32-9-240-3875
myriam.vanwinckel@rug.ac.be

Katsuya Yahata, MD, Associate Prof.
Dept. of Work Systems and Health
Institute of Industrial Ecological Sciences
University of Occup. and Environ. Health
1-1 Iseigaoka Yahatanishi-ku Kitakyushu city 807-
8555, Japan
phone: +81-93-603-1611, ext 2843
fax: +81-93-601-2667
yahata@med.uoeh-u.ac.jp

Subject index

Page No. in bold = main text;   f = see also pages that follow